# The Making of
# Modern English Society
# from 1850

# Development of English Society

Series Editor:

*Dorothy Marshall*
Formerly Reader in History in the University of Wales

The series will sketch the ways in which English society, seen as an entity, has developed from the England of the Anglo-Saxons to the England of Elizabeth II. Each volume is a separate study of a period of significant change, as seen by a specialist on that period. Nevertheless it is hoped that, taken as a whole, the series will provide some answers to the question 'How did we get from there to here?'

*Future titles will include*

The Later Middle Ages to the Accession of Henry VI *by E. J. King*
From Revolution to Revolution 1688–1776 *by John Carswell*
Industrial England 1776–1851 *by Dorothy Marshall*

# The Making of Modern English Society from 1850

*Janet Roebuck*

Department of History, University of New Mexico

Routledge & Kegan Paul

London

First published 1973
by Routledge & Kegan Paul Ltd
Broadway House, 68–74 Carter Lane,
London EC4V 5EL
Printed in Great Britain by
Western Printing Services Ltd, Bristol
Copyright © 1973 Janet Roebuck

ISBN 0 7100 7473 5

# Series Editor's Preface

It is a truism that 'of the making of books there is no end' but, at least with regard to the study of history, there are two cogent reasons why this should be so. One is that each decade sees the examination of more and more source material as the increasing flood of research continues to rise. This in itself can necessitate the revision of older views and older certainties in the light of new knowledge. But even if no new material were available there would still be a need for new books because every generation asks its own questions and demands its own answers that make, or at least attempt to make, sense to contemporaries. The nineteenth-century student of history was concerned mainly with the world of politics, with the growth of the constitutional monarchy and of religious and personal freedom. Then with the turn of the century men began to ask different questions, questions concerned with the industrial society in which they lived, and Archdeacon Cunningham produced his pioneering work, *The Growth of English Industry and Commerce*. For the first decades of the twentieth century the emphasis was on economic rather than social developments, though to begin with there was no very clear distinction between them. As economic history became more technical there also emerged a growing interest on the part of the non-specialist public in the everyday life of their ancestors, and the success of G. M. Trevelyan's *Social History* demonstrated how widespread the appetite for this kind of information was. Meanwhile the growth of the welfare state incited more and more people to ask questions about the history of the society in which they lived. How, for instance, had the relationships between the various layers which comprised it altered over the centuries? How far was social structure determined by economic factors? To what extent did the distribution of wealth within a society determine its form of government, both national and local? To what extent were ways of thought and attitudes towards religion, social problems, changing as the structure of society changed? The questions are endless.

It would be presumptuous to suggest that this series on 'The

Development of English Society' can even begin to answer them. Its
aim is the much more modest one of sketching out the major ways in
which English society, seen as an entity, has developed from the England of the Anglo-Saxons to the England of Elizabeth II. Each volume
is a separate study of a period of significant change, as seen by a specialist on that period. Because each period presents different problems
there can be no uniform pattern of treatment. Each author must make
his or her own decisions as to where to place the emphasis in each
phase of development. Nevertheless it is hoped that, taken as a whole,
the series will provide some answers to the question 'How did we get
from there to here?' This series is not therefore intended for specialists
or to add to the volume of existing research; it is designed primarily for
students whose courses, one hopes, will be enriched by a greater understanding of the main trends and developments in English society. It is
intended to be a background book, not a textbook, and as such the
series should appeal to that increasingly wide circle of readers who
while not wanting to be bombarded by too much detail and too many
facts, are interested in tracing back to its roots English society as we
know it today.

The story of the development of English society after 1851 is one of
great interest because of its relevance to modern problems but also of
great complexity, because there are so many strands which must be
woven into it. The task of the historian who attempts to delineate
even its main features is a difficult one. There are too many threads
to follow and too much evidence of every kind, often contradictory
and biased, to be evaluated. The most that is possible within the com-
pass of a volume of this size is to pick out and concentrate on the
dominant threads that together make up the complicated fabric of
modern English society. Even then there will be differences of opinion
as to the selection. In her contribution to this series Dr Roebuck has
laid her main emphasis on the development of an urban class society
in which, under the pressure of two world wars, the state has played
an increasing role and which has seen tremendous improvements,
both material and cultural, in the standard of living of the great mass
of the people. It may come as a surprise to many readers to realize how
much has been accomplished in this field and how great the changes
in English society have been since 1851.

# Contents

# Figures

Certain facts and figures can show us, in a very concentrated and succinct form, the state of the nation and the condition of the people. These have been kept to a minimum and the five graphs listed here will be found highly informative.

# Acknowledgments

The author and publishers wish to thank the following for kind permission to reproduce in this volume the works cited, or extracts from them:

Miss Sonia Brownell and Secker & Warburg for *The Collected Essays, Journalism and Letters of George Orwell*, ed. by S. Orwell and I. Angus.

Cambridge University Press for *Abstract of British Historical Statistics* by B. R. Mitchell and P. Deane.

Frank Cass & Company Ltd for *London Labour and the London Poor* by Henry Mayhew.

Chatto & Windus Ltd and Oxford University Press for *The Uses of Literacy* by Richard Hoggart.

Dobson Books and Doubleday & Company Inc. for *Bagehot's Historical Essays* ed. by Norman St-John Stevas.

Heinemann Educational Books Ltd and the Macmillan Company for *The Worker in an Affluent Society* by F. Zweig.

Macmillan, London and Basingstoke, and Harper & Row Publishers Inc. for *Winds of Change, 1914-1939* by Harold Macmillan.

The Executors of the Estate of Harold Owen, Chatto & Windus Ltd and New Directions Publishing Corporation for 'Dulce Et Decorum Est' by Wilfred Owen, from *The Collected Poems of Wilfred Owen*, ed. by C. Day Lewis.

Oxford University Press for 'Dipsychus' by A. H. Clough, from *The Poems of Arthur Hugh Clough*, ed. by Lowry, Norrington and Mulhauser.

Penguin Books Ltd for *New Grub Street* by George Gissing and *Sybil* by Benjamin Disraeli.

Routledge & Kegan Paul Ltd and Humanities Press Inc. for *Family and Kinship in East London* by Michael Young and Peter Willmott.

Sidgwick & Jackson Ltd, Dodd, Mead & Company and McClelland & Stewart Ltd, Toronto, for 'Peace' by Rupert Brooke, from *The Collected Poems of Rupert Brooke*.

Thames & Hudson Ltd for *Taine's Notes on England*, trans. and ed. by E. Hyams.

University of Chicago Press for *The English Common Reader* by R. D. Altick. The Estate of the late H. G. Wells and Dodd, Mead & Company for *Tono Bungay* by H. G. Wells.

# Chapter 1

# Introduction: the Changing Shape of Society

By 1850 the social effects of industrialism had crystallized out to produce a society which most contemporaries felt was basically sound and stable. It was very much a class society in which rigid social distinctions were still made on the basis of income and birth. Its upper layers, which enjoyed high incomes, high birth, or both, lived lives of solid comfort which contrasted sharply with the acute poverty of the mass of the people. England had achieved a precise balance of rural and urban forces but this balance, which helped sustain the apparently stable equilibrium between tradition and progress, was to be upset in the following century as the forces of industrialism and urbanism took over and dominated the shaping of society. In 1851, on the one hand, Hippolyte Taine, French writer, traveller and acute observer of mid-nineteenth-century England, declared that 'The whole countryside seems to be a fodder factory. The mere anteroom to a dairy or a slaughterhouse . . . ' (*Notes*, 127). Agriculture was a prosperous occupation and a socially significant force because it sustained many traditional social forms and observances. On the other hand, England's face had by this time been pockmarked by the industrial towns, which could only be considered even tolerable by those subscribing to the opinion of some northern industrialists that 'where there's muck there's brass'. The balanced nature of English society at this time could be seen in the achievement, in 1851, of a rural/urban population balance with half the people living in the country and half in the towns.

The growth of towns over the previous half-century had involved the movement of vast numbers of people, not only from country to town but also from region to region. Late-eighteenth-century and nineteenth-century industrial processes were based on steam power and coal, and industrial towns therefore grew up on the coalfields of Wales, Northumberland and Durham, and on the flanks of the Pennines in Lancashire and Yorkshire. None of these areas had been very densely populated, or of great national or social importance, when the national economy and social structure was almost entirely

1

grounded in agriculture. As industrialization progressed and the raw materials in these areas became more valuable, the population's centre of gravity shifted away from the farming districts of central and southern England and moved north and west towards the coalfields. Throughout the nineteenth century only London, for centuries a large and ever-growing trading, manufacturing, administrative and financial centre, and always the largest city in the nation, provided a real counterweight in the south. New towns and cities sprang up on the coalfields as industrialization took hold, and by the middle of the nineteenth century England was the most urbanized nation in the world. Because England was the pace-setter and because there were no real precedents for such rapid and widespread urban development, there was little effective planning involved in the early expansion of the industrial towns which evolved haphazardly according to the dictates of geography and profit. The social consequences of unplanned city growth were unknown and, inevitably, no steps were taken to avoid or solve the many problems involved until the 1830s and 1840s, and only a very few improvements had been effected by the 1850s.

Many black pictures have been painted of the abysmal conditions in which townsmen lived, but life in the country offered no really desirable alternative to working people. The conditions of the great bulk of the people, variously called the poor, the working, or the lower classes, had always been bleak, squalid and miserable, and they had always lived perilously close to the edge of survival. The poor agricultural labourer had as few personal possessions as his industrial counterpart; his house was just as poorly built and under-equipped, unconnected to water or sewer systems; his food and clothing were little better. Indeed, Disraeli's description of the small rural town of Marney in 1845 almost exactly followed the mid-nineteenth-century descriptions of living conditions in industrial towns.

> Before the doors of [the crumbling cottages of the workers] . . .
> ran open drains full of animal and vegetable refuse, decomposing
> into disease, or sometimes in their imperfect course filling foul
> pits or spreading into stagnant pools, while a concentrated solu-
> tion of every species of dissolving filth was allowed to soak
> through, and thoroughly impregnate, the walls and ground
> adjoining.
>   These wretched tenements seldom consisted of more than two
> rooms, in one of which the whole family, however numerous,

were obliged to sleep, without distinction of age, or sex, or
suffering. With water streaming down the walls, the light distinguished through the roof, with no hearth even in winter . . .
(*Sybil*, 60.)

The miserable living conditions of poor families were bad enough in
single households and small rural communities, but when these same
conditions were multiplied by the thousand in large towns, the sum
of their little evils proved to be much worse than simple addition or
multiplication might suggest, and the factories added their foul contributions to the resultant mess.

The conditions of most industrial towns were so appalling that they
seemed to many people to be a hell on earth. The smoke-belching
factories crouched beside the foul canals and rivers which supplied the
water for both factories and people, and also acted as the main sewer
which was expected to carry off all kinds of refuse including industrial
and human excrement, dead dogs and cats, and the blood and bones
of slaughterhouses. Around the factories clustered the small, mean,
terraces of workers' houses which curved across hills and through
valleys, the jutting ribs on the diseased bodies of these towns. Prosperous people lived as far out in the country as they could, emulating
the aristocracy which clung to traditional country homes, and avoid-
ing the stench and ugliness of the overcrowded industrial hives. By
1851 it had been recognized that the industrial towns presented many
problems; government and private reports had been made on the
nature of the problems, and some statutory powers provided for the
improvement of any town which cared to use them. In the 1840s and
1850s some civic authorities began work on improvement schemes
and opened the attack on urban anarchy, but improvement was slow.
For example, in 1858 the stench of the Thames, never pleasant, was
so bad as to force the Commons to adjourn. The real issue involved
in urban improvement was not the foundation of an aesthetically
pleasing urban civilization, but survival. The death rates in the nation
(see fig. 1) and especially in the towns were appallingly high, and
epidemic diseases such as cholera, typhus and typhoid stalked the
townsman throughout his short life.

Pollution and environmental destruction, which came to be seen
as serious problems in the middle of the twentieth century, were just
as acute in the mid-nineteenth century as they were to be a century
later. Indeed, by the standards of the mid-nineteenth century, the
towns of the mid-twentieth were remarkably clean and pleasant.

Early industrial towns were also appallingly noisy. The factories, mines and mills, with their massive machinery, great steam engines and shift-changing hooters and whistles, generated a great volume of sound, as did contemporary transport. The picture of a well-groomed, high-stepping horse pulling a hansom cab or carriage may have considerable appeal in retrospect, but in reality, when the horse was a major carrier of goods and people, the picture was not so attractive. Few horses were high-stepping, matched thoroughbreds; in fact, most horses used for everyday transport or for carrying heavy loads were broken-down old hacks, one tottering step away from the knacker's yard and the glue factory. The clatter of hooves on cobblestones and granite 'sets', or blocks, made a tremendous din. Wooden paving blocks reduced the noise a little but they were slippery when wet and horses often fell, sometimes causing traffic jams. The noise was so disturbing that well-to-do people whose houses bordered busy roads tried to protect sick members of their households from it by spreading straw on the road to muffle the sound of hooves. Horse droppings made up much of the filth which accumulated on roads and benefited only the few poor people who were lucky enough to have a small patch of garden and found street sweepings a useful fertilizer.

The Victorians were enchanted by the railway, the symbol of industrialism rampant, and in a great burst of enthusiasm and investment covered the country with a closely packed network of lines, the very profusion of which would plague their heirs a century or so later. The train made people and goods more mobile, made possible a closer economic and social connection between town and country and region and region, and promoted the development of suburban sprawl. It also produced noise, smoke and dirt which added to the output of the factories and domestic fires and helped dictate the appearance of the people. The 'typical townsman', whatever his class, generally wore dark clothes because they were the only ones which would not look grimy and unkempt after a few hours' wear, and a hat was valuable protection from the steady downpour of grit, smoke and soot. The few scraps of light cloth which were allowed to protrude from the dark wrappings were so difficult and expensive to keep clean that contemporaries judged a man's social status by the cleanliness of his linen.

The wide gap between rich and poor was reflected by marked differences in their appearance. Only rich people, members of the upper and middle classes, could afford clean linen and elegant clothing, and, because their clothing was such a clear indicator of social status, most of them paid great attention to it. The majority of the people were too poor to buy either good clothes or cleanliness. Their clothing was coarse, of poor quality, generally ill-fitting and dirty. Some of them wore cast-off clothing which might have been clean and attractive before it left its original owner and began to sink down the social scale, getting dirtier and more ragged as it descended.

People for whom existence was a struggle spent, of necessity, little on clothing because most of their income was spent on food. They could barely afford shelter and such accommodation as they could find was generally in bad condition and poorly equipped. Water, when not drawn from a polluted nearby river or well, could be had only for short periods of time from a public standpipe in a courtyard or at the end of a street; and bathrooms were non-existent in poor houses whose only sanitary facilities were outdoor privies, which were generally shared by several families. Very many lower-class homes lacked even the basic pots and pans necessary for cooking the cheap and nourishing dishes which middle-class philanthropic ladies recommended for the poor. The diet of the majority of the people bore no resemblance to Mrs Beeton's stomach-stretchingly ample 'simple family meals' and consisted of food which merely filled bellies and had a satisfyingly strong taste. The diet of the lower classes consisted mainly of bread with a few flavourings. The small quantities of sugar and treacle, fats (a little butter, mainly meat drippings and suet), bacon, meat and cheese, tea, and pickles which the poor could afford helped make the bread more appetizing but usually were not large enough to have much nutritional value. The limited funds of working people allowed them to eat little or no fruit, few vegetables except potatoes, and little meat except bacon and sausage. The diet of the masses was neither very appetizing nor nutritious, and that of the poorest elements allowed little more than short-term, bare animal survival at a not very efficient level.

In the course of the following century the mass of the people came to enjoy a much higher standard of living, and the huge gap between the wealthy minority and the poor majority gradually closed. Many social changes were closely related to changes in the economy, whose shifts and fluctuations, both short- and long-range, were reflected in social movements. The long-range shift of the economy away from a concentration on heavy capital goods and exports towards a stress on consumer goods and the satisfaction of a domestic mass market played a major part in helping to raise living standards in the century after 1850. In general terms, in 1850 the British economy flourished by producing such basic materials as coal and iron and by manufacturing heavy equipment such as railway lines and rolling-stock, ships and steam engines, and cotton and woollen textiles for export. In the second half of the nineteenth century, new inventions and production techniques, many of which were developed by nations which were beginning to overtake Britain's lead in industrial innovation, began to change the direction of the economy. The competition from other nations, which was becoming acute by the First World War, and the stagnation of world trade which followed the disruption of the international economy caused by that war, forced Britain to adjust her economy to the new demands of rapid, assembly-line, mass production and sale. Essential to the success of the new economy was a large group of people who could afford to buy the many consumer goods it produced. The adjustments were not made consciously or as part of a programme to ensure economic survival but, as the economic pattern changed, the mass of the people had to become more prosperous because the established prosperous minority could not alone buy goods in the quantities necessary to ensure economic survival and continued expansion. By 1950 British economic prosperity depended, to a very large extent, on the production of such consumer goods as household and electrical equipment, textiles made from man-made fibres, and motor cars.

The problems involved in such major economic, technical and social changes drew the government into more and more sections of national life until the government itself became a major agent of social change. Just as the emergencies of the high death rate and the epidemic diseases of the early industrial towns had drawn national and local government into their planning and regulation, the emergencies of two world wars, economic crises, and increasing concern for social justice drew it into new areas. By the end of the nineteenth century the government was already involved in many of the forces which affect social development, such as primary education, the regulation of hours and conditions of work in many industries, and the establishment of minimum standards of sanitation and food purity. By the turn of the century, too, the poor masses were the enfranchized masses, the bulk of the electorate, and politicians were forced to respond more readily to their wishes, desires, needs and fears. Better mass education, more effective union action, the spread of socialist ideas and a change in the direction of thinking on social reform theory all increased the pressure on the government to put more effective and wider ranging social planning into operation (see fig. 2). Spurred on by two world wars, socialism, technical advances and acute economic problems, in the twentieth-century government interference in many of the processes of social development increased markedly. By the mid-twentieth century it was actively involved in economic planning, regional development, land use, housing regulation and building, higher education, health care, old age, sickness and unemployment benefits, transport and communications, and many other fields which helped determine the shape of society. The direct action of government was an agent of social change, as was the indirect action of the tax system which had to be established to raise the money to pay for increasing social services.

The presumed stability of the society of 1850 did not last long and the equilibrium of tradition and progress, rural and urban social forms, was soon upset. The momentum of the forces which had made Britain a half-urbanized nation by 1850 was sustained. By the turn of the century 80 per cent of the population was urban and the forces of change which sprang from industry, technology and town unquestionably dominated the processes of social development, even of the rural minority. The influence of tradition and a deferential society long outlived the practical pressures which had spawned them, but as the pace of change accelerated their hold weakened ever more rapidly. Better transport and communications promoted more cultural and social uniformity across the nation; education and economic changes which opened up new occupations led to increasing social mobility; adjustments in the social functions of women intensified changes in the basic social unit, the family. Considering that so many changes took place so rapidly in the forces which change society, social change was surprisingly undramatic. There were no dawnings of new millennia and no revolutions—the rate of social change simply accelerated as time passed and as more new forces were brought to bear on society. The quickening pace of social change was marked by two notable periods of acceleration, the two great wars of the twentieth century. In wartime the essence of current trends was distilled by the heat of national emergency, and the distillate, more potent than any peacetime product, boosted the rate of change.

The class structure changed slowly and although the same three basic social labels in use in the mid-nineteenth century were still being used a century later, they no longer meant the same things. In the mid-nineteenth century the aristocracy was still a powerful force, economically, politically and socially. As agriculture entered a chronic depression in the 1870s, the forces of tradition which preserved the aristocracy's pre-eminent social position were challenged by new materialistic forces, and as the promise of democracy was fulfilled by the limitation of the political power of the Lords in the early twentieth century, their power and significance waned. By the middle of the twentieth century aristocratic status no longer necessarily implied economic security and a life of leisure, and the aristocracy was of only limited social consequence because the majority of the people looked elsewhere for social leadership. The entrepreneurial, property-owning, prosperous middle class of the mid-nineteenth century, the class which had operated the mid-nineteenth-century industrial system, waned as the economic system on which its prosperity was founded ran into difficulties and was superseded by the new, more sophisticated and complex system. The First World War and the depression which followed severely damaged the already declining fortunes of smaller manufacturers and by the mid-twentieth century this old-middle class, as it may be called, was but a shadow of its former self and its control over the shaping of society was minimal. Moreover, between the mid-nineteenth century and the mid-twentieth a major change occurred in the social status of white-collar workers—professional men, clerks, administrators and paper-workers of all kinds. As the economic, governmental and social systems became more complex, the number of people who ran them increased. By the end of the nineteenth century this group, which was neither traditional middle class nor working class, was an important element in the social system and was already helping to determine the shape of society. In the twentieth century the number of people in this group increased rapidly, and by the middle of the century they had taken over a social position similar to that which the entrepreneurs had occupied in the mid-nineteenth century. This group was larger than the old-middle class had been, but it set many of the social patterns that the masses strove to emulate. Many people worked hard in the hope that this would enable them, or their children, to join its ranks, and it became, in effect, the new-middle class.

In the mid-nineteenth century the majority of working-class people, who made up the bulk of the population, were poor, inadequately housed and badly fed, and had a shorter life-expectancy than the upper classes. In the second half of the nineteenth century they began to feel some of the results of industrialism—real wages went up, diet improved, literacy rates rose, the franchise widened, unionism and socialism grew in strength. By the first decade of the twentieth century they had the power and self-confidence to bring enough pressure on the government to usher in a new era of social reform. The First World War strengthened their pride and self-confidence, and, although the Depression affected many of them badly, the twenties and thirties were good decades of rising living standards for the workers employed in the new industries. The Second World War and the establishment of the welfare state in the 1940s marked working-class coming-of-age as an important shaper of social development, and in the middle years of the twentieth century the majority of working people enjoyed a high degree of prosperity and a style of life which was very similar to that of the new-middle classes. Between the mid-nineteenth century and the mid-twentieth, working-class living standards rose to an unprecedentedly high level and the working classes were gradually accepted as full members of the industrial/ democratic society. In simple terms, they became richer while the minority which had been rich in the mid-nineteenth century became poorer, and the social structure reflected these financial shifts with a withdrawal of people from the extremes of high and low status, prosperity and poverty. Gradually the mass of the people were collected and consolidated into a broad, modestly prosperous mainstream, in which new-middle and working classes became so intermixed that it was often difficult to make a meaningful social distinction between them.

Attempts to assess and describe alterations in the fabric of society over this century are complicated by the many changes which took place in contemporary social yardsticks, i.e. the means by which people at any time assess their, and society's, present position in relation to past realities and future desires. Changes in the economy and in government policy, the continual striving towards higher standards, the eternal determination of parents that their children should be given a better life than they had had, all led to a constant revision of 'desirable' living standards and of attitudes to them. In this century ✳ social goals were revamped more often and more rapidly than in any preceding century, and one generation's 'good life' became the lowest tolerable minimum standard of life for the next; by the mid-twentieth century the revamping process had speeded up and was taking place in less than a generation. The development and use of new yardsticks can be briefly illustrated by the changing attitudes to unemployment and changes in the standard of life of the unemployed. The chronically unemployed and underemployed of the mid-nineteenth century, living on or over the edge of starvation, clad in tatters, with little hope for the future of their children and no help for pain, seeking shelter in any nook and cranny or in the harsh, bleak embrace of the workhouse, would have found joy in the relatively good food, clothing and housing of the unemployed in the depression years and have been astonished by the amount of aid of all kinds upon which they and their children could draw. On the other hand, mid-twentieth-century social planners, reformers, politicians, citizens—anyone concerned with the present and future—cannot but regard the conditions of the poor in the early 1970s as a social shame and a national disgrace for which some new remedy must be found despite the fact that, by the standards of the depression years, they have a very high standard of living indeed. New yardsticks developed slowly until the new, higher standard became the contemporary 'normal' and, in time, a minimum base on which to build for the future. Society at any given time must, therefore, be assessed in relation to past realities as well as to the plans for the future which were being made by contemporaries.

Between the mid-nineteenth century and the mid-twentieth the population grew (see fig. 3) and became more urban, more mobile both socially and geographically, more rapidly and fully informed about what was going on in the nation and across the world, while more people were educated to higher levels. The majority of the people became more prosperous (see fig. 4), owned more possessions, enjoyed a greater variety of foods, better health and health care, more leisure and more security. The population's centre of gravity faltered in its northerly and westward movement at the end of the nineteenth century, and in the early twentieth century began to move south again, drawn by the developing new industrial areas in the midlands and around London. While the drift to the cities continued throughout this period, there was also a drift of people away from the centres of cities and more and more people lived in suburbia. Suburban growth promoted the expansion of the urban sprawls which, by the mid-twentieth century, linked many established city centres with almost continuous belts of building into conurbations. The mass of the people also came to look more alike and to live in more similar surroundings as the proportion of the very rich and very poor was steadily eroded and the vast majority came to live within a broad 'middle group' in society.

By the mid-twentieth century other nations with greater resources had overtaken Britain in the industrial race and the nation was much less securely prosperous than it had been a century earlier, although the majority of its people were much better off. It was uncompromisingly an industrial and urban nation but neither the industries nor the towns were as dirty, unpleasant, and unhealthy as their nineteenth-century predecessors had been. Agriculture was a much less important occupation than it had been in 1851, and there was less land to farm because the sprawl of building (see fig. 5) had eaten up, and continued to eat up, large slices of what had been green and pleasant land a century earlier. To the network of wrinkles that the railways had placed on the face of the nation were added those of the expanding road and motorway network, planes dragged their tails of noise over the land, television aerials sprouted from the rooftops, and the hearts of the young beat to rhythms which boomed from radios and record-players everywhere.

Despite the great acceleration in the rate of building which took place after the Second World War, urban development was much more rigidly controlled and well planned than it had been, and large areas of rural England, although crossed by busy roads and power lines, continued to survive. Farmers had a new lease of life, granted by government subsidies, planning and sales boards, and a shift in concentration to the production of perishable and luxury goods in which foreign competition was less fierce. Of necessity, many farmers adopted the techniques of industry to make farming more efficient and to cope with the scarcity of rural labour. Keeping an adequate labour force on the land had long been a problem, but once the siren song of the city issued from every radio and television set and was transmitted by every advertisement and newspaper, it became an all but impossible task.

Rural England assumed a new importance as a playground, providing recreation areas for the urban masses who flocked to the countryside on holidays and at weekends. The townsmen fled the towns in search of fresh air, exercise, quiet, and an attractive change of scene. Like motorized lemmings they headed for the seaside and the country in small family cars, sometimes giving up in despair before they arrived at their destinations, sometimes arriving only just in time to begin the journey back, and all too often finding that thousands had arrived before them, packing too many bodies into too small a space, scattering beer cans and litter and destroying what they had come to find. Much of rural England also became tourist England, the playground for the prosperous of many lands who made country excursions from their bases in cities. Foreign visitors, especially Americans, came to pay their respects to the past, to people picturesque settings with historical ghosts, and to take photographs for after-dinner slide-shows on winter evenings at home. Britain, the industrial leader of the nineteenth century, admired for her progress and prosperity, became a stage in the European tour, admired and respected for her traditions, ancient monuments, country houses, and other reminders of golden ages past. In the early years of the twentieth century the earnings from 'invisible exports' declined, but in the middle years of the century foreign earnings from the all-too-often highly visible temporary imports, the tourists, began to seem a promising replacement.

Remnants of nineteenth-century industrial England also continued to survive. In many of the old industrial towns the mean little terraced houses survived while waiting for a merciful death at the hands of slum-clearance planners. Many old factories, with soot-blackened chimneys, tiny windows and grim façades also struggled on, some still trying to operate despite their great burdens of antiquated machinery and outdated production methods. The railways continued to play a vital role as carriers of goods and people, but the Beeching axe lopped many branch lines from the system in the 1960s. The effective network of lines was reduced, and many previously busy stations were left as deserted and dilapidated gravestones which marked the passing of the great railway age. The smoke-belching engines which had made such a vigorous contribution to the life of mid-nineteenth-century England were museum pieces, shined, silenced, and retired to a few feet of track between old steam pumps and decaying early looms. The new railway engines used the fuels of the twentieth century, diesel oil and electricity, and ran on the welded track which took much of the hypnotic rhythm out of railway travel. Many people continued to live in the refuse the nineteenth century had left behind, but their numbers were decreasing rapidly as slum clearance proceeded and it began to seem that the day might not be far away when a row of two-up-two-down houses and an old factory might be as much of a tourist attraction as Anne Hathaway's Cottage.

Mid-twentieth-century England was a suburban land, a land of housing estates and wide, divided roads fringed with clean factories. The harsh lesson of nineteenth-century town-building, namely that unplanned urban development resulted in appalling living conditions and a high death rate, had been well learned and the people of the mid-twentieth century made plans before they built. The main beneficiaries of the planning were working people, more and more of whom, as a result of it, lived in semi-detached houses, on housing estates, or in flats in multi-storey blocks. Local government authorities provided an efficient sewer system, few homes lacked running water, and a domestic hot water system was regarded as one of the basic necessities of everyday life, as was a bathroom in every home. Contemporary basic housing units were designed to be light, airy and comfortable and to have access to some nearby open space. Planning extended beyond individual dwellings and basic sanitary services to encompass entire development areas, in which housing estates were planned from the first as whole communities. Broad planning lines were even established across the whole nation, providing for industrial, residential and green belt areas. Nevertheless, slum clearance proceeded relatively slowly in many places and a large minority of people still lived in housing which was well below contemporary 'normal' standards. Urban growth also had its dark side. It produced human problems of its own, such as the insecurity of some high-rise flat dwellers, the loneliness of old people who lived in little flats and houses far away from their children, and 'urban neurosis', a vague feeling that cities were unsatisfactory and disturbing living places.

The cheap, efficient transport of bulk goods and the nationwide need for good, cheap housing combined to give the country a much more uniform appearance. Mass-produced bricks and cement blocks were the cheapest materials available in almost every district, even where local stone was available, and slate, clay tile and asphalt roofing materials were also nationally available. Windows, doors, fireplaces and other building components were produced in standard sizes and styles in factories and shipped wherever they were needed. As a result, regional building materials, and the styles they dictated, played a less important part in determining the appearance of each region. The red-brick, slate-roofed, semi-detached house and the cement slab and glass block of flats became just as common in the Cotswolds and the Lake District as they were in the home counties or in the Pennine towns.

Just as the railway engine was a symbol of the mid-nineteenth century, the internal combustion engine was a symbol of the mid-twentieth. The family car was a fairly common possession by the 1960s, and the large number of cars and commercial road haulage vehicles made the improvement and construction of roads a vital issue. The growing number of people travelling by road choked city streets and made diversions, one-way streets, and bypasses necessary. Motorways were built to provide for increasing long-distance transport, and increasing pressure produced a continued need for the construction of these major highways. The development of air transport had less effect in England than it did in nations with large land masses, but it did exert some influence on society by bringing more of the world, especially Europe, within reach of larger numbers of people for both business and pleasure. The transmission of news was speeded up by the communications satellite system which made it possible for sound and pictures to be transmitted from almost any part of the world into almost every home. The mass of the people, not just a privileged tiny minority, could see the vital run or goal at the moment it was scored, watch statesmen meet and experts debate, and wonder at the opening of a new world at the moment the astronaut's foot touched the surface of the moon. All the major joys, sorrows and troubles of mankind became the common property of Englishmen who, like the people of other lands, shared in the many common and simultaneous experiences which were helping to dissolve the regionalism, not only of the nation, but also of the world.

England in the mid-twentieth century was, in almost every way, more uniform than it had been a century earlier. There were still many social differences and distinctions of all kinds but they were less rigid and more easily surmountable than in the past and the huge class gulfs had closed. Mass marketing and retail store chains removed many of the regional and class distinctions which had been based on dress, diet, and household furnishings and equipment. Most people could afford clean, attractive clothes and a nutritious, interesting, and varied diet which included frozen and fresh vegetables, fruit, meat and prepared and packaged foods of all kinds. Accents were less important than they had been and possibly less pronounced, more people were well educated, more people had pleasant houses and clean jobs which provided them with an adequate income and a good deal of leisure time. The colonel's lady and Judy O'Grady could no longer be distinguished by their everyday dress, and even distinctions of dress between the sexes became less clear-cut as men began to wear more colourful clothes and women to wear trousers.

# Chapter 2       The Structure of Mid-Nineteenth-Century Society

The two decades between 1850 and 1872 were the golden years of the nineteenth-century industrial economy, the years in which England was the 'workshop of the world' and had no serious industrial rival. During these years the skeleton of the railway network was fleshed out, the iron, coal and textile industries continued to prosper, while new industries such as engineering and chemicals developed into large-scale concerns. Agricultural production levels rose and farmers too enjoyed this period of prosperity. This was a time of economic well-being, a time when the position of the rich and the well-off was consolidated and when a few of the benefits of industrialism first began to seep down to the poor masses. There were some bad patches, such as the Crimean War and the Indian Mutiny, which revealed inefficiency in the army and suggested that British overlordship was not gratefully accepted everywhere, but these were small shocks and did little to affect the overall optimism of the period.

By this time industrialism was maturing and its operations were in the hands of a second and third generation of managers, men who were confident, experienced, and competent. The economy was still fluid enough, however, to allow the able and ambitious innovator to get ahead without treading on too many toes, for the process of industrial maturing had not yet produced ossification and a crippling adherence to tradition. There were few serious problems for the prosperous sections of society, only occasional slack periods in business, and it was only in the later 1860s that some far-sighted, pessimistic individuals were beginning to feel a little concern about the future and to worry about the economic competition which was bound to come as other nations developed their own industries and agricultural potential. To most people, however, the economy and the social system it supported seemed sound and continued prosperity almost inevitable.

By now people were becoming accustomed to industrialism and to the changes it brought. Change was no longer regarded as a disturbing force, as it had been in the past, but as a desirable sign of progress.

15

There was little discussion about policy as the nation went about its profit-making business, but when questions of policy were raised there was general agreement along liberal lines, especially about that primary doctrine of economic liberalism, free trade. The financial security of the middle and upper classes was the backbone of this confident liberalism of the golden age. With agriculture not yet facing the competition of large quantities of cheap, imported food and industry in possession of a *de facto* monopoly of the world's production of manufactured goods, Britain could easily afford a free trade policy.

Mid-century schemes of thought were built upon and conditioned by past progress and current prosperity. The prosperity the upper classes enjoyed at this time owed much to the fact that Britain had been the first nation in the world to 'progress' by industrializing, that is, to make practical, visible and profitable advancements by the mechanized manipulation of the material world. Successful people were aware, however, that their prosperity, with its by-products of material comfort and social standing, was not generated by some extra-human force but was the result of individual hard work and determination. Therefore, hard work and its attendant qualities were promoted to the status of moral virtues. The equation of hard work and moral worth was not new for it coincided with, or even pre-dated, the development of Protestantism, but the rapid growth in the power and influence of the middle class which came with industrialism strengthened the section of society which most ardently subscribed to the idea. Increasing middle class influence on society led to this idea becoming firmly interlocked into the moral and social code of the nineteenth century. The hard-working middle-class manufacturer, although generally lacking in meekness, inherited the earth; he mastered it and shaped it, and its system of values, more or less to his own liking. Such men were preoccupied with business and with the practical, tangible things this involved, things whose value could be assessed in precise terms. The practical business system of debits and credits could be, and was, extended to other areas. There were also, ready to hand, whole philosophies with which this value system was compatible, notably utilitarianism and positivism. Practicality, profitability and 'success' thus easily made the transition from the field of business to the *mores* of society.

The essence of the prosperous, confident, hard-working, and materialistic society which the middle class played an important part in shaping was distilled in its testament of faith in itself, the Great Exhibition of 1851, the forerunner of all later world fairs. The Crystal

Palace, Paxton's huge creation which was to house the Exhibition, was as unprecedented, as innovatory and in many ways as grotesque, as the society of its day. Standardized, interchangeable iron and glass sections, designed for easy erection and dismantling, were the basic elements of the structure. Nothing of this vast size in these unusual materials and components had ever been built before, and even many of its admirers were more than slightly apprehensive about the soundness of the building. The scepticism which preceded its construction only served to make the finished product all the more remarkable when it was duly, and stoutly, assembled over the living, mature elms in Hyde Park. The exhibits it housed were officially divided into four classes, raw materials, machinery, manufactured goods, and the fine arts and sculpture, but the chief items of public interest were British industrial machines and the goods they produced. Foreign and cultural exhibits provided an artistic, delicate counterpoint which emphasized the main, massively mechanical, theme of the Exhibition. In spite of the colourful concessions to internationalism, this was unashamedly Britain's tribute to herself, to her own industrial achievement, to her pride in her mechanized monopoly of world industry.

Prince Albert, the Queen's consort, soberly sponsored the Exhibition and the delighted Queen officially opened it. Members of respectable society followed the lead of the royal family and visited the Exhibition on Tuesdays, the 'quality' visiting days when admission cost one guinea, a handsome price to pay for being solemnly delighted in their turn. Entrance was not, however, the exclusive prerogative of the wealthy. On all days except Tuesdays the entrance fee was reduced to one shilling to allow the less prosperous sections of society to view the wonders, and the railway companies also provided special cheap excursion trains. Many thousands of lower-middle and upper-working-class people responded to these practical inducements to join the great pilgrimage to the shrine of industry. By the time the Exhibition closed, over six million people had paid over £356,000 to see the show. The tribute to enterprise and industry made a suitably impressive profit.

The Exhibition was more than show and chauvinism, it was also a social experiment. It was the first occasion on which large numbers of the lower classes had been encouraged to participate, *en masse*, in an 'official occasion'. Members of the upper and middle classes would not have dreamed of visiting the Exhibition on 'cheap days', and very few working-class visitors expected to rub shoulders with their social superiors. But despite the very clear-cut social distinctions implicit in the entrance fee arrangements, the fact that the lower classes could visit the same place as their betters, see the same things and presumably feel a similar pride, was a great social step forward. There had been a good deal of concern about the way in which the visitors from the great, largely unknown, and much mistrusted working classes would behave. This concern proved groundless, and it was observed that the workers did not destroy or damage the exhibits, riot, or hold drunken brawls or debauches beneath the great elms and soaring iron pillars. In fact, they behaved in a fashion remarkably similar to that of their betters, being properly awed by the building, soberly admiring the exhibits, and generally showing a high degree of social discipline. The cleanliness, neatness, sobriety, and good behaviour of the masses was much praised, even by *The Times*, and in the end was cited as a further sign of the advancement and superiority of the nation as a whole. Working-class appearance at the Great Exhibition did suggest that, by mid-century, at least the better-paid sections of the working classes were beginning to benefit from industrialization and to come to terms with life in the mechanized world. Their labour gave them the money necessary to visit the Exhibition, and the railway, the great carrier of industrialism, took them there. The tales of wonder the visitors took home helped broaden the social and geographical horizons of others, while the huge attendance figures testified to the downward percolation in society of the admiration of material values and of the comfort and prestige material possessions brought with them.

SOCIAL RULES AND SOCIAL CLASSES

Although pragmatism and practicality had a strong influence, society continued to follow many of the forms of a social organization whose economic system was beginning to wane. Throughout the agrarian centuries which had preceded industrialization, Britain had an aristocratic hierarchical society, grounded on respect for one's betters and paternalism—on 'knowing one's place'. Because there was no great socio-political revolution to break the ties to this past structure, hierarchical forms persisted and the landed aristocracy continued to be a force to be reckoned with.

Even in pre-industrial times it had been possible to move up and down through the social ranks. Social mobility increased with industrialism, but a sense of social order, stability, and ranking was nevertheless strong in mid-century society. The 'average' man of the mid-nineteenth century was much more likely to accept without question his inherited social rank and to defer to his 'betters' than his descendants would be a century later. A deeply rooted respect for rank and a strong feeling of the obligations of authority were the bases for much of the social behaviour of the mid-nineteenth century. People in the higher levels of society expressed their sense of responsibility for their inferiors in a variety of ways. The upper- or middle-class lady of the house generally felt obliged to watch over the moral welfare of her servant girls and was exhorted to take this duty very seriously by such household experts as Mrs Beeton. Many aristocrats continued to act on their traditional obligation to rule and run the country and attend to the well-being of its people. Many prosperous people made brief sorties into slum districts carrying food and biblical tracts in little baskets, while even an occasional factory owner felt an obligation to care for the welfare of his workmen. Such actions were grounded on and testified to the general acceptance of the inevitability of a hierarchy of social classes.

The cult of respectability, which was so much a part of the mid-century social scene, was also at least partly founded on the hierarchical structure of society. 'Respectability' is a difficult term to define because it covered such a wide variety of attitudes and behaviour. It included social acceptance by people one respected, the possession of good manners, ownership of the trappings of comfort, conformity to accepted social norms, regular attendance at an acceptable church, avoidance of public participation in proscribed activities and, if possible, good breeding. The great stress on respectability by the middle classes can be accounted for, to some extent, by their insecurity in the established hierarchy. Aristocrats were securely respectable because of the very nature of their social position, unless they behaved quite outrageously. They were born with respectability, or at least bought it with their titles, while the middle classes had to work hard for any social recognition they were accorded. Respectability was, for them, a hard-won trophy to be polished with pride, and, to preserve its value, the price they had paid for it was the entrance fee they demanded from all others who wanted to join their ranks. Throughout the nineteenth century there were 'new men' rising in the ranks, men whose very rise threatened the social position of the industrial and commercial middle classes who were themselves barely secure in the social structure. To preserve their hard-won but still insecure status, the middle classes insisted that new recruits be respectable. While money alone could not buy respectability, it could buy the paraphernalia necessary for social position—a house, servants, elegant horses and a carriage, entertainment, generous donations to church and charities, and clean linen. The social value of money combined with practical business sense to transform the hard work and self-discipline which had earned the money into social as well as quasi-religious virtues. A hard-working man acquired some respectability from his labour alone, even if he had little to show for it, while any man who was ostentatiously idle lost some of his respectability no matter how wealthy he was.

In such a stratified society, snobbery was bound to appear. Members of all but the very highest class strove to emulate the appearance and behaviour of the class immediately above, to pretend to the world that they were 'better' than they were. This was part of the whole process of trying to rise in the ranks, and it promoted a curious cohesiveness in this basically divided and sub-divided society. Because the pace-setters of each class aped the class above, eventually all socially ambitious segments of society came to share certain similar standards, aspirations, and behaviour patterns, with the result that they had more in common than might have been expected. For example, aristocratic homes had halls cluttered with an accumulation of family portraits, armour, and hunting trophies; middle-class houses had entrance halls with decorative models of knights in armour, realistic pictures, and stuffed stags' heads; socially ambitious artisans and their wives looked for a house with an entrance passage wide enough for a hat rack, umbrella stand, and a reproduction of a painting such as Landseer's *Stag at Bay*.

### THE ARISTOCRATS

Despite the economic, political, and social advances of the middle classes, the aristocracy remained vitally important, continuing to dominate government at all levels from the cabinet to the ranks of the Justices of the Peace. The middle classes had risen to the status of voting junior partners in government with the Reform Act of 1832, but the power of the House of Lords was not to be broken until the early twentieth century, and it was not until the middle of that century that a man would be obliged to renounce his hereditary title in order to take an active part in politics. In the nineteenth century a title, together with the influence and connections of an aristocratic family, was still an important asset in politics.

The social significance of the aristocracy was far greater than its very limited numerical strength might suggest. Every socially ambitious member of the middle classes would rather have been an aristocrat than not, and, not having been born into the charmed circle, many sought to edge closer to it or to bluff or buy their way in. Taine, who visited England in 1859 and 1862, noted the large number of aristocratic estates which still remained in the country and remarked: 'Not only are the most ancient estates kept in being by virtue of the law of primogeniture; but in addition almost every self-made rich man's ambition is to own an estate, establish his family in it, and enter the ranks of the local gentry' (*Notes*, 137). The importance attached to rank was a relic of the old, long-established social system. Many of the qualities which made up respectability were those which, in the past, had been exclusive to the aristocracy. Breeding, gentlemanliness, bearing, natural authority, the ability to rule, judge, and care for others were all qualities aristocrats were presumed to have and which the status-seeking middle classes coveted. Just as British workers wanted, not to overthrow the middle classes, but to share in the kind of life they enjoyed, the middle classes wanted, not to destroy the authority and prestige of the aristocracy, but to join its ranks. In the case of both classes, the ambitious wanted, not a new society, but a better place in the existing one. Implicit in this ambition was a respect for those who already occupied the coveted 'better places'. In 1859 the contemporary commentator Bagehot observed that

> Our higher classes still desire to rule the nation; and so long as this is the case, the inherent tendencies of human nature secure them the advantage. Manner and bearing have an influence upon the poor; the nameless charm of refinement tells; personal confidence is almost everywhere more easily accorded to one of the higher classes than to one of the lower classes. (*Essays*, 308.)

The aristocrats did not exercise their traditional social and political leadership simply by virtue of the inertia of the old social forms and the power of tradition. Most of them were very rich. Agriculture continued to be profitable until the early 1870s and many aristocrats participated, as they had always done, in commercial ventures. In addition, the traditional landowners derived enormous economic benefit from the new kinds of land use brought by industrialization. Industry needed supplies of raw materials, especially coal and iron ore; railway companies needed land for lines, stations, and yards; shipping companies needed docks; factory owners needed sites; wealthy manufacturers wanted country estates of their own; the expanding towns needed commercial and residential building land. Landowners could profit by satisfying these needs, either by selling parcels of land outright for a high price or by leasing or renting land and buildings. Urbanization, industrial and population expansion, all offered opportunities for the intelligent landowner to secure or improve his financial standing, and many aristocrats made the most of these opportunities. For example, 92 per cent of Lord Calthorpe's estimated income of £122,000 a year was said to come from his holdings in the rapidly expanding Birmingham suburb of Edgbaston.

Members of this respected, monied class led lives of leisure and ease punctuated, in many cases, by civic and social endeavour. London remained the centre for their formal and splendid social occasions, and most aristocrats maintained a house there which they occupied during 'the season'. However, the country was still their real home, and most of them, of both sexes, maintained an interest in its activities and its people. In both town and country the aristocrat was cosseted by a team of servants—cooks, butlers, valets, maids, grooms, coachmen, and footmen. Ancestral homes were adorned with the necessities and comforts of their own time as well as with the treasures of the past, and anyone who was uncertain about style could follow the Queen's lead into the realms of over-ornate, often grotesque, interior decoration. The aristocrats were, as always, a mixed lot. Some led exciting lives, some were dissipated, some insane, but the basic pattern of life of many of them was not markedly different from that of the prosperous middle classes. Aristocrats also were supposed to adhere to Christian values and apply the moderate virtues, as the well-behaved royal family demonstrated and insisted upon. They, too, were concerned with family, church, good works, prosperity, and hard work for some worthy cause. The lives of some aristocrats were not necessarily enjoyable and were often probably very boring and stiflingly restricted. Many of them were snobs, not in pretending to be better than they were, but in vigorously rejecting the idea that others were as good. They denied others entrance into their most exclusive ranks by stressing breeding as a necessary entrance qualification. Breeding was something no one, even those who could buy a title, could buy but which all established aristocrats had, and it was, therefore, an ideal barrier against the rising tide of *nouveaux riches* and an automatic control which preserved the exclusive character of the topmost layer of society. The growing upper-class absorption with, and middle-class interest in, genealogy, heraldry, and the contents of *Burke's Peerage* was an indirect result of this form of snobbery.

THE MIDDLE CLASS

The extremes of the middle class ranged from enormously wealthy industrialists who were not quite socially acceptable to the aristocracy but who may have had sons who were being educated with the sons of aristocrats and would be accepted by them, to shopkeepers and small businessmen with one or two employees who worked long hours to maintain their little homes and solitary servants. With such a wide range of prosperity, social standing, and occupation it is difficult to generalize about this as a single class. There were, however, features common to all sections of the population that could be called middle class.

All members of this class were concerned with success and respectability and the outward show that went with them. Hence there was a good deal of emphasis on material comforts, the keeping up of a prosperous appearance, and all segments of this class strove to make the biggest status-enhancing display out of however much, or little, they had. The compulsion to present visible evidence of success and respectability led the richest members of the class to buy country estates and send their sons to public schools. Taine saw what the game of respectability and social advance meant in the poorer middle-class suburbs:

> The well mowed lawns, the little iron gates and painted façades
> and symmetrical plots are reminiscent of nice clean toys. The
> ornamentation of the houses is in bad taste . . . all [designs]
> borrowed from times and places equally remote, all of it fresh
> and neat and incongruous, an equivocal and trumpery luxury
> like that of a newly rich self made man who, trying to look smart,
> looks bedizened. (*Notes*, 220.)

Surroundings such as these were part of the 'appearances' the lower middle classes were trying to keep up, and each trumpery luxury advertised respectability to the outside world. At the lowest fringes of the middle class the pathetic little status symbols were often purchased at great personal cost. Many a modestly prosperous domestic façade hid an empty larder and a cold fireplace.

Hard work was a vital part of the middle-class code, but only work outside the home was respectable. Domestic labour was shunned and delegated to servants. A servant was a necessity, not only because the keeping of a large family house placed a heavy burden upon its mistress, but also because it was impossible to be properly middle class without a servant. The employment of at least one servant was an absolute necessity for middle-class status, and it was the employment of servants which separated the middle from the lower classes. Servants were the merit badges of Victorian middle-class society. The presence of a servant was a constant reassurance to the ambitious middle-class family that they were important, that they were respectable, that people would do their bidding, that others were lower on the social scale than they, and that others would pay them the compliment of imitation by aping their manners and wearing their cast-off clothing. A servant was a living symbol of success and social attainment, a reassurance of the social position of the master, and evidence that the class system continued to operate.

### THE LOWER CLASS

This was by far the largest group in mid-century society and, like the middle class, it embraced a vast range of occupations and prosperity levels. At the upper end of the scale were prosperous skilled artisans who might, in the near future, be able to hire one or two workmen, establish a small business, move to a 'respectable' neighbourhood, hire a servant, and join the lower ranks of the middle class. At the lower end of the scale was the sediment of human society—the physically disabled, the mentally deficient, and the social misfits who were unable to find work and were reduced to short, grim lives of homeless begging or crime. A large section of the people lived at a level just above these dregs, the lowest level at which a human being could function as an active social animal. Poorly paid manual workers with large families whose employment was insecure generally had to spend more than they earned to stay alive. A variety of classification schemes could be applied to the lower classes, including the basic distinction between rural and urban poor. One could make distinctions between the 'dregs of humanity', the poor, and the artisans, or between the comfortable poor whose income more or less balanced expenditure and the miserable poor who were always hungry and in debt. A contemporary distinction, the one on which the workhouse system was supposed to have been based, was between the 'deserving' and the 'undeserving' poor. This classification scheme, based on the doctrine of work, suggests how deeply the notion that work for its own sake was a moral virtue had penetrated into social thinking. The deserving poor were those who worked when they were able and would have been respectable if they could but were prevented from attaining this goal by no fault of their own. The undeserving poor were the chronically unemployed, the idle who ignored the commandments of society and sinned against the god of work.

The life and work of the rural poor had never been the idyllic romping in sylvan groves sometimes imagined by romantics, and in the mid-nineteenth century the lives of those who remained on the land were much the same as those of their ancestors. The agricultural labourer worked long and hard and was no more free or secure in his job than his urban counterpart. While the factory worker was subject to the demands of the shift, the machine, and the fluctuations of the markets, the farm labourer suffered the whims of the weather and the vagaries of his employer. Sickness or injury was a devastating blow to both rural and urban workers, for few in either group had the necessary margin of income to save money or buy insurance in case of hard times.

Some rural workers, especially those with special, valuable skills such as caring for cows and sheep or operating farm machinery, were generally well treated. A few fortunate ones enjoyed an adequate wage and decent living conditions simply because they worked for philanthropic, paternalistic employers. The less fortunate, including most casual labourers, often lived in abject poverty in miserable conditions, and their cold, ill-repaired, dank little hovels were as bad as anything in the 'primitive past'. They were also undernourished. The notion that the farm worker was better fed than his urban counterpart because he was 'closer to the soil' was romantic nonsense. A few agricultural labourers were able to grow some of their own food but the cost was generally high; occasionally a piece of 'potato ground' was given in lieu of a portion of money wages; sometimes workers rented a piece of ground from farmers. Many employers paid part of their workers' wages in kind, allotting inflated money prices to the doles of cider, beer, or bread they bestowed on their less than fortunate employees. Often workers got food or drink they neither wanted nor needed or which, had they been paid entirely in cash, they could have bought more cheaply. The proximity of agricultural labourers to the source of food supplies did not help them obtain better, more, or cheaper food because few farmers were willing to sell even milk and eggs in the small quantities the workers could afford. It was not worth their trouble to take a pint of milk from the pail or a few eggs from the crate destined for town in order to sell these things to local people. Given the lack of country comfort, it is not surprising that so many workers migrated from the country to the towns.

By the middle of the century 'town labourer' had become almost synonymous with 'industrial worker', but it must be remembered that a large number of urban people worked in service occupations, supplying the needs of the urban population. Thus 'town labourer' also included such people as milk-carriers, bakers, butchers, coal-men, lodging-house keepers, street sweepers, hawkers, and publicans. Factory-workers, coalminers, and iron-workers were, of course, central to the existence of the industrial towns where works, factories, mines, and mills dominated life in a physical as well as an economic sense. They filled the air with noise and dirt, blackened rivers and streams, and generated the sprawl of soot-smudged little houses and mean little streets and yards as a neglected wound builds up a spreading, ugly infection. The lives of the workers were very much dominated by the industries of their town or city. The factory horn or whistle, signalling the beginning and end of shifts, divided and ruled their nights and days. The work shift, twelve or even eighteen hours long, was broken only by short and infrequent breaks for rest and refreshment. Food, generally bread and an occasional piece of cheese or bacon, was brought from home and eaten in the factory, mill or mine, often while the labourers were still working or were cleaning machinery. The work was long and hard but wages were meagre. Men could not hope to keep large families on their pay alone, and their wives and children often had to work too to help support themselves.

Poverty, a chronic problem in towns, had many and deep roots. Many industrial towns, especially the medium-sized and smaller ones, were economically dependent on a single industry. Any slow-down in trade which brought shorter hours or the closing of local industries meant that the whole industrial population became unemployed and unemployable. Such unemployment, and underemployment, quickly spread to the service occupations in the town as the money supply dried up. In addition to unemployment, old age, sickness, physical disability, accidents, low wages, large families, and the death of a family's chief wage-earner were all major causes of poverty. Whatever the cause of their poverty, there were only two basic alternatives facing the poor: to try to struggle on in hunger and hope until something better turned up, or to go into the workhouse. The workhouses, which had been reorganized by the Poor Law Amendment Act of 1834, were supposed to work along utilitarian lines and divided the poor into two groups, the deserving and the undeserving. There was supposed to be one kind of establishment for the deserving poor, where the young, the old, the sick—the worthwhile poor who were victims of circumstance—would get humane treatment, and a different kind for the undeserving poor, where the idle, the wastrels, and the drunks—the worthless wretches who were responsible for their own poverty—would be encouraged to go out and find work. In practice, special facilities for the deserving poor were not set up, and all suffered the harsh treatment designed to spur the able-bodied indigent to find outside employment. The system worked, but it worked too efficiently. The workhouses were called 'Poor Law Bastilles' by the poor, who hated and feared them, often preferring death to official poverty. The religion of work had its vision of heaven—prosperity, servants, respectability, and a house in the country—but to give incentive to the slackers, it also had its vision of hell—life in the workhouse.

The poor could only afford to live where no one else wanted to live, in the least desirable part of any town, in the decrepit houses, surrounded by malodorous courtyards and alleyways covered with stagnating puddles and rotting refuse, which stood beside the blast furnaces or railway lines, on the banks of reeking rivers and canals, beneath the shadow and the smoke of the factory chimneys. Overcrowding added a further blight to these miserable slums. The very poorest families could not afford a whole house, even in these districts. The best they could hope for was one room in an apartment house, possibly a room big enough to allow them to sub-let a few square feet of floor space to help pay their rent. In these poor districts sanitary facilities did not exist; there were no water taps or dustbins and few privies. The poor lived, and generally very quickly died, amidst their own refuse.

The urban death rate was high, which was not surprising in view of the miserable living conditions and the lack of adequate health and safety regulations. Throughout the 1850s, 60s and 70s the national death rate was over twenty deaths per thousand people. (In the mid-twentieth century, when the population was 'older', the national death rate was around eleven per thousand—see fig. 1.) The death rate in towns was often much higher than the national average and higher still among the poor and children under five. Disease and the prospect of an early death were spectres which hovered over the lives of people of all classes, but their shadows were especially dark over the lower classes, who succumbed in large numbers to such diseases as cholera and typhoid which were directly linked with poor living conditions and inadequate sanitary facilities.

The conditions of the poor masses both at work and at home were miserable beyond the imagination of most of their mid-twentieth-century descendants. There was little opportunity to escape for a few hours, for few of the lower classes had much time or energy left after work for recreation, and even fewer had money to spend on entertainment. For those whose work was long, hard, and ill-paid and whose cramped rooms offered no comfort, the most popular recreations were those which offered escape. Some, who were lucky enough to live near a theatre and who had a little spare money, sometimes went to hear songs, to sing, to watch acrobats, and to hurl orange peel and insults at the performers. However, the local gin or beer shop was the main recreation centre for most of the urban and many of the rural poor. There they could escape from both work and home, meet friends, talk or sing, and find a temporary escape in a drunken stupor.

However, to be a member of the lower-class majority of the people was not an automatic sentence to life in a dark cellar with a pile of soot for a bed and an early encounter with death in some frigid workhouse. Some of the working classes enjoyed decent living standards and attempted to 'get on in life'. The homes of the more prosperous skilled workers, the élite of the lower classes, were often pleasant and, apart from the lack of a servant, very little different from those of the lower middle classes. Such houses were clean and neat, had some of the less expensive comforts of the day, furniture, curtains, rugs, a fire, candles, soap, well-stocked food shelves, and perhaps a few books. Those who could boast of such homes were the 'respectable' working classes, the industrious and thrifty who did not despair of the future and might even be aspiring to something better in the future for themselves or for their children.

By the 1850s there were signs that conditions were improving a little, that life for the mass of the people was not quite so bad as it had been. The 1850s and 60s were, on the whole, prosperous years with few prolonged periods of high unemployment. Crime, poverty, and drunkenness were still major problems, but many contemporaries felt that they were a little less prevalent than they had been a decade or so earlier. Some of the more prosperous workers were joining friendly societies and beginning to save for the future; some of the more highly skilled workers were trying to organize trade unions in an attempt to improve their wages and conditions of employment. There were signs, too, that at least the better-off workers were coming to be accepted as reasonable, responsible members of society.

SOCIAL INSTITUTIONS

Staid Englishman, who toil and slave
From your first breeching to your grave,
And seldom spend and always save—
And do your duty all your life
To your young family and wife . . .

Clough, *Dipsychus*, scene V, 28–32 (1850).

The middle classes placed great emphasis on the importance of the family, and, as they set much of the social tone of the age, anyone who hoped to be accepted as respectable worked hard to build and support a solid family background. The model member of mid-century society was the man who came closest to achieving the twin ideals of middle-class life—a successful, prosperous business and a solid, respectable family life. Taine grasped the essence of the family ideal:

The ideal . . . is a dry, stoutly roofed, well-heated house; evenings tête-à-tête with a faithful wife, who must be a good housekeeper and neatly dressed. The rosy cheeks of well-washed children in clean linen, the sight of a good, clear fire, an abundance of furniture, utensils, ornaments useful or otherwise agreeable, well set out, well polished . . . [and, inevitably,] respectful servants. (*Notes*, 61, 65.)

This ideal of the family, mundane and materialistic as it might seem, was endowed by contemporaries with romantic overtones so sweet as to be sickly. In an age when 'love' meant marriage and good economical housekeeping, the notions associated with love and romance were inevitably attached to the home, the perfecting of which was the highest personal goal to which anyone could aspire. Thus, the establishment of a home and family became the ideal of romantic youths of both sexes. Although the saccharine ballad *Home, Sweet Home*, the great hymn of praise to domesticity, was enormously popular in the 1870s and later, it perhaps expresses best, with all its banality, the domestic romantic ideal which was so characteristic of mid-century middle-class society.

The importance attached to the home had its roots in practicality as well as in romance. Sober men of business and industry laboured long hours; the dictates of the code of respectability did not allow frivolous pleasures; drinking was frowned upon; theatregoing was of only marginal acceptability. Hence the home was a man's main refuge from business and competition and the chief recreation centre for

respectable people. At home, neither his wife nor his children expected him to do much except issue orders to the servants. In his home
the middle-class husband and father was master, and, no matter what
his standing was in the social hierarchy outside, at home he was respected, his orders were obeyed, his word was law. At home the ambitious or insecure man could act out his hopes and fantasies of power
and prestige. For lower-middle-class men who worked for someone
else, home might also represent an escape from the humiliating
observation of a social or business superior and be a place where a man
could enjoy the ego-boost of giving orders instead of taking them.

Great emphasis was placed on the 'comforts of home', and in this
respect, too, interest in the home probably gained a great deal from
its contrast with work. There were few comforts and amenities in the
offices of even quite prosperous gentlemen, and many of them were
probably encouraged to lavish money on their homes not only to
enhance their social prestige, but also to build a comfortable refuge
from the discomforts of the office or factory. In addition, the Victorian
middle classes were enchanted by the number of things their prosperity made available to them, and industry was producing an ever-
increasing range of household commodities. The product of all these
forces was the claustrophobic clutter and massively overstuffed
'comfort' of the typical mid-century middle-class home. There was
a profusion of overstuffed couches and low-sided chairs designed to
accommodate ladies wearing fashionably voluminous skirts. Elabo-
rately decorated stands of all designs and sizes supported a wide
variety of knick-knacks, vases, figurines, and wax fruit and flowers
immured in glass-bell tombs. Pianos, ornate barometers, bookcases,
and complicated wallpaper designs abounded. Fringes with bobbles,
horsehair and brass trimmed the furniture; pictures of monarchs of
glens, of limp and virtuous maidens and of solid, but no less virtuous,
Queen Victorias adorned the walls.

Family life involved a good deal of ritual, many predetermined
activities occurring at inflexibly established hours. The major events
were the dispatching of the master to work, welcoming him home
again, and preparing and serving his meals. There were also the rituals
of shopping, ordering the meals, and child care, of family reading,
music-making and church-going. Visits to and by an assortment of
relatives were red-letter days in the family calendar, as were the annual
holiday excursions. Long-term planning also revolved around the
family. Grandparents and unmarried sisters and aunts had to be
provided for, and an inheritance for the children built up. Sons had

to be given the best possible education and good marriage prospects found for daughters. The mid-century middle-class family looked at itself and its life in a fashion rather similar to that of the medieval church; the cast might change but the sets and the ritual came from the past and were expected to continue on into the endless future. The faith was one of pious domesticity, the home was the temple and the routines of family life were the forms of service.

The middle-class domestic ideal was supported by a variety of practical forces. Economic realities strengthened the hierarchical character of the family. The husband/father was king of his castle not only because he wished to be and because the domestic ideal said he should be, but also because he was generally the only, and always the major, provider for the family unit. Respectable ladies did not work for financial gain, and by the time a middle-class son was in a financial position to challenge his father he was also capable of establishing his own home and generally did so. Father/husband paid the piper and this gave him the practical as well as moral right to call the tune. The corollary to this, and a further support for family solidarity, was female subservience. The respectable female always, for reasons of financial survival, belonged to some male. In youth she was her father's daughter, economically supported and governed by him; in adulthood she could marry and be supported and ruled by a husband or remain single and be supported and ruled by a brother. Middle-class women lacked the economic independence to break out of this system and, in fact, few seemed inclined to do so. Women were expected to run their homes and supervise their servants and children, do a little charitable and church work, entertain their friends and make sure that they and their homes remained fashionable and a credit to their husbands. The bearing and rearing of a large family was also time-consuming and reinforced a wife's dependence on her husband. High infant mortality, the expectations of society and her husband and, above all, the lack of effective contraceptives, ensured that a healthy married woman would bear a large number of children. The active years of female youth and maturity were spent in catching a husband, bearing and raising his children, and running his home. Thus respectable women functioned in society only in so far as they were part of a family unit. Home and family were at once their job, their social life, their economic support and their *raison d'être*.

Beneath the apparently placid surface, there were many forces which strained this system. The subservient economic, legal, and social roles of women made practicality the major consideration in choosing a mate. Often the husband was chosen by the bride's father, but, in looking for a mate, even the girl herself was likely to take into consideration a man's capacity as a 'good provider', knowing that the man she chose would be her economic support for the rest of her life. Many emotional and temperamental mismatches were produced by this system and, beneath the respectable surface, many lives must have been spent, at best, in quiet, desperate, loveless misery. It was no accident that this was the great age of prostitution, female 'vapours', and other symptoms of domestic and personal *malaise*. A further source of strain was the ambivalent attitude towards women. On the one hand they were seen as delicate creatures, frail and emotional, to be treated with gentleness and respect. They were expected to be pure, untouched by the harsh realities of life, and only slightly lower than the angels. On the other hand, they were expected to bear an enormous number of children, keep a large household running smoothly, and manage the lives of servants, dependent relatives, and total strangers when necessary. These two views of the nature and function of women, while not diametrically opposed, could only be reconciled if women were also acknowledged to be sexually and emotionally functioning human beings, but in respectable society no one was generally acknowledged to be a sexually functioning being and scant attention was paid to emotional needs.

In the education of the young a conspiracy of silence surrounded sex and sensuality as schoolmasters and preachers condemned without giving information or advice. Sex was something whispered about in oblique terms by daring children behind the woodshed. The romantic visions of the age were couched, not in personal terms, but in public platitudes in which marriage and home were prominent, and little or no recognition was given to emotions or physical contact beyond the furtive holding of hands between piano duets. By the time they reached maturity respectable men and women regarded sex as something which was disreputable, degrading, at best amoral. Sex was not supposed to be indulged in by members of polite society except as necessary to produce children, and it was never discussed. This silence inevitably introduced an incongruous note into an age when a big family was the rule. In an attempt to restore harmony, the stork became a member of every family. The tale of the stork could, however, have done little to alleviate a bride's fear of her husband or to ease the pain of childbirth. It did not resolve the guilts or relieve the conscience of a husband who did his joyless 'duty' by his wife for the sake of home and family and sought personal pleasure and solace

outside his home with 'ladies of ill repute'. All this combined to produce one of the springs from which flowed the stream of Victorian
hypocrisy. Among those who railed against immorality were many
who patronized prostitutes and were deemed considerate of their
wives for doing so; there were many illegitimate births and 'baby farms'
in an age when female purity and the sanctity of the family were
heavily stressed; on the absurd side, there were polite requests for the
'limbs' of a chicken at dinner parties and the dressing of furniture
legs in 'modest' little trousers.

The aristocracy was less devoted to this home and family ideal than
the middle class, but it did have some influence in their ranks. It was,
after all, the ideal espoused by the leading family in the nation. The
aristocracy had long had a family concept of its own, but this owed
much more to ancient dynasticism than to recent middle-class
notions. The importance of home and family was not, therefore, a
novelty in aristocratic circles, and it was not necessary to emphasize
it so much. In addition, the aristocracy was a little less prudish than
the middle class, although there were some people in the upper
classes, including the Queen herself, who might be considered leaders
in this field. The lower-class family differed from the middle-class
ideal in many ways. The all-important servants were missing, as were
the middle-class comforts. Lower-class women kept house themselves,
and many of them also held jobs and contributed to the family
finances. The home was less important in working-class life because
poor people had little leisure time and only a few had welcoming or
comfortable homes. As in poor families wives and children were
expected to earn money when they could, the husband/father was de-
prived of much of the economic power which sustained the notion that
a man's home was his castle and its inhabitants were his to command.

A second social institution which exercised an important influence
on the lives of mid-century Englishmen was religion. Britain was, at
least publicly, an extremely devout nation. Bibles were chained in
many conspicuous public places, including railway stations, and
religious tracts appeared everywhere—distributed as Sunday school
prizes, placed in workhouses, prisons, and schools, handed out in
stations, or simply tossed from carriages into the street. On Sundays,
servants were excused from duty to attend church; middle-class
families, dressed in their best, drove to church, often attending all
three services. There were fewer trains on the Lord's Day; games and
other forms of entertainment were forbidden, and time not spent
in church was supposed to be spent in 'serious' reading and meditation.

Even the most sober amusements were denied by the Sabbatarians. For example, in 1856 proposals were made to open the British Museum and the National Gallery after church on Sundays and to offer band concerts in the parks in the afternoons. These proposals were damned from pulpits and blocked by influential congregations. London had to wait another forty years for them to be put into effect. By limiting the range of activities available on Sundays, Sabbatarianism thus reached into the lives of most of the people, even of the majority who did not go to church. It even influenced the literary output of the nation by generating a demand for 'morally uplifting', 'thought-provoking', and often appallingly banal stories for Sunday reading.

Religion was a popular topic of conversation among respectable people. Most of the talk, both from the pulpit and among the members of the congregation, was concerned less with doctrine and philosophy than with attitudes and behaviour. Clergymen preached about, and their congregations discussed the way in which a 'religious' man should behave, what ideals he should espouse, how he should treat other men and interpret God's will on earth. The churches emphasized the virtues of obedience, temperance, brotherly love, social and personal harmony, and stressed the tenet that the patient endurance of suffering and hardship was a virtue which would be rewarded in the next world. These beliefs, put into practice, provided an extremely valuable social cement. They helped support the status quo, discourage revolution, and uphold the existing structure and forms of society. It is possible that many 'religious' people supported the church because they realized the value of its teachings as a social insurance policy. It is also possible that some of the missionaries who went into the slums were motivated as much by the desire to persuade the 'godless masses' to adopt a conservative creed as by the desire to save their souls.

Religion formed a vital part of the way of life and thought of the middle classes, many of whom wore their religion like a uniform which testified to their respectability and rank. The respectable middle-class man was expected to take his family to church at least once every Sunday, to give his servants time off to attend, to appear, at least, to be paying attention to the preacher, to applaud the missionary efforts in the slums, and to see that his family read 'improving literature'. At least a display of observance of the most public facets of religion was necessary for social standing and advancement. For a sincere man, any degree of unbelief, from atheism to an occasional reservation, could end in disaster. If he spoke unwarily or neglected to observe the expected forms, he might be ruined socially or professionally. Given the penalties for deviation from the norms, it is not surprising that most of the unbelievers and doubters resigned themselves to hypocrisy. A factory owner might escape the consequences of unconventional religious behaviour, especially if he lacked social ambition, but for the doctor, the lawyer, or the banker the risks of nonconformity were simply too great. The religious devotion of the age was thus, to some extent, superficial and cloaked much that was far from being pure and spiritual. 'Religion' was closely bound up with all manner of material and practical considerations, and the forms of religious observance did much to add to, not to offset, the hypocrisy which abounded.

By no means all or even a majority of the people regularly observed the formalities of organized religion. The Religious Census of 1851 showed that only a minority of the people in England and Wales attended church at all, at least on the Sunday of the Census, and there is no reason to suppose that this was much different from any other Sunday. The national average attendance at the three services on Census Sunday ranged from 17–28 per cent of the rural population to 10–23 per cent of the urban population. Formal religion seemed to be a matter of tradition and class. Henry Mayhew, who interviewed all kinds of people in London in his mid-century survey, talked to a scavenger who expressed an attitude which seemed to be common among the working-class majority of the people.

> I never goes to any church or chapel, sometimes I hasn't clothes
> as is fit, and I s'pose I couldn't be admitted into sich fine places
> in my working dress. I was once in a church, but felt queer, as
> one does in them strange places, and never went again. They're
> fittest for rich people. (Peter Quennell (ed.), *Mayhew's London*, 365.)

The fierce commercial competition in which many middle- and upper-class men of the age engaged made it difficult for them to follow the gentler paths of Christianity in their daily lives, but this was a time of great philanthropic activity when the desire to improve the lot of the less fortunate was much in evidence. Philanthropic drives were produced by a number of forces, both religious and social. The religious and social codes of the middle classes gave many of them an enormous sense of self-righteousness which very easily became moral indignation when they found others not living by their rules. This reinforced a deeply felt sense of fair play which was genuinely offended when the unfortunate or helpless were seen to be suffering unduly or treated harshly.

Some philanthropists and philanthropic movements were untainted by selfish motives, but they were rare. Working for or giving money to the poor or socially depressed was a mark of social standing in a self-conscious class which proudly emphasized its own material wealth and religious conscience. Philanthropy was a necessary entrance qualification for any group which considered itself both wealthy and Christian. Many 'good works' were also tinged with self-preservation, for although the poor masses were pitied, they were also a little feared. The urban masses especially were an unknown quantity, a bubbling, seething pool of humanity at the bottom of the social ladder which might one day boil over and topple that ladder and the people clinging to it. Many people gave to charity in the private or public hope that a slight improvement in the conditions of the poor might stop them boiling over.

However mixed the motives of many philanthropists might have been, they did do some valuable work. Philanthropy supported hospitals, dispensaries, and schools for the poor; it dispatched food into the slums; it distributed Bibles and religious tracts; it supported lecture courses for workmen, and, perhaps most important, it helped generate and support legislation for the improvement of conditions in mines, factories, and towns. In its grander moments it even built whole new towns like Saltaire. Sir Titus Salt was a wealthy woollen textile manufacturer and the Liberal M.P. for Bradford from 1859 to 1861. He felt that working-class living conditions in and around Bradford were calculated to deprave and debauch, and determined to remove his workers from temptation by housing them in a new town, built to his specifications around his factory. The work on the town began in 1851, and by the time of the 1871 census the town held over 4,000 people. It still stands, solid respectability oozing out of every grey stone wall, a monument to nineteenth-century paternalistic philanthropy. Sir Titus, however, may well have had mixed motives for providing a town for his workers. A title, a seat in Parliament, and an experiment in town planning seem to suggest conscious social climbing, and the name of the town reflects a sense of self-importance, the enjoyment of the exercise of economic power, and a desire for immortality. Sir Titus's motives may not have been entirely selfless, but the textile workers in the neat houses which bordered the orderly streets of Saltaire were certainly much better off than their counterparts in the stinking back-alleys beside the foetid canals of nearby Bradford.

How did the lower classes, the recipients of charity, feel about all this? The mass of the people left few records and spoke out very little in print—the voice of the people was rarely heard until the twentieth century. However, from the limited information available it seems that they shared many of the same attitudes as the upper and middle classes about problems of unemployment, poverty, charity, and the general structure and nature of society. At least, they used the same set of terms and broad concepts. Except for the very few radicals among them, the working classes did not blame 'society' for poverty; they blamed individual incompetence and impersonal, unavoidable circumstance, as did their social superiors. Like other sections of society, they were very conscious of social order and social stratification, as was implicit in the phrase 'people in our station of life'. Phrases such as this were used with pride by the upper and middle classes and with awareness of their lowly station in life by the working classes. The vast majority of people of all classes simply accepted that society was hierarchical and deferential, and, although some of the poor might have resented the charity of the rich, the majority gladly received what their betters gave.

# Chapter 3　　The Later Nineteenth Century: Society in Flux

In the last thirty years or so of the nineteenth century the British economy, like the world economy, became more sophisticated and its machinery more complicated. Newly industrialized nations began to emerge as serious competitors on the world market, and the steel age was born with the development, in the 1850s, of the Bessemer process, which made it possible to produce good, cheap steel in large quantities. More sophisticated and specialized machines began to out-produce the old, massive but rather simple, steam-powered machines and began to threaten their survival. The system of the organization of production based on owners, manual labourers, and a few skilled workers began to evolve into a more complicated managerial system composed of shareholders, managers, office workers, and machine operatives, which in its turn helped promote the growth of a more complex social system.

In these years the decline of agriculture, which had been only relative up to the 1870s, became absolute and chronic, causing great distress to those sections of society which derived their income from agricultural sources. Before this time the slow progress in agriculture had simply been overshadowed by the rapid advances in industry, but after 1872 the slowly climbing graph of agricultural advance turned sharply downward, and there was a decline in farm production and income which began a depression which would last for decades. By the end of the seventies it was obvious that no short-term explanation such as bad weather or poor marketing conditions could explain the decline, and farmers had to face the fact that their depression was likely to be prolonged. By this time the nations of the 'new world' had begun to exploit the potential of their vast areas of virgin soil, and the growing international railway network and better, faster, trans-oceanic bulk shipping allowed them to export their large surpluses easily and cheaply. Meanwhile the population of Britain continued to grow and to become increasingly urban while villages stagnated as the agrarian labour force declined—1 male in 6 was employed on the land in 1851, 1 in 10 in 1881, and 1 in 20 in 1911. Paradoxically, while both farm profits and rural population were declining, the pay and conditions of agricultural labourers began to improve as farmers, hard-pressed though they were, had to make an effort to keep their best workers from moving away to the towns.

There were no tariff barriers to protect English farmers who, because of their limited land area and high rents, could not hope to compete with the flood of imports at low prices. Townsmen preferred cheap food to expensive food and cared little whether it was domestic or foreign, and the agrarian interest was by now politically too weak to overturn the policy of free trade which had become a part of national mythology. Because the government offered them very little aid, farmers had to cope as best they could with falling prices, foreign competition, and a shrinking labour force. Under these pressures many farmers turned to the production of highly perishable goods such as vegetables, poultry, milk, and flowers. By the 1880s the golden age of agriculture was undoubtedly over, and future prospects looked bleak.

There was clearly no great depression in industry as in agriculture, for production levels did not decline but actually increased in some fields. Nevertheless, a feeling of gloom spread as profits began to fall; the future seemed less bright than it had in the middle years of the century, and the owners and managers of business and industry worried themselves into a feeling of depression. Again the basic cause of the trouble was foreign competition, which came mainly from Germany and the United States, bigger countries with greater resources and much larger productive capacities than Britain's. By the last decades of the nineteenth century these rising industrial powers were not only satisfying their home demand but also producing industrial and agricultural surpluses which were put on the world market in competition with British goods. Britain's comfortable *de facto* monopoly of the world market vanished and was replaced by increasingly formidable competition. Up-to-date machines and techniques enabled foreign factories to produce goods more efficiently and cheaply than British industries and, as a result, British firms had to cut their prices, and their profits, to compete.

The economic changes inevitably brought about many changes in society. For one thing, new industries and production techniques created the need for new skills and gave rise to a whole battery of new occupations. In this period of social change what was to be virtually a new social class, the white-collar workers, began to emerge. Such people as clerks, typists, draughtsmen, accountants, low-ranking civil servants, and local health inspectors were clearly not 'workers' in the currently accepted sense of the term. They were not employed in factories, mines, or ironworks, did not come home sweaty and grimy from a hard day of physical labour, nor did they normally work shifts. They worked regular, if long, office hours, wore suits and fairly clean linen, and returned home with little more than a few ink stains to show that they had done a day's work. Although white-collar workers resembled the middle rather than the working classes, they were not middle class because few of them owned property or capital. They were employees, not employers, and their income came from weekly or monthly wages, not profits on sales or investments. The income of many of these people was low; some of them made less than some highly skilled artisans with their rough clothes and dirty faces, and many certainly could not afford to hire servants or maintain established middle-class standards. However, the white-collar workers shared the middle-class craving for respectability and tried to imitate middle-class appearances as far as their means would allow. Even for the moderately well-off this often meant a good deal of penny-pinching, as the novelist George Gissing suggested in his description of the life of a middle-class widow in the 1880s: 'Whereas she might have lived with a good deal of modest comfort, her existence was a perpetual effort to conceal the squalid background of what was meant for the eyes of her friends and neighbours' (*New Grub Street*, 269).

It is difficult to fit this new class neatly into the established social structure, for it covered a tremendous range of incomes and variety of occupations. At the prosperous end of the spectrum could be found well-paid, high-ranking civil servants, quite possibly the sons of gentlemen. Many of these had been educated at minor public schools, and with the combined income from small investments and salary could maintain the material standards necessary for middle-class status. At the opposite extreme were young board school (see below, pp. 55–8) products who worked long hours in small, uncomfortable offices. Subject to the slightest whim of superiors or employers, they received little pay although they were expected to meet the costs of keeping up at least a respectable personal appearance, with clothing in reasonable repair and white collar and cuffs. The lowest level of white-collar work offered little security because low-grade clerks were easily replaced. Their only necessary skills were reading, legible writing, and elementary arithmetic and, as the Registrar General observed in his 1891 Report, 'The increased diffusion of education has apparently flooded the country with candidates for clerkships'.

By being neither lower- nor middle-class and yet something of both, this new group opened up the possibility of the establishment of a new bridge between the classes. At first this bridge was narrow and rickety and allowed only a few to make the journey across the gulf, but as government and civil service activities expanded and commerce and management became more complex, the bridge became wider and more stable. In the twentieth century the business- and capital-owning Victorian middle class would shrink to form only a tiny percentage of the population, while the white-collar group would expand to become the middle class of the mid-twentieth century.

The inclusion of a growing number of females among the white-collar workers was also significant. In 1871, 2 per cent of all clerks were female; by 1881 this had increased to over 3 per cent, and by 1891 to over 7 per cent. The employment of women owed a great deal to the invention and increasing commercial use of the typewriter. The Registrar General reported in 1891 that most of the females classified as clerks in the census were probably 'typewriters'.

The number and size of the professions also increased in the second half of the nineteenth century. As the economy became more sophisticated, the number of specialized tasks multiplied and the jack-of-all-trades was replaced by a whole series of experts—engineers, architects, chemists, electrical engineers, and the like. The experts soon developed feelings of speciality and responsibility and showed a desire to maintain standards of practice and training. Undoubtedly, in doing so they were also inspired by a desire to control and restrict the supply of their particular skill and to translate their special economic and technical roles into social prestige. The need for the maintenance of status and standards promoted the formation of professional associations such as the Institution of Electrical Engineers in 1871 and the Institute of Chartered Accountants of England and Wales in 1880. The formation of new professions and professional societies was a symptom of deepening economic sophistication, and their growing number and importance pointed the way to the mid-twentieth century when the professional men would become the meritocrats, the aristocracy of the white-collar, new-middle class.

TRANSPORT AND COMMUNICATIONS

The growing technical sophistication which played an important part in changing occupations also produced many changes in transport and communications which would have vitally important social consequences. In addition to the increasing volume of things carried, which included the foreign agricultural produce which injured farmers and helped improve the diet of townsmen, there was also a considerable increase in the speed with which information could be transmitted. The first international telegraph cable was laid across the Channel in 1851, and the first trans-Atlantic cable was laid in 1866. The expansion of the national and international telegraph network effectively shortened distances and began to 'shrink' the world. News reporters could get their reports home within hours and thus give overseas news a new immediacy. The more rapid transmission of information affected diplomacy and military activity, gave a boost to the development of a more sophisticated international commercial system, widened the horizons of many people, especially newspaper readers, and speeded up the pace of life. The world came to lie, not over the horizon and over the sea, but on Everyman's doormat, and its joys and sorrows became his own. As The Times, commenting on the laying of the Atlantic cable, put it, 'America cannot fail to live more in Europe and Europe in America . . . For the purpose of mutual intercourse the whole world is fast becoming one vast city' (30 July 1866).

The development of mass communications began in 1896 when Alfred Harmsworth's Daily Mail gave birth to the modern popular press. In the first part of the nineteenth century the only really widely distributed daily newspaper was The Times, which was not designed to appeal to a broad range of people, much less to barely literate readers. It was not cheap and, as a result, one copy was likely to be read by several people. Although the hiring out of newspapers was illegal, it was widely practised, and many London newspaper men hired out copies of The Times at 1d per hour on the first day and later posted them to their country subscribers, many of whom passed them on to friends and neighbours after they had read them. The forerunner of the popular daily paper was a periodical, Tit-Bits, first published by Newnes in 1880. This was a 16-page penny magazine filled with illustrations, light fiction, amusing scraps of information, and letters from readers.

In the 1880s other, similar, magazines were published, and the first popular newspapers bore a closer resemblance to them than to the established daily press. They were cheap, priced at ½d to appeal to a wide but relatively poor market, and their stories were short, their headlines eye-catching, and overall they were designed for barely literate readers with short attention spans. The first generation from the board schools must have made up a large part of their circulation. The editors of these newspapers shortened news reports, making them into 'lively stories', and, in the process, consciously or unconsciously presented many pre-digested, ready-made opinions to their readers. Popular newspapers had little measurable effect as generators and mouthpieces of 'public opinion' in the late-nineteenth century, but they were building up the large body of readers which would give them a great deal of influence in the twentieth century. Their sales grew rapidly. For example, the *Daily Mail*'s average daily sale in its first year of publication was 202,000 copies; three years later it was 543,000.

The second part of the nineteenth century also saw the birth of the cheap popular book. This was facilitated by a number of events, including the repeal of the duty on paper in 1861, the use of high-speed presses imported from the United States in the 1860s, and the expansion of the railway passenger service. As time passed, larger numbers of people travelled by train either regularly or on special occasions. Once the novelty had worn off and the pleasures of window-gazing were exhausted, travellers looked for something else to do during the enforced period of inactivity, and many of them found that newspapers and books filled the bill. Railway companies realized the need for station bookstalls at an early date and allowed disabled employees or their widows to sell books, but these vendors sold the lowest type of reading matter, which was much criticized as being likely to have an adverse effect on public morals. In an effort to make bookstalls more respectable, the companies leased fewer to their dependants and more to W. H. Smith & Sons. By the end of the sixties, Smith's had acquired a virtual monopoly of station bookstalls and had introduced a new institution into the lives of the reading and travelling public. A visit to Smith's came to be almost as essential a part of a train journey as a visit to the ticket window.

Newspapers and magazines were sold on bookstalls, and publishers were not slow to see the opening for the sale of cheap, attractive, easy-to-carry, paperbound books. A whole series of 'libraries' of such books was developed, initially to appeal to first-class passengers—the first volume in Murray's *Library of Railway Readings* consisted of selected articles from *The Times*. The range soon widened and by the later 1850s the 'yellow backs', so called because they were characteristically bound in glazed yellow paper, crowded the bookstalls. Some series were reprints of older works and some were original, so-called 'railway' novels. In addition to fiction, there were non-fiction works and topical books on, for example, the Crimean War and the Indian Mutiny. Most of the books sold for one or two shillings and, although they were more expensive than newspapers, they provided more reading matter. The bright display of books in the mundane background of the station, the ease and cheapness of buying them, and the lack of pretension in their binding made them familiar objects and helped remove the mystique which had always surrounded books in the past. Books ceased to be altarpieces in temples of prosperity and became the everyday possessions of the common man.

Much popular literature was blatantly escapist, and there is no doubt that many of its readers simply wanted entertainment and temporary relief from drab and difficult lives. Others, however, sought self-improvement, information, or a means of continuing their education, and their needs were satisfied by publications such as *Cassell's Popular Educator*. This was first published in 1852 and was a combination of an encyclopaedia and a set of self-instruction courses. Published in a large number of parts at 1d an issue, it included an illustrated history of England, an illustrated family Bible, and teach-yourself-language courses such as the one Thomas Hardy used to teach himself German. By the early 1860s the *Popular Educator* was selling between 25,000 and 30,000 copies a year.

The wider diffusion of information had profound effects on many aspects of national life. For example, political reporting in the popular press had a great impact on politics, political campaigns, and party structure, and it is possible to see the popular newspaper as being no less necessary a prerequisite for the development of modern democracy than the extension of the franchise. The newspapers, magazines, and books helped create a broader awareness of social problems and of the need for social change by making condensed versions of government and private investigations and reports available to the public. The fact that the new press deliberately aimed its wares at a broad market ensured that this information reached readers who might otherwise have been unaware of the facts about social strain and injustice and uninformed about the suggested solutions for social problems which were being put forward. The growth of the local as well as national press ensured that readers came to know more about people and about the way other people lived. What had previously been gossip and had had only a limited circulation could be formalized and widely distributed by newspapers, and the fear of adverse publicity undoubtedly affected the public behaviour of at least some people.

Taine saw publicity as a force which helped sustain socially approved standards of behaviour and retarded the development of more relaxed standards ' . . . in the provinces, everybody's business is known to everybody else and the . . . fear of publicity and the newspapers . . . acts as a sort of policeman' (*Notes*, 80–1). It is unlikely that this social 'policeman' ever troubled the lower classes much, but Taine was probably correct in assuming that it did influence, to some extent, the behaviour of the members of respectable society.

Physical as well as cultural horizons were widened in the second half of the nineteenth century. The main framework of the railway system was already completed by 1851, but it was filled in in the latter part of the century. For example, the length of track increased from 4,600 miles in 1848 to 13,600 miles in 1870. In the same period travelling conditions were improved with the introduction of better signalling and braking equipment, steel instead of iron lines, sleeping cars, and the replacement of the old open third class carriages by covered ones with more comfortable seats. From a relatively early stage, the railway had been a democratic form of transport, for in 1844 an Act had been passed which created the 'Parliamentary Train'. Railway companies were obliged to provide one train each day, running in both directions along each line, which had to stop at all stations and carry third class passengers for 1d per mile. As more lines were built and competition grew keen, the railway companies began to lower their fares to attract more passengers, to provide more excursion trains at weekends, holidays, and special occasions, and, from the 1870s, to attach more third class carriages to trains. Excursions and cheap third class tickets brought occasional journeys to the sea, country, large town, or special event within the reach of many maidservants and factory hands who had not been able to afford to travel for pleasure before. Some of the rural working classes who travelled by train bought one-way tickets to town and made their homes and new lives there; those already established in towns could enjoy the pleasant scenery and clean air of the countryside on their days off. For most working-class people, travelling was still something special, but it was no longer beyond the bounds of possibility, no longer a miracle, and journeys over the horizon, previously undertaken only by the wealthy and adventurous, came within the reach of large numbers of people.

Railway expansion fostered the development of the suburbs around large towns where many white-collar workers found homes. Some suburbs developed as distinctive railway communities. These were nucleated settlements which had the station as a core and which expanded to the limit of walking distance all around it. The station, the creator and centre of the community, attracted retailing and service establishments, while the residential section grew up beyond this commercial nucleus. Although the edges of its old nucleated community are now blurred by later developments, Surbiton provides a good example of this pattern. Charles Booth, in *Life and Labour of the People in London*, which he compiled in the 1890s and which was published as a multi-volume survey at the turn of the century, described Loughborough Junction, an inner suburban area heavily influenced by the railway:

> . . . nowhere have the possibilities of locomotion a greater effect upon the character of the population than here. There is an all night service of trains, and the tired compositor . . . returning to his home, encounters the meat salesman as he goes forth to work . . . there are Covent Garden Market men, signal men and railway porters from Snow Hill, who all keep unusual hours, while West End shop assistants, Board School teachers, and City clerks go in and out in the ordinary way. (*Life and Labour*, ser. 3, v. 6, 50.)

In suburbs such as these, which grew up around the station, the railway was woven into the whole social fabric and dictated the broad outline of the lives of the inhabitants.

While railway building benefited people who could afford to live in the suburbs, it was often detrimental to the poorer sections of society. The building of lines and stations in the centres of already established towns and cities involved the clearing of much slum property. While slum clearance was generally desirable, it was of no immediate benefit to the poor who had lived in the slums which were cleared, because no attempt was made to re-house them, and they could not afford to move to the new suburbs the railways created. The people who lived in urban slums did so from necessity, not from choice. They could not afford better housing, and when they were displaced they simply moved to other slum areas where rents were low and added to the overcrowding there. Railway travel was a necessity for some people, a joyous adventure for others, but life beside the line, even in the suburbs, was a pleasure for no one. Passing trains were dirty and noisy, a constant irritant in the daily lives of those who lived beside the line. The 'railway age' foreshadowed the 'automobile age' in that it increased mobility, stimulated suburban growth, and forced the less fortunate elements of society to come to terms with the problems of high noise levels and dirty air.

Short- and medium-distance urban road transport advanced with the introduction of horse-drawn omnibus and tram services in many places in the second half of the nineteenth century. The rich had their horses and carriages, the moderately prosperous used railways and omnibuses, but the majority of people still walked wherever they had to go. In both town and country people walked considerable distances as a part of their daily routine. Rural people had always walked, and continued to do so, but the amount and extent of urban walking would be surprising to the modern observer, and probably horrifying if it were suggested that he should regularly undertake such hikes. Many townsmen thought a walk between home and work of half an hour, an hour, or even longer nothing extraordinary. Life was made easier and safer for urban walkers by the more general use of gas lamps in the streets in the second half of the nineteenth century, and some electric lights began to be used by the 1880s.

The penny post, introduced in 1840, was an important addition to the nation's communications facilities. Its immense success was partly due to its cheapness, partly to its being introduced at about the same time as the railway made nationwide rapid delivery possible. Despite the decrease in cost from 1d to $\frac{1}{2}$d in 1880, postal revenues increased 50 per cent in the 1880s, a vivid illustration of increasing volume and success. The post was simple, cheap, reliable, and useful. Young workers away from home could keep in touch with their families, friendships could be sustained through long absences, and the cheap postal service may well have given many people the incentive to learn to read and write or to use and develop the elementary skills they had learned in their short time in school.

The Post Office became more than a mere letter-carrying agency at an early stage. The first telephone exchange connected ten London offices in 1879, and *The Times* forecast a great future for the infant communications service, predicting 'What has been done for ten stations will soon be done for a vast number besides . . . Ease, rapidity, certainty, and privacy of communication are the great advantages which the novel method will secure' (8 September 1879). The introduction of the Post Office Savings Bank in 1861 pointed to the time when the Post Office would become a vital link between government and people and an important part of the welfare state machinery which would deal, for example, with the payment of all kinds of allowances from family allowances to old-age pensions.

The fund of common experience shared by the English people was enriched by each of these developments in transport and communications. More and more people came to accept travel and a wider first-hand knowledge of their own country as a normal part of life, and anyone who cared to do so could find out from their reading a great deal about the rest of the world, other people, and other classes in their own country. Ever larger numbers of people read the same, or similar, things, saw the same books on station bookstalls, read similar news stories at breakfast or on the way to and from work. As a result, many of the differences of experience and knowledge which had always distinguished the social classes began to fade. Obviously, the reading and possession of books, previously a fairly reliable guide to class, could no longer be used as a social yardstick unless hedged with qualifications as to the type of book, binding, and price. Such changes, small as they were individually, in sum began to blur existing social divisions and were among the many developments which began to melt class society into mass society.

THE EXPANSION OF URBAN SOCIETY

Mass society was urban, not rural. In the second half of the nineteenth century, towns became the place where the majority of the people lived, and the social structures urban living fostered inevitably determined the current and future shape of society. By 1891, 72 per cent of the population was urban, and, before the century closed, some urban areas had almost reached the conurbation stage of development, generally regarded as being characteristic of the twentieth century. This was noticeable, for example, in the cases of some northern industrial towns, such as Liverpool and Manchester, whose spreading suburbs were engulfing surrounding towns and villages and almost forming one huge, connected built-up area. The extent and size of the 'typical town' expanded generally. A man of the 1890s who said he lived in a typical town would have had in mind a much larger and more heavily populated area than  a man making the same claim in the 1850s. London continued to outstrip all other towns, as it had for centuries, and remained by far the largest urban area in the country. By the turn of the century, its suburban sprawl was slopping over the Registrar General's official boundary.

Although certain forces and features were common to the growth of all towns, no two exhibited exactly the same growth pattern or grew in exactly the same directions for precisely the same reasons. However, some generalizations can be made without oversimplifying the picture too much. By the second half of the century most town centres housed fewer people than they had in the past, as industrial and commercial establishments took over. Few people chose to live in noisy, dirty town centres, and most people who could afford it moved as far away from the centre as they could. Therefore, at any given time, in any given town, the general residential pattern was for the richest people to live on the outermost fringes of the town, for the poorest, who could afford nothing better, to live closest to the centre, and for the rest to live somewhere between the two extremes. These processes led to the development of a residential and class pattern of concentric rings, like the growth rings of a tree, which was modified by a variety of local geographical and economic forces. The precise pattern of any town was determined by such factors as natural features of the land, the character of industry in the area, the pattern of transport facilities, and the presence of already established communities in the surrounding area.

Industrial and commercial establishments were also growing larger and more complex. The 'typical' industrial unit at the end of the century was, like the typical town, much larger than it had been in 1851. There were fewer of the old-style commercial businesses as the small offices with one or two quill-penned clerks supervised by the owner ran into difficulties and were replaced by larger offices with typists, clerks, accountants, managers, boards of directors, and stockholders. The expansion of towns and improved transport widened the market area available to their central shops, and, to take advantage of this, many central shops began to use more sophisticated and profitable retailing practices. The small shops run by the owner, his family, and an assistant began to go the way of the small factories and offices, while the large department stores began to take a larger share of urban retailing. A similar process operated in almost every urban institution and even affected schools. By the end of the century there were some one- and two-teacher schools still to be found in some towns, but the number of multi-teacher, high-enrolment establishments was large and growing.

As the towns sprawled and the jobs within any one business became more diversified, it became less and less likely that people who worked together would live in the same area. By the end of the century, some members of any group of urban employees were likely to live within walking distance of work while others came in by omnibus or tram from widely scattered areas, and still others came by train. The precise location of their homes depended on the particular town, the kind and character of the transport facilities, and the range of incomes and occupations of the workers in the establishment concerned. Whatever the details of the pattern, its effect was to loosen the bond of community which had tied people together in the past and still continued to do so in rural areas where work area and home area still roughly coincided. Some urban people continued to work with their neighbours even in the twentieth century, but it was less and less likely that they would do so, and this meant that many changes began to develop in old patterns of social relationships. For example, more and more people were likely to have one set of friends at work and another at home. There might be a few people common to both groups, but in many cases they no longer coincided completely and in some cases did not coincide at all. In short, the common society of work and leisure, inevitable in small rural communities, was broken up, and this fragmentation weakened all the social bonds the community had previously possessed. Working companions did not have to know what kind of house a man had, whether or not he had a respectable home, whether he was a regular churchgoer, a habitual drinker, or a wife-beater. The people next door did not have to be told what he did at work or at the office, if he was incompetent, if he was esteemed by his co-workers or shunned by them. With the increasing size of industrial and commercial firms and growing specialization of function, the ties between employers and employees were also weakened. A worker in a large factory might never see his manager, an assistant in a department store catch only rare glimpses of its owner, the board school teacher might never know the members of the board or live in the same district as the children he taught. Many of the threads which had bound people together in a community of interest were weakening and beginning to fray, opening the way for what twentieth-century social commentators would call a sense of alienation, loneliness in a crowd, the 'facelessness' of modern man.

The character of society in the expanding suburbs especially was coloured by this increasing isolation, as well as by the continuing desire of every suburbanite to be a country squire rather than a townsman. Taine observed that

the townsman does everything in his power to cease being a townsman, and tries to find a bit of country in the corner of a town . . . From this derives the plan of immense streets, silent and devoid of shops, in which each house, surrounded by a plot of green, is isolated and contains only a single family. (*Notes*, 220.)

Most suburbanites seemed to be convinced that an Englishman's home should be a castle, but although they built their castles, they could not create the communities to surround and sustain the social life of the castle. Castle-building, therefore, merely created row upon row of red-brick, hedged and fenced social fortresses in which each family was walled off, protected from, and totally independent of its neighbours.

The church, traditionally a unifying element in society, had only a limited effect in the rapidly expanding towns. Many of the new towns had grown up independently of any church, and when churches were built they were generally late-comers, not cornerstones of the community. Many religious groups attempted to bring God to the towns, sending missions into the slums and exhorting the more prosperous suburban dwellers to build churches for themselves. The missionary efforts did produce some positive results; there were some genuine conversions, and a few churches, notably the Methodist, did provide true community centres. Generally, however, the church no longer functioned as a community centre and there was little parallel between parish and community. Certainly few urban churches were social mixing devices, bringing all social classes together around a common focus of faith and local interest.

The pattern of much nineteenth-century social reform was determined by conditions in towns and in the factories which had spawned them. Outbreaks of epidemic disease in the sprawling, unplanned, and insanitary towns sparked off investigations into urban living conditions in the first half of the century and helped generate support for the Public Health Act of 1848. By mid-century some public health provisions were being made in districts which had set up local boards of health under the terms of the 1848 Act, but in 1858 the national co-ordinating Board of Health was dissolved, and for many years public health was left to the civic pride, or panic, of individual towns. One potentially useful piece of legislation was the Torrens Act of 1868, which allowed local authorities to compel owners to improve insanitary dwellings. As was the case with most other such permissive legislation, few local authorities cared to use it. There was more public health reform in the 1870s, the impetus for which came partly from individual towns and partly from Disraeli's 'Ministry of Sewage'. Birmingham, the most notable example of civic progress, made great strides forward between 1873 and 1876 under its mayor, Joseph Chamberlain. In these three years the city was, according to Chamberlain, ' . . . parked, paved, assized, marketed, Gas-and-Watered, and improved—all as a result of three years' active work'. Disraeli's government gave more consolidated power to the local authorities. For example, the Public Health Act of 1875 required them, instead of merely allowing them, to appoint medical officers of health, and the Artisans Dwellings Act of the same year empowered them to pull down slum buildings and to build new housing under certain conditions. Public health reforms were thus introduced, slowly and erratically, but as the century progressed the falling death rate showed that progress was being made. In the 1850s the national death rate was between 21 and 24 deaths per thousand; by the 1890s it had fallen to between 17 and 19 deaths per thousand people. Moreover, this decrease took place at a time when the population was still growing and the towns were continuing to expand, both conditions which would have tended, all other things being equal, to increase the death rate.

The local health and sanitary authorities, in acting as agents of public health reform, also became minor and inadvertent agents of social change. Charged with the task of improving conditions in unhealthy areas, they initially concentrated on the worst ones, not on the prosperous, ratepaying districts. Improvement schemes were inevitably financed by the major ratepayers, many of whom supported the health improvement projects because they realized that diseases such as cholera, which spilled out of the slums, were no respecters of person or class. In improving the worst districts, the local authorities lifted the standard of living of the poor a little by setting and maintaining minimum sanitary standards. Before the local health authorities were established, the working classes had no recourse if repairs or cleaning were needed and the landlord refused to do anything, but the establishment of the authorities gave them new hope. Local government officials were relatively powerful people who could be asked for help, and, although they often did little, they also occasionally effected visible and striking improvements. At the individual level, public health reforms might mean little more than giving up the habit of throwing refuse into the street and forming the new habit of placing it in a dustbin in the confident expectation that the bin would be emptied by the servants of the local authority. Changes such as this were small and mundane, but they did symbolize the fact that the lower classes no longer had to resign themselves absolutely to living in dirt and degradation. In general, the work of the lower authorities began to dissolve the marriage between poverty and filth, whose children were a high death rate, hopelessness and social disgrace.

Social reformers also concerned themselves with the regulation of working conditions in mines and factories. Concern about this began to be expressed in the first half of the century and was originally centred on women and children. A landmark was passed with the Ten Hours Act in 1847, which limited the weaker sections of the labour force—women and juveniles (young people under 18)—to ten hours' work a day and a total of fifty-eight hours a week. The labour of women and young people was a necessary support for the work of men, and so any limitation on the length of their working day affected the working day of the men too. In 1864 the terms of this Act were extended to include some other industries, and the enforcement was made somewhat more effective. In 1878 Disraeli's government passed a consolidating Factory Act, which established regulations for factories and workshops, although many concerns, notably the notorious 'sweatshops' which were the objects of a good deal of public indignation in the 1880s, escaped regulation. Improvements in the mines followed a similar course, the initial concern for the welfare of children and women resulting in a general improvement of hours and conditions for all workers. An important step was taken in 1850 when government inspectors were appointed to see that mine regulations were enforced. The initial shortage of inspectors, poor standards of inspection, and lack of adequate powers were eventually dealt with and enforcement was tightened up. Despite many faults in legislation and enforcement, it was quite clear that by the end of the 1870s the state had assumed some responsibility for regulating the hours and conditions of a large number of the people. In 1880 the Employers Liability Act recognized the responsibility of employers for insuring workers against the risks of their occupations. Again, there were many exempted occupations and laxity of enforcement, but this was a sign that henceforth the state expected employers to be responsible for the prevention of occupational hazards.

By the end of the century government itself, at both national and local levels, was becoming a major employer and as such was taking a lead in the improvement of working conditions. For example, by the end of the century the 10-hour day had gained general acceptance and the 8-hour day was the next goal of many labour leaders. Between 1889 and 1897 the 8-hour day was adopted in over 500 establishments including almost all municipal gasworks and government dockyards and workshops. In its various capacities as legislator, as enforcer of statutes, and as employer, the government was already one of the workers' best allies in their fight for better conditions.

EXPANDING EDUCATION

A little learning may or may not be a dangerous thing, but it has certainly proven to be a social solvent. In simple agrarian societies an individual can survive, even prosper, with the skills passed down the generations and a little native wit. In an industrial society more highly technical skills are necessary not only for earning a living but also for gaining social prestige. When industry matures into a more complex stage, the old skills become outdated and the untaught individual becomes as helpless as a child. Even if the uneducated individual can find work, it will certainly be poorly paid and carry only the lowest social status. Hence education is a necessary qualification for full membership in an industrial society, and the more sophisticated the industrial system and the more complex the society, the more necessary is education.

Elementary education first aroused official interest, for it was here that the most basic and obvious needs lay. The national government took its first halting, rather feeble, actions to aid education in the 1830s when it began to give small grants to religious educational societies and attached education clauses to the early Factory Acts. In all too many cases, factory 'schools' either did not exist in practice or were merely rest periods for tired young workers, but by the 1850s government inspectors were returning more encouraging reports, maintaining that some good was coming from the education clauses. In 1862 the 'payment by results' system was introduced for schools receiving government grants in an attempt to ensure that the nation would benefit from the investment. Standards of attainment for children of various ages were established, and teachers were paid according to pupil attendance and the number of children who met the required standard. This system reduced the costs of education a little, but was much criticized because it encouraged teachers to mass-produce large numbers of minimally trained students. Once the brighter children had learned enough to pass a test, they were left to their own devices or to help other children, while the teacher coaxed, bullied, or beat the slower children into learning their quota. Pupils had no incentive to learn and teachers none to teach anything beyond the required minimum; for bright children school became a trial by boredom; for slow children it became a place of pressure, if not constant terror. Children who could not pass the test were often spirited away to other schools on inspection days, and attendance books were often altered to bolster the salaries of teachers. This stultifying mechanical system lasted for thirty years and made school almost as much a blight as a blessing for generations of pupils and teachers. Even after the system was abandoned, the ghosts of the principles behind it lingered on into the twentieth century in the shape of a system of secondary school and university entrance qualifications based on public examinations.

In 1858 a Royal Commission produced a complacent Report on the state of education and noted with satisfaction that about one in every eight children attended some kind of day school, although only about 40 per cent of the children enrolled in grant-aided schools were in school more than 176 days each year. However, other people were not so content with the state of education. Some manufacturers held that a little education seemed to make better workers, workers who could read notices, lists, and instructions and who seemed to take a greater interest in their work, although they were often also more active in demanding better pay and conditions. By the later 1860s a few people were beginning to worry about foreign competition, and to feel that other nations that had, among other things, better popular education than England, were taking the lead in technical innovation. These people believed that it would be good for the country if the government provided for a more effective and complete system of national basic education. The Reform Act of 1867 introduced another element into the education question by expanding the franchise to give household suffrage in urban constituencies. With this expansion, politicians faced the prospect of having to woo an electorate which included a large number of illiterate and under-educated people, and, having given them the vote, many decided to support the campaign to give them a basic education. All these forces combined to produce the support necessary for the passage of the Forster Education Act in 1870.

The Act, named after its sponsor, William Forster, provided for the division of the country into school districts, each of which was to have an elementary education system adequate for the needs of its population. Where existing religious schools provided too few facilities, a school board with the power to levy rates to pay for more schools was to be elected. The local boards were given the power to waive fees and require school attendance at their discretion. The controversial issue of religious instruction in the new secular schools was solved by an uneasy compromise which required that religious education be given but also required that it be non-sectarian. This Act, often hailed as a great stride forward in the development of a national education system, was a compromise document with many weaknesses. Much that should have been mandatory was left to the discretion of the individual school boards, and primary education was not, in fact, made compulsory until the passage of another Act in 1880.

Although the Forster Act was an important step towards the formation of a system of national compulsory education, it did not create a new system, and the education of the masses received no great boost in the 1870s. National literacy statistics in the Census Reports have certain limitations. They refer to people married in the year concerned, who were deemed literate if they signed their name in the register instead of making a mark. The definition of 'literacy' is, therefore, very limited and, furthermore, the statistics refer only to the marriageable age range of the population. The 'literacy' level of the population as a whole was probably lower than they suggest.

*Literate population of England and Wales*
*as a percentage of the total population*

| Year | Males | Females | Year | Males | Females |
|------|-------|---------|------|-------|---------|
| 1851 | 69.3 | 54.8 | 1881 | 86.5 | 82.3 |
| 1861 | 75.4 | 65.3 | 1891 | 93.6 | 92.7 |
| 1871 | 80.6 | 73.2 | 1901 | 97.2 | 96.8 |

(Registrar General's Returns, from Altick, *Reader*, 171.)

Despite their shortcomings, the literacy figures do suggest several interesting points about education in the second half of the nineteenth century. First, the literacy rate was rising before the Forster Act came into operation, and there was no great acceleration in the rate of increase in the 1870s. The Act can be seen, therefore, less as a startling innovation than as a mopping-up operation which brought educational opportunities to children who had so far been denied them. Had the Act not been passed, the steady climb of the literacy rate might have slowed down or stopped towards the end of the century and the increasing social mobility that education tended to promote would have been reduced. Second, the figures show that although the female literacy rate was initially well below that of males, they were almost equal by 1901. This suggests that in the early and middle years of the century girls received less education than boys, while by the end of the century they received more or less the same basic education. This change points to both the mid-century subordinate status of women and to the relationship between education and economic and social advancement. Boys were better educated than girls because parents assumed that boys would eventually have to support a family, whereas girls would marry and be supported by their husbands. The money available for education was naturally spent on boys, who needed it to boost their adult economic and social status. The rapid increase in the female literacy rate came in the same half-century as the expansion of respectable female employment and the beginning of the female emancipation movement, lending further support to the idea that education was a basic requirement for full membership of a complex industrial society.

Since there was no state-supported secondary education at this time, few of the lower classes had much more than a simple primary education. The institutions of higher learning open to them were few and usually poor. For example, Mechanics' Institutes, of which there were 610 in England in 1850, were originally intended to be educational institutions, but by the end of the century the few that survived had virtually abandoned their educational functions and resigned themselves to being social clubs. Some middle- and upper-class charitable institutions and individuals organized lecture courses, generally short-lived, for workers. Workers whose thirst for learning was so great as to sustain them through hours of sitting on hard chairs in their best clothes after work in some sombre hall could hear talks on such topics as 'On the apparent contradictions in chemistry', 'Principles of English liberty historically considered', 'Hamlet' and 'On explosive compounds'. Few of the topics were suitable for people with only a very rudimentary education whose paramount need was for training and information of a more basic and pragmatic kind. Some workers had a good deal of self-education, and many were probably given the incentive to learn when they came under informal, but practical, pressures to do so. The desire to read popular newspapers and magazines and the need to write to absent relatives and friends may well have given some people the incentive to learn to read and write, and increasing opportunities in lower-grade white-collar jobs may have increased this drive. By the latter part of the century it was becoming fairly clear that economic status could be improved by education, and awareness of this must have generated some new demands from people who were previously indifferent.

The nature and value of education and the wisdom of extending it to the lower classes had long been debated, and in the latter part of the nineteenth century the debate continued. Some people felt that the downward extension of education would act as a social stabilizer by transmitting the values of the ruling classes down to the ruled. This idea worked to some extent. School board members and teachers were generally drawn from middle-class ranks, and the values they consciously or unconsciously imparted to their charges were also middle class. Other people feared that increasing popular education led to moral decay and pointed out that the newly literate working classes were gleefully reading penny dreadfuls instead of 'literature' and were being exposed to 'undesirable' and 'unsuitable' subjects through their reading of popular newspapers.

Middle- and upper-class children, especially boys, generally did receive some formal secondary education, and in this respect the educational system ran in parallel with and reinforced the existing class and socio-economic structures. The traditional secondary education institutions, the grammar and public schools, could not keep pace with the increasing demand for secondary education in the second half of the century. By the mid-1870s the civil service qualifying examinations and the entrance examinations for the professions, the armed services, and the universities had produced a battery of seventeen examinations from which a boy could choose. To provide training for these examinations many new private schools were established, ranging from the good but expensive to the relatively cheap which simply ground out low-grade exam-passers. Tradesmen and artisans who were ambitious for their sons often made tremendous efforts and great sacrifices to scrape together school fees so that the next generation could have the opportunity to leap the educational barriers and enter the promised land of the white-collar workers or lower middle classes. Established middle-class families also strove, at a more expensive level, to buy their male heirs a respectable education, for this brought with it such economically and socially useful assets as influential friends, contacts, and polished manners.

FEMALES AND FAMILIES

Better education, easier travel, and more openings for respectable female employment meant that by the 1890s female emancipation was becoming an increasingly serious social issue. The single most important step in the direction of increasing freedom for women was their achievement of economic independence through the exercise of their own earning capacity. As long as there were no 'respectable' jobs for women, they were tied to home and family, and their very dependence perpetuated the myth of their subservience and innate inferiority. During and after the 1870s, the social barriers against respectable female employment began to weaken as the range of jobs available widened and as more 'ladies' took them. Female typists were employed in ever-increasing numbers, trained nurses played a vital role in the improvement of medical practice, the new board schools hired women teachers, in the 1880s the lower ranks of the civil service were opened to women—especially in the Post Office—and the new department stores offered employment of a marginally respectable kind. It was still not common for respectable females to work, even by the end of the century, but it was possible for them to do so and to become economically self-sufficient without losing respectable status. By the close of the century the doors of institutions of higher learning were beginning to open a little to allow a few women a restricted glimpse inside. Advances towards legal equality included the setting up of the Divorce Court in 1857 and the passage of Married Women's Property Acts from the 1870s on. Before these Acts were passed the control of a woman's property passed to her husband on marriage, an ironic reversal of the property pledges of the marriage service. With the passage of the various Property Acts women gradually acquired more legal control over their own property and, by implication, a little more control over their own destiny.

Better education and, above all, the availability of respectable employment inevitably meant the disappearance of many of the old patterns of life which went with the traditional female role. Obviously, a girl who lived in the suburbs and went to work every day by train could not always be accompanied by some guardian or male protector. Sheer practicality forced working women to break the old taboos on travelling alone, and this in turn opened the way for married women to travel without an escort. The number of ladies travelling alone had become so large by the late 1880s that in 1888 the Great Western Railway introduced ladies-only compartments. In the latter part of the century, too, outdoor sports became more popular. A social code which presupposed that females were delicate creatures with weak constitutions was incompatible with their participation in such sports as bicycling, tennis, rowing, and cricket. Many respectable ladies were determined to pursue their sporting interests, and the old social code had to give to allow them to do so. Ladies joined gentlemen in many leisure-time activities, and the inevitable relaxation of established formal patterns of behaviour and address under the pressures of competition tended to persist after the game, which helped promote a generally less oppressively formal social atmosphere. The practicalities of work and play helped change fashions of dress. Discounting passing fads, the general trend in this period was for women's clothes to become simpler. The stiff, billowing clothing which had been tolerable and even appropriate when women were mere ornaments was just not practical for a more active life of work or sports, and as women became more active clothing came to reflect their new role by allowing for more freedom and comfort.

White-collar employment offered respectable women an acceptable alternative to marriage as a means of economic support. While there was no wholesale rejection of marriage by women, the mere fact that an alternative now existed was bound to affect the character and status of matrimony. For example, the ability of respectable ladies to support themselves dealt a great blow to the notion that the family was the one and only economic, and hence social, survival unit. Existing social codes revolved, to a great extent, round the focal point of the family, and therefore any change in its functions, or attitudes to them, was bound to affect social patterns.

Two other blows which fell upon the traditional middle-class family ideal were the development and increasing use of effective methods of contraception and a rise in the level of material ambitions and expectations. These new forces contributed to a decline in the size of the socially acceptable family which began in the 1870s and 80s, when respectable people began to have fewer children than in the past. The sustained fall in the infant death rate in the latter half of the nineteenth century meant that it was no longer necessary to 'over-produce' children to be sure of having some descendants after disease and death had taken their toll. As women found more interesting things to do outside the home and came to enjoy more freedom, many of them were less inclined to spend such an overwhelmingly large proportion of their active adult lives in husband-chasing and child-bearing and rearing. In the last part of the century the marriage rate began to fall a little, as was evident in London, for example, from the 1870s on. This may have been due in part to an 'older' population or to changes in economic pressures, but it did suggest that slightly less emphasis was being placed on marriage than in the past. The decline in family size was first evident among the middle classes who, at mid-century, had been the stoutest upholders of the idea that the family was the fount of all earthly joys. In the 1870s, at a time when family limitation became a really practical proposition thanks to more effective contraception, middle-class prosperity began to falter, while at the same time the number of material status symbols proliferated and a man came to expect, and to be expected, to reach solid economic and social ground before he married. While the economic position of the middle classes was becoming increasingly shaky and the whole fabric of their social life was being pulled by new strains, real wages were continuing to rise, bringing the additional danger of upward social pressure from below. One of the products of this complex series of shifts and social pressures was the re-ordering of priorities. Faced with a choice of maintaining their social position and fulfilling rising material expectations, or the production of a large family and the acceptance of relative material poverty and social decline, many middle-class families chose higher living standards and paid for them with the economies a smaller family made possible.

The declining marriage and birth rates were both symptoms and causes of the changing role of the family. The profusion of social functions of the mid-century ideal family could not be fulfilled by the smaller family unit, and the smaller the family unit became, the less central was its role in social life. The rearing of a small family took less time—fewer hours each day and a shorter proportion of the life-span of the parents—and smaller families produced fewer relatives who had to be visited and cared for. The shrinking of the family sector of social life left more time for other pursuits outside the home and also led to a greater emphasis being placed on the quality, rather than the quantity, of family interpersonal relationships.

CHANGING PATTERNS OF SOCIAL LIFE

The role and status of the church, that other pillar of respectable mid-century society, also changed in the second half of the nineteenth century. Apart from brief and restricted flares of activity such as the Oxford Movement and the founding of slum missions, the churches showed little dynamism in the second half of the century, a time when they needed all the vigour they could muster if new challenges were to be met. Intellectual developments either contradicted the teachings of the church, as did Darwin's work, discounted it, as in the case of Marx, or simply ignored it, as did the work of the increasingly influential body of scientists. Some churches reacted by condemning all scientists and thinkers and thus alienated large segments of the educated population; others seemed caught in a paralysis of indecision. In the main, the churches found no effective means of responding to challenges and continued along well-established lines of missionizing and moralizing, activities which appealed to ever-smaller segments of the population. The religious compromise of the Forster Education Act ensured that all children had some religious education, but its compulsory and non-sectarian nature helped make bland passivity seem a major part of the Christian ethic. All too many children found that 'school religion' consisted of morning assembly, with its hymn, prayer, and school notices, and religious instruction classes in which they learned to recite the Lord's Prayer, read the books of the Bible, and draw an interminable number of maps of the journeys of St Paul. The materialism which contributed to declining family size also helped reduce church attendance. As possessions and economic standing assumed a greater importance as status symbols, church attendance was no longer such a necessary part of the process of keeping or gaining social status. As the years passed, clergymen increasingly bemoaned the absence of the 'godless middle classes' from their congregations. As congregations shrank, collections grew smaller, and the respect accorded to the local parson began to fade, fewer able and ambitious men were inclined to make their career in the church. As this downward spiral continued, the churches became more and more debilitated and less capable of keeping up with, let alone taking advantage of, the ever-increasing pace of social change.

The enfeeblement of the churches led to a decline in Sabbatarianism, which was accelerated by the expanding range of attractive alternative Sunday occupations. Maidservants, artisans, office-workers, even members of the middle classes, found it much more pleasant to indulge in rural frolics at weekends than to go to church. At weekends the townsmen began to return to the country, picnicking, painting, or 'rambling' for pleasure along paths their rural grandfathers had walked of necessity. The more daring and youthful members of both sexes enjoyed the fresh air from the height of their bicycles. As the century drew to a close, the weekend exodus of people to the countryside swelled, and more and more people came to sing their secular Sunday hymns of praise to the joys of the open air, exercise, and rural beauty. The foundation of the National Trust in 1875 symbolized the growing awareness of the countryside and rural monuments and testified to a desire to preserve the better parts of the past and present for the future.

Rural recreational activities were not the only ways in which a new joy in physical health and exercise was expressed. Outdoor sports of all kinds became very popular: the rules of Association Football were formulated in 1863, the Rugby Union was founded in 1871, the rules of lawn tennis were finally revised to form the basis for the modern game by 1877, and the Hercules of cricket, W. G. Grace, played his legendary games between 1870 and 1886. It is significant that these sports began to become popular in the last three decades or so of the century and that in their 'modern' form they were undeniably mass sports. Although they could be enjoyed in the countryside, and cricket on the village green was regarded by some people as the most enjoyable form of the game, these outdoor sports, unlike the more traditional ones such as hunting and fishing, were sports which could be enjoyed by townsmen. They were the sports of mass man and also spectator sports which allowed even the weakest and least graceful individual to enjoy the vicarious thrills of physical expertise. Attending important matches contributed to the enjoyment of those who actively participated in these sports in their leisure time and gave an additional edge to street-corner football with half-brick goals, and to cricket matches with piled coats for wickets and a board bat.

In the second half of the nineteenth century English society began to take on a slightly more homogeneous appearance. In its last decades the people began to look more alike. Fewer farmworkers wore traditional smocks, and more began to work in shirt, jacket, and trousers; except among miners, boots began to replace the traditional clogs of urban workers; more working-class women wore hats or scarves instead of shawls, and fewer of their children went about without shoes. More people travelled on a regular or occasional basis; more people were literate and better informed. The growing number of white-collar workers began to blur the lines of social distinction between the middle and working classes. There were more opportunities for respectable women to gain the financial independence which formed the practical groundwork for the female emancipation movement and brought them a degree of social freedom which was closer to that which their working-class sisters had, of necessity, long enjoyed.

Old distinctions of behaviour which had been used to characterize class groupings in the past were being eroded as people came to behave in more similar ways. For example, many mid-century social observers had commented on the number of drunkards in the streets and had deplored the drunken ways of the lower classes; near the end of the

century similar observers were noting the decline in public drunkenness and commenting on the improved behaviour of the lower classes
in this respect. At mid-century the middle classes were, by and large,
church-going while the lower classes were not; by the end of the
century clergymen were sighing over their declining middle-class
congregations. These two examples illustrate the ways in which the
middle and lower classes were beginning to move closer to a common
behavioural pattern. Class distinctions were still deeply marked and
there were very many differences between the classes, but the important fact remains that the differences and distinctions were becoming
less, not more, socially significant.

Meanwhile, the cities continued to grow and to house an ever-
larger proportion of the population. By the end of the century almost
80 per cent of the people were townsmen, and most of them were
town-born, children of the streets, not of the fields. Despite the growth
of towns, the conditions of town life had improved. Most town-
dwellers, whatever their class, began to expect minimally decent
sanitary facilities, including access to piped, fairly clean water, regular
rubbish collection, and clean streets and yards. 'King cholera' was
dead, and even the occasional walks of his ghost struck little real terror
any more. Dark and dangerous streets became fewer as the ordered
army of street lamps advanced into all parts of town, making life safer
for the law-abiding citizen and more difficult for the thief. Inequalities
and injustices, poverty, misery, dirt, and darkness continued to exercise their social tyranny, but new champions were emerging who
would begin a new campaign in the war against them. There were
many symptoms of social disturbance, including continued emigra-
tion, a growing jingoism in opinions about the Empire, the selfconscious flaunting of established social codes by some of the upper classes
in the 'naughty nineties', and concern about the economy, but some
symptoms of disturbance were inevitable at a time when so many
aspects of national social life were beginning to change and to suggest
the shapes they would assume in the twentieth century.

In the latter part of the nineteenth century, too, some people began
to re-evaluate social objectives. A few reforming measures were passed
between the mid-seventies and the end of the century, but the last
two-and-a-half decades were a slack period for social reform legislation. By the mid-seventies virtually all that could be done, according
to the assumptions of the great nineteenth-century reformers, had
been done. Cities had been cleaned and improved, hours and conditions of work improved in many occupations, the political system had

been dragged over the threshold of modern life by the great Reform Acts, and an elementary education system had been established. In short, the work of nineteenth-century utilitarianism and evangelicalism had been pretty well accomplished. Between the end of this phase of social reform and the opening of the twentieth-century collectivist phase was a period of gestation in which little legislation was produced while new philosophies of reform were being developed and changes made in the assumptions on which social reformers based their plans.

In the last two decades of the century surveys were being made and information published which helped build up a body of new material on which a new kind of social conscience would grow. Many of the most stimulating investigations and reports of these years were made by individuals and groups who were more interested in social justice than in utilitarian principles. The investigators included Charles Booth, who conducted the survery for *Life and Labour of the People in London* between 1886 and the end of the century; Sidney and Beatrice Webb, Fabian socialists who were responsible for massive and detailed research into the background of many nineteenth-century social and administrative problems; and the Fabian Society, the intellectual arms of socialism, which published a good deal of evidence of social injustice together with some propaganda and many proposals for reform in the *Fabian Tracts*.

In the 1870s and early 1880s some social critics portrayed the English working man as docile and apathetic, hardly likely to change the social framework in which he lived. Some critics concluded that the downward transmission of middle-class values had worked all too well and that the workers were simply paler, poorer copies of the middle classes. In the later 1880s and in the 1890s, however, working men did begin to take a more active interest in movements such as socialism and trade unionism which, through their interest in the life, work, and status of the working classes, looked towards further social change. The friendly society and co-operative movements, after a slow and often erratic start, had become relatively powerful by the end of the 1880s. By then the 32,000-odd friendly societies with nearly seven million members who paid an annual average contribution of 5s each had accumulated enormous gross assets. Co-operation, an early concept of utopian socialism which had had only a limited success in Robert Owen's own time, grew rapidly in popularity in the latter part of the century after the formation of the national co-ordinating organization, the Cooperative Wholesale Society. The value of the annual net sales of this organization, which had been £52,000 soon after its foundation in 1864, came to over £11,500,000 in 1874.

In 1871 the Trades Union Act gave unions sufficient legal status to enable them to function effectively, and the 1870s saw the formation of a new type of trade union comprised of semi-skilled and unskilled workers. Distinguished from the older unions by the lower level of skill and pay of their members and their lower subscription rates, such unions included the Tea Porters and General Labourers Union, formed in 1887, and the Gas Workers and General Labourers Union, formed in 1889. The formation of new unions and the increase in work stoppages in the last two decades of the century indicated that more workers were becoming interested in fighting for better pay and conditions and that the unions were becoming increasingly militant. Skilled workers had earlier formed unions and attempted strikes, with little success, but by the end of the century semi-skilled and unskilled workers, such as dockers and match-girls, were striking for better conditions. Many working days were lost in strikes, 30,440,000 in 1893 alone, and the prevention of these stoppages came to be seen as one of the most serious problems facing industry.

This burst of labour activity was the product of so many social and political changes that it is difficult to single out one cause, or even one general set of causes, as being responsible for it. One explanation has been that the 'depression' stimulated unskilled workers to organize for their own protection and to strike for their own betterment by demonstrating to them that they were the first group to suffer in hard times. The simplicity of this explanation is appealing but there is no evidence to support it. This 'depression' was, in industry and trade, a crisis of confidence and a stagnation of profit which hurt the middle class most, not a slump of falling production and increasing unemployment. Employment did fluctuate and there were some short-term falls in real wages, but between 1850 and the mid-1890s the income and standard of living of the working classes improved considerably, and life was better for most workers in the 1880s and early 1890s than it had been in the past when there had been little union activity. Real wages rose from an index value of about 120 points in 1870 to about 175 by the end of the century, an increase of nearly one-third within thirty years (see fig. 3). Any explanation of increased worker activity based on the idea that the workers were rebelling against the adverse economic effects of the 'depression' will not, therefore, fit the facts.

The reasons for the increase in agitation certainly must be sought in improving, not deteriorating, working-class conditions. The cliché that it is not the really oppressed, downtrodden, and suffering who revolt but those who have begun to enjoy a few improvements in their standard of living fits this case. By the late 1870s and the 1880s the worst evils of the early stages of industrialism had been removed, and some of the benefits of industry had begun to seep down to the masses since 1850. By the end of the century many of them had tasted enough of the fruits of relative prosperity to make them desire more, while their social and economic advances had given some of them the confidence and the money to sustain short strikes in support of their higher levels of expectation. Thus increasing labour activity, the expansion of unionism and the growth of socialism bore little relationship to the 'depression', except perhaps in that the precise timing of some of the agitation may have been determined by short-run economic fluctuations. They were more closely related to, or 'caused by', rising real wages, improved living and working conditions, the stronger legal position of the unions, more education and information, the extension of the franchise, and the host of other social changes described in this chapter. The labour disturbances were progress pains, a social blemish created by processes of maturing and improvement, much like the scab that forms over a healing abrasion. It was at this time that the working classes really began to associate agitation, unionism, and government legislation with their own living standards, and this association was one which would help determine much of the shape of English society in the twentieth century.

# Chapter 4    The Edwardian Years

The years between the turn of the century and the outbreak of the First World War were years of confusion and contradiction, years when, as H. G. Wells wrote in *Tono Bungay* in 1908,'. . . all the organising ideas have slackened, the old habitual bonds have relaxed or altogether come undone'. The gold and the glory of the nineteenth-century Empire lingered; the monarchy and aristocracy were more news-worthy, if more scandalous, than in the days of the old Queen; London was still the financial capital of the world; Britannia, from the bridge of a Dreadnought, still ruled the waves. There were, however, omens of changes to come: economic problems continued; foreign competition grew more intense and threats and fears of war mounted; violence spread at home; socialism gathered strength from a new awareness of poverty and social injustice; the nineteenth-century political system seemed to be succumbing to a creeping paralysis. National expenditure rose as spending on social services and arma-ments increased; real wages began to fall, and this combined with a variety of other forces to produce serious unrest and a number of strikes. Moving towards political maturity, the working classes showed an increasing determination to use their franchise for their own bene-fit, and the growth of the Labour Party, which had 42 members in the Commons by 1914, added to the disruption of the established two-party system. A strange tension built up, often marked by hysteria and irrationality, which culminated in the outburst of exhilaration and relief which greeted the declaration of war in 1914.

The relative economic decline which began in the 1870s deepened as competitor nations began to develop new industries which England had neglected. Nevertheless, the economy was still sound enough to produce an interlude of prosperity between 1909 and 1913, which suggested that the battle was not yet lost and that with some effort a new phase of economic success might begin. There was a strong feeling that readjustments were necessary, that a change was due and already in the air. As *The Times* stated (23 January 1901),

Others have learned our lessons and bettered our instructions
while we have been too easily contented to rely upon the methods
which were effective a generation or two ago . . . The command
of natural forces that made us great and rich has been superseded
by newer discoveries and methods, and we have to open what
may be called a new chapter.

The Astronomer Royal declared that the new century began in
1901, not 1900, and Victoria, almost precisely on this official cue, died
a few days after the century that her reign had dominated. The simultaneous demise of the old century and its figurehead gave a sharper
edge to the ruminations about the past and the apprehension about
the future which the passing of any chronological milestone seems
to produce. Some people were optimistic, feeling that change had to
come and that the clean sheet afforded by a new century and a new
monarch would aid its coming. Other people sensed change in the air
but were apprehensive rather than heartened.

Even before the death of Victoria, changes were evident in the upper
ranks of society. Many people had felt for some time that the old
social standards of morality and the old philosophy, with its ration-
alism, evangelicalism, and utilitarianism, were out of date. By the turn
of the century formal social codes had become ossified, values had
been replaced by mere observations of form, and behind this façade
society was already changing. Some indication of the direction the
changes were taking had been given in the 'naughty nineties', a decade
in which many people from the upper levels of society had been
almost selfconsciously decadent by Victorian standards. The new
monarch, Edward VII, seemed to promise a genuine relaxation in
formal standards because, as Prince of Wales, he had been a leading
figure in the hedonistic movement. He had reacted against his overly
strict upbringing by embarking on a life of pleasure in adulthood. In
the early 1870s, when divorce was still far from respectable, he was
involved in a divorce case; his affair with Lily Langtry was public knowledge; his weekend parties contrasted sharply with the strict Sabba-
tarian practices of his mother. He was, nevertheless, dignified on
official occasions and became an impressive and popular king. Those
of his people who were ready for a relaxation of formal standards of
social behaviour welcomed his easy-going, good-natured self-indul-
gence. After all, 'affairs' had always existed at all social levels, many
people enjoyed gambling and horse racing, and the majority of the
people had not gone to church even in the 'good old days'. Edward's

more relaxed way of life brought him closer to his subjects because, as *The Times* (7 May 1910) said on Edward's death,

> They liked to see him taking his pleasure with a zest greater than their own. As sportsmen themselves, they were pleased to have a Sovereign who had won three Derbys . . . They liked to have a King who . . . looked after his estates and his tenants, bred and exhibited prize cattle, and shot his pheasants and partridges like other country gentlemen.

Edward's popularity rested on his combination of humanity with monarchy in the best traditions of lusty, wenching, sporting, but dignified English kingship.

The aristocrats were still rulers of society and retained their political power until 1911, but their shibboleths were changing. In the mid-nineteenth century when it had been possible to rise from humble beginning to considerable wealth, wealth alone could not be relied upon as a mark of the highest social distinction, and many aristocrats had therefore stressed birth and lineage as necessary additional qualifications for admission into their ranks. With the depression in agriculture and the stagnation in profits from industry, new fortunes became rare, and so wealth became the privilege of the few. As it became scarcer, wealth was more heavily emphasized and displayed by the upper ranks of society; this was an age of expensive horses, yachts, and motor cars. The great industrialists and traders who could afford the expensive, prestigious toys were accepted by the few who had the equipment to play the game and were allowed to join it. The 'beerage' had arrived, as far as 'society' was concerned, as had rich Americans. The Victorians had patronized Americans; the Edwardians accepted the wealthy ones and even admired them, maintaining, for example, that American women were more attractive and wittier than English ones. Whether or not this was true, the fortunes of many an aristocratic family were certainly improved by the marriage of a son to an attractive, wealthy American girl who was charmed by the prestige of a title and rich enough to support it in grand style. The aristocracy recognized the economic realities of life and, of necessity, became 'Americanized' long before the middle and lower classes.

These changes in social standards brought no social levelling, and class distinctions were as sharp as they had ever been. The upper ranks of society simply adjusted the bases on which they made class assessments—wealth was much more important and all else was much less important than it had been in the past. As the 'society' magazine,

*Queen*, said, 'There is only one society sin nowadays—that is to be poor' (quoted in Crewe, *Privilege*, 93). H. G. Wells commented on the increasing social importance of money in the upper social ranks in his account of the life of the hero in *Tono Bungay* with his uncle and aunt.

> We became part of what is nowadays quite an important element in the confusion of our world, that multitude of economically ascendant people who are learning how to spend money. It is made up of financial people, the owners of businesses that are eating up their competitors, investors in new sources of wealth . . . it includes nearly all America as one sees it on the European stage.

These new, rich, social climbers 'discover suddenly indulgences their moral code never foresaw and has no provisions for, elaborations, ornaments, possessions beyond their wildest dreams' (225).

The living standards of the mass of the people at this time were much better than they had been in the mid-nineteenth century. For example, by the end of the first decade of the twentieth century the average consumption of fruit, vegetables other than potatoes, eggs, and meat was higher than it had ever been before. The average consumption of meat between 1903 and 1913 was one-third higher than it had been in 1881, and the consumption of tea had more than quadrupled since the mid-nineteenth century. Nevertheless, the social reformers were busy re-defining social standards and they emphasized the relative poverty of the mass of the people. Despite the social changes of the previous half-century, which had begun to narrow the gaps between classes, the gulf between the rich and the poor seemed to yawn wider in these years because relative wealth and relative poverty were increasingly visible on both sides. However astute the hindsight assessment of long-term trends by historians, contemporary opinion, if not always more accurate, is always more influential in effecting social changes in the period concerned. Many contemporaries at this time were pointing to social gulfs and emphasizing the still miserable conditions in which the majority of Englishmen lived. For example, in 1902 Sir Frederick Maurice stated that 60 per cent of the male population was unfit for military service, a statement later supported by the Army Medical Service; social surveys suggested that almost one-third of the population was living at starvation level. Although the poor were much better off than they had been, standards of expectation had risen and the social reformers of the early twentieth century were in the process of raising the generally accepted standard of what was socially desirable, tolerable, and just. They were anxious to define and delimit social problems and propose new ways of solving them, and so they stressed the many inequalities and injustices, not slim degrees of improvement, hence the apparent increase in poor conditions and social inequality in these years.

The changes in the criteria of social assessment which had begun to be made in the last years of the nineteenth century started to bear fruit in the early years of the twentieth. Undesirable conditions which traditionalists saw as side-effects of poverty and personal incapacity the new reformers saw as the direct results of faulty social arrangements. The nineteenth-century social reformers had been concerned mainly with the ending of the waste of human resources, with economy, and with the humanitarian treatment of women and children. The new reformers were more concerned with social justice and the human rights to decent living conditions and a fairly secure life. Mere survival and the physical ability to work were not considered adequate bases for a satisfactory life by the new reformers who maintained that all people were entitled to a minimally decent life. They were concerned not with the moral virtues of work but with the social sins of unequally distributed wealth. An important difference between the old and the new reformers was that the new insisted on a much higher base level of tolerable living conditions: they wanted the people to have a general level of life which would support human dignity, not just simple animal survival.

The utilitarian philosophies which had influenced nineteenth-century social reform were replaced by the more socialistic philosophies which were to colour twentieth-century social reform. This new approach was implicit in such works as Booth's survey of London, Rowntree's study of York, and Sir Leo Chiozza Money's *Riches and Poverty* published in 1905, which clearly pointed out the unequal distribution of national income and supported a more equal one, more government planning, and more social services. A new realization of the importance of analysis was also implicit in these works, which were more detailed, methodical, and statistical than the earlier social investigations.

Concern about the distribution of national wealth was given added depth in this period by the end of the long-term rise in real wages. The slow-down in the rise of real wages began in the mid-1890s and continued through the first decade of the twentieth century, a time when the rich were flaunting their wealth more ostentatiously than ever before. This helped to emphasize the differences between rich and poor and stimulated additional interest in investigations into the distribution of national wealth. The results of these investigations, such as that conducted by Money, were startling. They revealed that $2\frac{1}{2}$ per cent of the population controlled two-thirds of the national income, leaving $97\frac{1}{2}$ per cent of the population to struggle through life on the remaining third. These facts supported the contention that the current social system was unjust and placed an unfair burden on the poor majority of the people. Fears that national wealth was stagnating, or even declining, simply made the situation worse, for a serious decline would have a drastically different effect upon the poor and the rich: starvation for the masses and fewer racehorses and yachts for the wealthy. More and more people came to the conclusion that the slices cut from the national cake should be more equal in size and more fairly distributed, even if such a change did mean that the rich would, inevitably, become poorer.

Booth took an income of 20s a week per family as his definition of 'poor', and considered any income below this as 'very poor'. According to these definitions he estimated that 22.3 per cent of the people of London were 'poor' and 8.4 per cent 'very poor'. Rowntree, in *Poverty: A Study of Town Life*, published in 1901, provided information about York and reached very similar conclusions. On the basis of the results of his investigations he concluded that between 25 and 30 per cent of the urban population of the United Kingdom lived in poverty, which he defined as lack of the income necessary to sustain life at an efficient level. Both surveys showed that low wages, rather than idleness or incapacity, were the main cause of poverty—a conclusion which linked their work directly with that of more general analysts such as Money. Booth and Rowntree also suggested that the irregular employment of men who could work and wanted to work was a much more important factor in poverty than idleness or incompetence. Other causes of distress were illness, old age, and the death of a family's main breadwinner. These dry, statistical pictures of the lives of the poor stirred the consciences of many people and began to trouble even some of those who had considered social reform an almost completed task. Their statistics provided the ammunition for those who would fight for reform, and thus they made a vital contribution to setting the goals of twentieth-century social reform.

Despite the mounting interest in social questions, only a very hesitant start on social legislation was made before the war. The 1902 Education Act abolished the old school boards and passed their powers, with some additions, to county councils and boroughs. In

1904 a royal commission was established to enquire into the operation of the Poor Law, and four years later it presented a two-part report. The majority report was fairly conservative, although critical of the Poor Law system, and the minority report, whose authors included the noted Fabian, Beatrice Webb, was far more radical and innovative, but, apart from helping spread some new ideas, the Report produced little. In 1908 an Old Age Pensions Act was passed, but this was hardly innovative as Germany had had a similar scheme for decades. The Act provided for a pension of up to 5s a week (7s 6d for a married couple) for old people with an income of under £26 a year. This was not very generous even by Booth's standards of poverty, but it was expensive enough to produce a Budget problem, especially when added to the cost of eight new Dreadnoughts. Lloyd George designed his 'People's Budget' of 1909 to raise more money by increasing death duties, taxing high incomes, and providing for the making of a land survey as the basis for a reassessment of land taxes. The latter, especially, was much resented by landowners, and the Budget was rejected by the Lords. The Liberal Party had become impatient with the Lords because they had rejected many Liberal Bills, and Lloyd George played on the Budget issue in an attempt to whip up popular support for the reform of the Lords. The constitutional conflict between Lords and Commons was resolved by the passage of the Parliament Act of 1911, passed by the Lords under the threat of the creation of a majority of Liberal peers. The Act specified that the Lords could no longer amend or reject a money Bill, could delay other Bills only for two years if the Commons was determined that they should go through, and that the life of a parliament was to be reduced from seven to five years. The promise implicit in the extensions of the franchise, that the majority of the people should control government and legislation, was fulfilled by this Act which placed the elected House in full effective control of the legislative system.

In 1911 a Health Act was also passed which allowed poor wage-earners to join the 'panel' of any doctor enrolled in the scheme. These doctors were paid by the government, but hospital treatment continued to be provided only by charity and Poor Law institutions. By 1914 it was clear that a new phase of social reform had opened, but, considering the amount and vitality of social investigation and debate, the initial measures were surprisingly modest, and the pre-war reforms laid only a thin new skin over the old Poor Law system. Practical social reform was limited, but it was in these years that many essential building blocks were laid in the foundations of the welfare state. Higher standards were set; socialistic ideas became more widely accepted, and the reforms that were passed showed that the government could act to secure the new standards the social reformers were demanding.

Social changes were reflected in many symptoms of political *malaise* in the Edwardian years. At the turn of the century tenures of office were short as the established political parties moved rapidly in and out of office. The Irish question bedevilled politicians, even the determined Gladstone having failed in his mission to pacify that troubled country. The Liberal Party was divided on the question of Home Rule for Ireland, and both political parties began to crack as their right and left wings drew away from each other. In the early years of the twentieth century classical liberalism lost its dynamism, and while the socialist challenge gained strength, the Liberal Party developed deep rifts in its own ranks. The Conservatives, meanwhile, tried to hide their own bewilderment behind rhetoric and maps of the Empire.

The causes of unease ran deeper than simple political issues and were, at bottom, related closely to long-term social changes. Classical liberalism, the philosophy which underlay the policies of both the Conservative and Liberal parties for much of the nineteenth century, was the creed of the prosperous and self-confident, a set of middle-class ideas which reached its apogee when the middle class was strongest and most secure. Its reforms were made from the position of confident strength which made even-handed generosity no self-sacrifice. By the end of the nineteenth century, however, the middle classes were less secure than they had been and were more inclined to keep what they had rather than give it away in the name of liberalism. Hence, their support for reforming liberalism waned, while the Liberal Party found it harder to attract the votes of workers, who wanted social reform to continue. The purity of the creed of freedom and *laissez-faire* had always been somewhat sullied by the inclinations of the liberals to succumb to their humanitarian, evangelical instincts, and it had been their quasi-liberal reforms of the nineteenth century which helped start England on the road to collectivism. By showing that government interference could produce better urban living conditions, better working conditions and hours, and even purer food, the liberal social reforms generated a demand for more government action on the part of the lower classes, who were its chief beneficiaries. By the end of the century, this demand had grown to such an extent that the Liberal Party could no longer satisfy it while remaining even partly true to its classical ideals.

In the first decade of the twentieth century the Liberals found themselves on the horns of a dilemma. If they appealed to the working classes with a far-reaching programme of social reform, they would have to change much of their basic philosophy and would lose the support of their natural constituents, the middle classes; if they adopted a line-holding, non-reform policy, they might preserve middle-class support but would not attract mass votes. The development of the Labour Party added to their troubles. At the time there was no way of knowing what the Labour Party might be in the future. It might remain a small but useful ally of the Liberals, who provided the young party with shelter in the Commons, or might become a fox in the bosom of the Liberal Party which would gnaw at its vitals and eventually kill it. Half a century later it is easy to say that it was inevitable that the Liberals would decline as the Labour Party grew in strength, but contemporaries did not have the advantage of this perspective, nor did they know of the war and the depression to come. The Liberal Party continued to provide shelter for the 'Lib-Lab' MPs in the Commons, and the political situation remained fluid and perplexing.

In the first decade of the twentieth century the theoretical force of socialism united with the practical, often inarticulate demand of the workers for social reform. Both had their roots in the nineteenth century, intertwined with the growth of unionism, the expansion of the franchise, the new theories about the direction reform should take, and the emergence of the political arm of the labour movement. The major exponent of socialist theory was the Fabian Society, which had 800 members in 1900 and 4,000 by 1914. The Fabians held themselves aloof from the Labour Party for some time, displaying little faith in a workers' movement and aiming for a gradual take-over of government at all levels by the experts, the thinkers, the planners—in short, themselves. They insinuated themselves into government by collecting information, by planning, by serving on government commissions and as local government and civil service officers. Eventually a loose union of these theorists and the worker movement was formed in the field of practical politics, in which both parties were interested and involved. This, then, was a time when social change was reflected by political uncertainty, when the old social reform party of the past, the Liberal Party, was increasingly unsure of itself and when the reforming party of the future, the Labour Party, was too small and young to take or to force much effective action. Under the circumstances, neither the weakening old party nor the feeble young one was able to produce the far-reaching social reform measures the investigators and theorists of the time were demanding.

The Edwardian years were a time of lightness and gaiety as well as one of increasing social concern and political turmoil. The Edwardians seemed more pleasure-loving than their fathers and grandfathers had been, and they thought that enjoying life was a necessary and desirable part of living, rather than evidence of weak moral fibre and light-mindedness. W. E. Adams, writing in 1903, said that he could not imagine a world with little or no football, tennis, hockey, golf, croquet, and cycling, despite the fact that 'all the amusements and recreations . . . are the growth and invention of less than half a century. It is still true that life is not all beer and skittles; but it is much more beer and skittles than it was when our old men were in their prime' (*Memoirs*, 468–9).

In the Victorian period there was little conflict between writers and the censor because little was done which would challenge the established code, but the censor was there and a potential source of friction should anything new be tried. In the early twentieth century the censor was the defender of the established church, the supporter of the liberal political system, and the upholder of nineteenth-century 'moral values'. In the Edwardian years his task became more difficult because all kinds of literary and theatrical productions began to reflect social changes and to stray away from the old values and ways of doing things. The hard-and-fast lines of Victorian public morality began to crumble under the impact of developments such as Edward's well-known affairs, the change in the relationships between men and women, and the promotion of more progressive ideas about sex. One of the most innovative works in this period was Havelock Ellis's *Studies*, which presumed that sex was a fit topic of discussion for adults and was written for general, rather than specialist medical, consumption. The book was published in America, but in England the censor was victorious and publication was delayed until 1935. Playwrights, too, had new ideas and new ways of presenting them and they also clashed with the censor. The demand for 'serious' theatre grew, however, and the defenders of the old order found innovation harder to resist as playwrights such as G. B. Shaw, a socialist who did a good deal of research into poverty, insisted on writing plays which dealt with social issues and the problems of industrialism. For example, *Mrs Warren's Profession*, written in the 1890s, dealt with the problem of prostitution, and *Major Barbara* condemned war profiteering and the munitions industry. A landmark in the relaxation of censorship was passed in 1914 when Ibsen's *Ghosts*, a play which dealt with the topic of inherited venereal disease, was seen on the stage, England being the last European country to allow its performance.

## CONFUSION AND UNEASE

Winston Churchill sensed a peculiar feeling of restlessness in 1914 which he expressed as a strange 'temper in the air'. *Malaise*, unease or 'strangeness' was evident throughout the early years of the twentieth century, and it occasionally erupted into episodes of violence and hysteria which became more frequent as the years passed. Upheavals at home added to the worries caused by the troubled world situation. Concern about foreign economic competition was amplified by a growing anxiety about military challenges, especially from Germany. Under the aggressive, erratic leadership of William II, Germany became involved in a variety of international incidents, and William's encouragement of England's enemies, such as Kruger, was very disquieting. Improved literacy rates and popular communications meant that these incidents disturbed larger numbers of people than they would have done in the past. Concrete form was given to vague fears by the increase in German naval strength, which seemed a direct challenge to Britain, who felt that she had to control the seas not just to support the national prestige but to ensure national survival. Without freedom of the seas it would be difficult to secure the continued flow of trade which was essential for industrial production and the feeding of the people. Military and political leaders decided that the challenge of the German navy had to be met, and in response the Dreadnoughts were built. The most modern techniques were used in the building of these warships, which made all existing vessels obsolete. The popular cry for more Dreadnoughts, 'We want eight, and we won't wait', provided an outlet for, and expression of, the general feelings of unease and the desire for increased security.

The self-assurance of the mid-nineteenth century, of the days of Palmerston when Britain could at least appear to solve foreign problems by sending a gun-boat, was gone and a loss of national self-confidence was evident in the obsession with armaments and the profusion and popularity of invasion stories. The rapid defeat of France by Prussia in the early 1870s showed what modern military techniques could do, and many people began to worry about what this might mean for England. The Boer War kept up national interest in military matters, and in the first decade of the twentieth century, especially between 1906 and 1909, a large number of books were written about invasion and modern warfare, such as H. G. Wells's *The War in the Air* (1908). By the end of the decade the arms race was on in earnest, so much so that even ladies' 'society' magazines paid attention to it. In 1910, for example, *Queen* included among its staple fare of items about court and society functions a series of articles entitled 'Our Dockyards'. There were many symptoms of a national feeling of insecurity, including rumours that apparently sensible people had seen all kinds of mysterious lights in the sky and strange machines spying on various parts of the British Isles. Zeppelin stories became even more popular than flying saucer stories were to be in the 1950s. *Queen*, not normally given to the publication of anything disturbing, said, 'from various parts of the country we continually hear reports of mysterious aircraft having been seen at night passing over our towns' (quoted in Crewe, *Privilege*, 83). The stories of the mysterious flying machines had no factual basis, but they provided an outlet and an explanation for unrecognized fears and supplied villains the people could blame for their troubles. Over the centuries, England had become accustomed to inviolability; wars came and passed, nations fought and invaded other nations, but the British Isles, sheltered by the sea, had been safe from all such turmoil. Many people feared that this old assumption might no longer be valid, and the scare stories were symptoms of the attempt to adjust to the fact that the old secure isolation was no more, that the island *might* be invaded. This prospect was probably as terrifying then as was the prospect of atomic warfare in the 1950s.

The Empire, too, received its share of troubled attention. Throughout the self-confident, industry-building years, few people had given it much thought, and some of those who did think about it held that imperialism no longer had any point or profit. Towards the end of the nineteenth century new ideas about the Empire began to emerge, ideas which were symbolized initially by Victoria's taking the title of Empress of India, invented by Disraeli, in 1877. From the 1870s on the popular concept of the Empire became more and more self-congratulatory, romantic, even slightly hysterical, all of which was both expressed and amplified by the works of Rudyard Kipling, high priest of the imperial faith. He presented imperialism as a mission, which the British, the chosen people, were called upon to fulfil. By virtue of their innate capacity to organize and to improve, they were destined to bring the light of reason, government and progress to the inferior people of the world. It was their duty to rule and to bring 'civilization' to the dark areas of the world, to shoulder the 'white man's burden'.

His heroic stories of soldiers and administrators living difficult but exciting lives in exotic places were extremely popular and helped promote a jingoistic patriotism. Music hall songs, such as those noted by Booth, expressed and stimulated similar feelings and, in the early twentieth century, many people took a slightly hysterical, irrational pride in the fact that 'the sun never set on the British Empire'.

All this appealed to many people who were trapped in drab, grey towns and dull routine tasks. Immersed in the works of Kipling a man could escape from suburb or slum, browbeating boss or nagging wife, and imagine himself in some far-off exotic land where life was exciting and where he was the messiah of civilization, a leader, a master who was accorded every respect. He could read about the Empire and feel that he was important, not just an unrecognized toiler on the industrial ant-hill, but an Englishman, one of the lords of the world. The new imperialism was a way of bolstering pride when the world seemed to be sliding away and out of control and it offered an escape from routine and dissatisfaction.

At the same time, many men feared that England was sliding into a decline, and it was inevitable that parallels would be drawn between it and the Roman Empire. This idea was developed in a pamphlet by Elliot Mills, *The Decline and Fall of the British Empire* (1905). The great success of this work was in itself a symptom of unease; it was favourably reviewed by *The Times* and other newspapers, and sold 12,000 copies in six months. The workshop of the world was no longer a monopoly establishment; there was less and less peace to be found in the Pax Britannica; the Hun again seemed to threaten the civilizing Empire.

Little comfort could be drawn from the world situation, and the domestic scene had little security or ease to offer because all the disruptive forces which had been evident in the later nineteenth century gained strength in the new century. The new, freer attitudes of the upper levels of Edwardian society were instrumental in changing the ground rules by which the social relationships between men and women were conducted. Edward's affairs were no secret; for example, pictures of the King and Mrs Keppel were published openly in magazines with no attempt to disguise their friendship. In the past a married woman was expected to be above reproach, but Mrs Keppel clearly was not. The King equally clearly did not mind, and 'society' changed its standards to fit the circumstances. The married female Edwardian socialite could do virtually anything she liked, provided she was reasonably discreet and provoked no unpleasantness such as divorce proceedings. In the past a man had been sure of the sympathy of his fellows if his wife did not prove to be a model of virtue, and confident of their approval if he punished her suitably for her sins. Now, nobody in 'society' cared very much, and he might well be criticized for punishing her for what were now considered to be mild indiscretions. A man could no longer assume, with the support of respectable society, that his mate would stay loyal and virtuous in both deed and appearance, and the married state was weakened by the death of this assumption.

Young married women began to underplay their traditional role of prospective pillars of decorous society and to assume a new role as leaders of fashion and makers of new patterns of social behaviour. Many young men left England for long periods to serve in the armed forces or as imperial administrators, and while they were shouldering the white man's burden, their young wives were often left at home with little to do. It was still fairly difficult for a woman to entertain herself, and it came to be considered polite and considerate of her husband's friends to escort her to the theatre, to restaurants, and to sporting events. Most of these associations were entirely proper and courteous, but their very existence led to a relaxation of many old restraints. A woman was no longer expected to be chaperoned everywhere but could now move around freely, alone or in the company of either male or female friends. In this easier social atmosphere, some daring young women began to smoke publicly to symbolize their new independence, and fashions echoed the prevailing mood with less cumbersome clothing and lower necklines.

Some women felt that increasing social freedom was not enough and began to campaign vigorously for legal equality too. The Women's Social and Political Union was founded in 1903 with the aim of securing legal equality, especially the franchise, for women. At first the suffragettes heckled speakers at political meetings, carried placards, made speeches, and indulged in other noisy but harmless means of promotion, but after 1909 their campaign became more serious and more violent. Women as convinced and determined as the redoubtable Pankhursts proved themselves willing to undergo pain, suffering, and even death in the interest of their cause. In the years immediately preceding the war, the supporters of women's suffrage became more aggressive and began to adopt tactics similar to those used by the violent and incomprehensible Irish who were also demanding independence. Women rioted, broke windows, chained themselves to railings, knocked helmets off policemen and staged hunger strikes in prison and had to be force-fed. The movement acquired a martyr when Emily Davison sought publicity and found death by flinging herself under the hooves of the King's horse at Epsom in 1913. Such violence was startling and disturbing, and even men who applauded the freer social habits promoted by the 'new women' were unprepared for the activities of the suffragettes. It was one thing to escort a friend's wife to the theatre and to dinner and to light her cigarette; it was quite another to encounter 'respectable' women screaming like harpies and brawling like Irish navvies in the streets. Many women, too, were embarrassed by all this as the suffrage movement rocked and shocked society and disturbed the equilibrium of many homes.

The breakdown of the old philosophical certainties, which had begun in the second half of the nineteenth century, accelerated in this period. The grip of the church, which had traditionally helped define and support the moral structure of society, continued to weaken. Science, once a popular contender for the old position of the church, seemed less and less likely to fill its place as scientists pursued their investigations beyond the realms of common understanding and came up with no readily acceptable new certainties. The turn of the century brought a series of new and deeply disturbing discoveries. For example, the discovery of X-rays in 1895 and of radium in 1900 led scientists to new conclusions about the nature of matter— the atom ceased to be considered a rigid unit, and matter was reinterpreted in terms of energy. In general, the work of the scientists was leading into incomprehensible new areas in which everything seemed to contradict ideas based on the information men derive from their senses, the information on which 'common sense' is grounded. Darwin had already cast serious doubts on man's ancestry, and at the turn of the century the work of Freud was casting doubt on his rationality by maintaining that the conscious was only a small part of man's mind and that the uncontrollable unconscious determined many of his actions. As usual, contemporary scientific work had little impact on the masses, but to those who were aware of it and could understand it, its implications were disturbing. The best-educated and best-informed members of society, those who might have provided stability and reason in a crisis, were less capable of doing so because their world and their reason were being shaken too.

The scientific notions that were filtering down to the masses at this time were derived from older, less complex and more readily comprehensible work, but they offered little reassurance for faith in reason. That men were descended from apes was not a happy thought for those who believed that man was literally created in God's image; the notion that even strong men died from diseases caused by tiny unseen organisms, germs, was upsetting. The simplified versions of the theory of natural selection which had become fairly general knowledge by this time brought no comfort to people who were beginning to feel that natural but irrational forces were taking man's control of his own destiny away from him. This knowledge helped deepen, for example, concern about the physical and mental decay of the people. The census reports of the last decades of the nineteenth century showed a startling increase in the number of mental defectives. This was probably due partly to a change in phraseology and classification by the census-takers, partly to an increasing number of weak children surviving the deadly childhood years, and partly to the increasing interest in social questions of all kinds. To contemporaries, already worried about national decline and the future of nation and Empire, it seemed evidence of a fundamental weakness in the people. Controversy arose over the cause of mental defects with the advocates of heredity winning temporary ascendancy over the advocates of environment. Some people suggested that social reform should be aimed, not simply at the elimination of poverty, but at the ending of the fertile poverty which seemed to be increasing the number of social and economic incompetents. Along these lines, an organization of conservative reformers, the National Social Purity Crusade, launched a campaign in 1908 to raise the standards of social and personal 'purity', in the hope that this would somehow reduce the number of unproductive, substandard elements that society was producing.

At this time of intellectual and social turmoil and torment, the physical pressures on the people continued to increase. Although the rate of population increase was slowing by the end of the nineteenth century, the total number of people on the tight little island continued to grow. Meanwhile, the drift to the towns continued, and so the ever-larger number of people lived in an ever-smaller area. By this time the vast majority of people were concentrated into relatively small areas where a man could look forward to life as a tiny particle of the mass, to being unknown by most people, to doing work which could be done just as easily by any one of the thousands of people just like him. He was destined to live in a crowd, to work in a crowd, and to be buried in a crowded graveyard. Few townsmen could look forward to a life with much security or comfort, and although the conditions of life of the lower classes had improved over the previous half-century, most of them worried constantly about money and their jobs and found life a round of depressing drudgery, as was suggested by John Davidson:

> For like a mole I journey in the dark,
> A-travelling along the underground
> From my Pillar'd Halls and broad Suburban Park,
> To come the daily dull official round;
> And home again at night with my pipe all alight,
> A-scheming how to count ten bob a pound.
> John Davidson (1857–1909), 'Thirty Bob a Week'.

The feeling that life, when not positively unpleasant, was boring and dull provided fertile ground for the growth of escapism. Imperialism and its mythology was one means of escaping boredom. The Boy Scout movement provided a similar kind of escape and group identification, and there was a great response to it. Scout troops were started after the publication of Baden Powell's book *Scouting for Boys* in 1906, and in 1907 the movement was already large enough to stage a rally of 11,000 of its members at the Crystal Palace. There was only a limited need in urbanized twentieth-century Britain for people skilled at tracking, building fires in the rain, surviving under extreme climatic conditions, tying knots, and whittling wood to make rough furniture, but the movement provided, along with the benefits of fresh air and exercise, an excellent opportunity to escape from contemporary realities. While scouts played at being pioneers in the woods and fields, theatregoers found escape into the excitement and security of childhood in J. M. Barrie's play *Peter Pan*, the story of 'the boy who never grew up', first produced in 1904 and regularly thereafter. The wealthy continued to escape into a glittering world in which money and possessions were all-important, while anyone with a few pennies or shillings to spend could continue to seek solace in the countryside or in a book.

There was a continued, restless search for 'something new', and many forces which had been latent in the Victorian period came to the forefront in the early twentieth century. Even in the nineteenth century there had been a strong undercurrent of irrationalism and emotionalism which had found partial expression in the Romantic movement. A morbid pleasure in poems and stories of death and danger, a larger-than-life excitement in the dramatic pictures of hopeless love and utter despair, added a new dimension to humdrum lives. Other phenomena which spoke of irrationalism and hysteria in the nineteenth century were the many semi-mystical, emotional, charlatan 'sciences' such as palmistry, astrology, and phrenology. All these streams came together, mixed with other ingredients, and produced a curious, often curdled brew in the Edwardian years. The price of thrill-seeking was often high. As Adams commented in his *Memoirs* (1903, 599),

> There is a sort of degeneracy . . . in the everlasting craving for excitement. We make a business of pleasure, not a pleasure of business. Seriousness has gone out of fashion . . . Intellectual pastimes are but little patronized, while brutal sports are always sure of a large following.

The people wanted a change, something more exciting, and many drifted towards violence and irrational escapism. The demand for increased armaments, the jingoistic interest in the Boer War, the antics of the suffragettes, the strikes and labour violence which became more troublesome in these years, the continued violent conflict with the Irish, the desire to conquer 'uncivilized natives', and the obsession with invasion, taken singly can hardly be accepted as evidence of increasing violence in national life, but taken together and coming within a decade they do constitute a significant body of evidence suggesting an increasing interest in violence which was alarming by the accepted standards of the preceding half-century.

Anything which might generate excitement was seized on and amplified by the popular press. The 'new' press had from the start changed news stories to make them more appealing and to boost circulation. The press which gave its readers what they wanted, as opposed to 'straight' news, soon discovered that death, disaster, and hatred sold newspapers. One of the maxims of Alfred Harmsworth (later Lord Northcliffe), one of the most important shapers of the policy of the popular press, was that readers liked a 'good hate' and would buy more often and more frequently if their newspapers pandered to this taste. In 1898 his paper the *Daily Mail*, found that its exciting stories of Kitchener's Omdurman campaign boosted circulation. After this the *Mail* did all it could to whip up popular feeling about South Africa, and it was not above inventing or embellishing foreign news stories if there was little exciting fact around. The newspapers simplified everything for their readers, including the problem of who or what was causing all the discomfort, unease, and danger in the world. In the nineteenth century they had tended to blame France for all England's troubles; in the early twentieth century Germany became their ogre.

In many respects the outbreak of war in 1914 was merely the grand finale for all the preceding scenes of insecurity, violence, tension, irrationality, and confusion. The declaration of war with Germany was welcomed, greeted almost as dawn might be welcomed after a restless night filled with strange and disturbing dreams. The declaration of war also brought relief after the years of uneasy waiting and preparation for war. Implicit in the popular cry for more Dreadnoughts was the presumption that they would balance German naval strength and place Britain in a better position for conflict with Germany; the mysterious lights in the sky were generally presumed to be those of German airships; the Germans were seen as the most serious threat to British industrial leadership; the Germans presented a serious threat to the Empire; it was the Germans the popular newspapers saw as being at the bottom of all the problems which plagued the world. The outburst which greeted the declaration of war was not the shock reaction of a surprised people, but the expression of relief that the years of tension were over and that the nation, united in a common cause against evil, could set about removing the source of its ills.

Much of the previous distress and disruption had nothing to do with Germany, or indeed with any external irritant. Most of the trouble was internal, but because of its complex nature it was not easy to find the source of the trouble, and it was even more difficult to find remedies. Many people found it convenient to blame Germany and easier to fight the Germans than to undertake a complex, rational analysis of the situation. With the declaration of war the enemy was identified and the goal of defeating it set. Fighting any enemy, even the wrong one, was easier than living with constant tension and undefined fear.

Many of the men who were to fight the war saw it as an opportunity to cleanse by fire, to right the wrongs of the world and usher in the millennium. It was fulfilment for all who had sought escape and excitement in violence, and it was popularly seen as something glorious, a golden opportunity to break with the stale past and embrace all that idealistic and violent hearts had long desired. Such emotions were expressed by Rupert Brooke, one of the early war poets.

> Now, God be thanked Who has matched us with His hour,
> And caught our youth, and wakened us from sleeping,
> With hand made sure, clear eye and sharpened power,
> To turn, as swimmers into cleanness leaping,

Glad from a world grown old and cold and weary.
Leave the sick hearts that honour could not move,
And the half-men, their dirty songs and dreary,
And all the little emptiness of love.

Rupert Brooke (1887–1915), 'Peace'.

It was popularly imagined that the war would be a combination of sacrificial bloodletting, atonement for the sterile sins of the past, and a brief, colourful, exciting military tattoo. Some deaths were inevitable, but the shedding of a little blood was a necessary part of the drama and was therefore a part of the pageantry of honour and glory. England expected to work the poison out of its system. The boys would enjoy the lark and their women would enjoy the excitement, the bravery, and the sweet sorrow of a brief parting. Then the nation could get back to its legitimate business of being happy and glorious. People expected the war to end the years of turmoil. Instead it ended many thousands of lives and the world of long dresses, large flowered hats, croquet on the lawn, and honey for tea; and it put an end to the Indian summer of England's greatness.

# Chapter 5 The War Machine

The shock of the conflict of 1914–18 was compounded by the fact that it was a new kind of war and no one was prepared for, or had even anticipated, the enormous demands it would make on the nation and its people. The traditional form of warfare involved men and tactics, marches and battles, but modern total war primarily involves machines and economic production. The First World War proved to be a contest, not of which side could outshoot and outmanoeuvre the other, but which side could out-produce, out-supply, and simply out-survive, the other. There had been hints in the nineteenth century, such as the American Civil War, of the direction warfare was taking, but these went unnoticed or ignored. In any event, modern military equipment and techniques replaced the old forms only fairly slowly in the First World War. Many lorries were being used for military purposes by the end of the war, but in the earlier stages long distance transport was by railway, and the traditional load-carrier, the horse, was also used a great deal. Telephones and radios could be used to transmit military information and orders, but they were still unreliable in field conditions and human messengers were more dependable.

Technological developments had produced new and efficient weapons of defence. Field guns were bigger and more destructive, and the machine-gun and barbed wire were highly effective defensive weapons. Similarly effective offensive weapons, such as tanks and planes, were still in their infancy. This lopsided development of military technology produced a static, defensive war. Generals were slow to grasp what the new weaponry meant and they committed many tactical errors at a great cost in life. For example, British commanders retained their faith in the mass advance of foot-soldiers, and they ordered thousands of troops to advance on enemy trenches which were protected by barbed wire and machine-guns, with disastrous consequences. There were few glories in this war or dramatic, heroic advances and conquests; just trench-foot, lice, deafness from the pounding of the big guns, blindness and burns from mustard gas, and the misery of life in the muddy holes in the ground which were decorated with fragments of smashed guns and bodies. Giving one's life for one's country proved to be no noble and romantic sacrifice but an anonymous and meaningless demise amid the smell of fear and the stink of unwashed uniforms. It might come from an enemy shell in the Allied trenches, in a waterlogged shell-hole in the blasted, bloody earth of no-man's-land, or on the barbed-wire fringes of enemy trenches where bodies hung like rag dolls after an abortive advance. There was a great gulf between the original romantic ideas of war and the reality of it, which can be seen clearly in the contrast between the early and later war poems. For example, Rupert Brooke's ideas about the glories of war were a world away from Wilfred Owen's grim appreciation of the realities of a gas attack at the front.

> Bent double, like old beggars under sacks,
> Knock kneed, coughing like hags, we cursed our way through
>   sludge,
> Till on the haunting flares we turned our backs,
> And towards our distant rest began to trudge.
> Men marched asleep, many had lost their boots,
> But limped on, blood-shod. All went lame, all blind,
> Drunk with fatigue; deaf even to the hoots
> Of gas-shells dropping softly behind.
>                 Wilfred Owen (1893–1918), 'Dulce Et Decorum Est'.

Initially most people expected a short war and saw no need to change normal patterns of life. Under the slogan 'business as usual', people made their own adjustments to the war. By the end of 1914 the opposing forces were entrenched on a 400-mile front stretching from Switzerland to Ostend. The war had settled down to a contest of minute advances and retreats, and it was clear that it would not be over in a few weeks. As news, and some of the wounded, trickled back from the front, it was realized that this was no lark for a summer day, no game played by gentlemen with sharp swords as a brief diversion from tennis and cricket, but a grim, bitter, painful fight for survival. If the war was to be won, its demands had to be met, and possibly endured for a long time, so the nation set about meeting them under the direction of the only body large and powerful enough to organize all its efforts and resources—the government.

THE PROBLEMS OF SUPPLY

There were two basic supply problems, that of supplying men and that of supplying materials. The demand for both soon exceeded the supply, and there were many problems involved in the efficient allocation of scarce resources. At first it was hoped that needs would be met by the uncontrolled responses to immediate demands, and in the beginning soldiers were recruited simply by calling for volunteers. Patriotic appeals were made, dramatic posters displayed, and some women distributed the white feathers of cowardice to men of military age still in civilian clothes. Initially the call for volunteers was successful, but it was a shortsighted policy and wasteful of national resources because recruiting sergeants paid no attention to any special civilian skills which made men more valuable as workers than as soldiers. In the early stages of the war there were more soldiers than the arms, ammunition, and equipment with which to supply them, and men who were needed to maintain production and supply were thrown away as cannon fodder. For example, a quarter of a million miners volunteered and were allowed to join the army and navy in 1914, although they would have been much more valuable to the war effort at home producing coal. Also among the first to volunteer were many idealistic, well-educated young men, some of whom saw the war as an exciting adventure they could enjoy before they settled into sober and responsible careers. The educated élite, those with a degree, received a commission automatically upon enlistment. For all too many of these young men the war meant an impressive title and uniform, a brief whirl of pleasure, praise and pride before they left for the front, perhaps a fleeting thrill of command, and an early death. Even for this war of enormous casualties, the death rate among British junior officers was incredibly high; in proportion to the numbers involved, junior officers had three times the casualty rate of ordinary soldiers.

The waste of manpower resources inherent in the volunteer system was gradually appreciated, and in 1915 the government began to classify occupations which were necessary to the welfare of the nation and to forbid men in these occupations to join the armed forces. Towards the end of 1915 the flow of volunteers began to dry up while military leaders continued to demand more and more men. A part-volunteer, part-government coercion system was tried while the arguments of those in favour of a conscription system grew louder and more insistent. The whole idea of conscription was profoundly illiberal, and the belief in liberalism was strong enough to defeat several conscription Bills before practical pressures finally overcame it and conscription was introduced in the late spring of 1916. By this time there seemed to be no practical alternative to conscription;

national survival appeared more important than liberal principles, and it was more or less a question of accepting the inevitable. Conscription combined with the system of occupation classification and necessary exemptions to give the government virtually total control over the manpower resources of the nation and their allocation. The labour shortage was so acute that women were eventually brought into the war effort. In 1916 the Army and Navy founded women's corps to perform non-combat duties and to free men for active service. In the same year the Land Army was established as a means of organizing female labour for agricultural work, which became more important as food supplies dwindled. Women also served in more-or-less traditional roles as volunteers in hospitals and canteens, as nurses and knitters of socks, and in less traditional civilian roles, doing jobs which had, before the war, been reserved for men.

Just as the pressures of necessity had forced the government to acquire wider powers to control manpower, they also forced it to assume a greater control over supplies and their allocation. The need for government powers which went beyond peacetime controls was dimly recognized in the early stages of the war, and the Defence of the Realm Act was passed in 1914. This gave 'the King in Council' (in effect, the Cabinet) the power to make any regulations or requisitions necessary for the defence of the country. Later additions were made to the Act until eventually the government had the power to do almost anything under the heading of war emergency and national necessity. The cast of major characters engaged in this grim play, Tommy Atkins, the Kaiser and his Huns, was joined by a female player, Dora. By the mysterious alchemy of humour and humanity which has seemed to flourish in the inhuman war years of the twentieth century, the Defence of the Realm Act was transformed from a piece of emergency legislation into Dora, a human caricature. Dora assumed the form of a kill-joy maiden aunt who came to stay with every family for the duration. Dora did big, important, official things for the government such as requisitioning ships and raw materials, but she also did smaller, irritating things which plagued the everyday life of the people. For example, in Dora's name the early closing of shops was begun and blackout precautions and food controls introduced. The fact that the Act came to be endowed with human characteristics and that it and its effects were accepted with grumbling tolerance as a part of everyday life and folklore possibly played a part in the later peaceful acceptance of government collectivism.

Wars had always imposed demands on the military supply industries, and the demands of this war were greater than those of any previous conflict because its scale was so large, it involved more people, and its weapons were more efficient and sophisticated. A few relatively minor examples will serve to illustrate the enormous material consumption of the war. The Army needed large numbers of sandbags for the construction of defensive positions, the shoring-up of trenches and other work. In 1914 it estimated that it would need 250,000 sandbags a month; by the spring of 1915 it was asking for 6 million. The making of weapons ate up materials and labour, and once in service the weapons consumed vast quantities of ammunition. In the nineteen-day bombardment at Third Ypres in 1917 the Army used a year's production of shells by 55,000 British workers. Similarly enormous, unprecedented demands were made for supplies of all kinds—clothing, food, knives and forks, barbed wire, boots, bullets, transport equipment, and all the other trappings of modern war.

Neither industry nor society was prepared or geared for such a massive military effort, and the change from peacetime to wartime production could not be made overnight. There was no time to wait for industry to change over at its own pace, and normal market channels provided no guarantee that the right materials would get to the right industries in their order of national and military importance. It was clear that the machinery of the normal peacetime economy was incapable of meeting wartime needs, and that if the needs were to be met some special controls would have to be introduced.

Government intervention in the workings of the economy ran counter to all liberal economic ideals and, at first, it was slow and hesitant. In any case, wide-ranging government control was difficult to impose because it had never been tried before, and there were, therefore, no precedents on which to base any plans. At first, the government tried to introduce only very mild controls in limited areas to meet immediate needs, but the very complexity of the economy and the demands made upon it made such restricted control impossible to maintain. Any attempt to regulate one area of production involved a wide range of industries. For example, the demand for metals was enormous, but iron, the basic metal, could not be considered as an independent entity because its production involved ore, coal, limestone, and additives of various metals and minerals for special steels. It involved blast furnaces and coal mines, transport facilities and large numbers of iron and steel workers, miners, railwaymen and managers, unions and firms. Any controls on the flow of raw materials and iron and steel affected both other industries and exports and imports. So, any interference produced a long and tangled chain of effects, many of which also had to be controlled at the national level.

The government did not set out to regulate huge segments of the economy, but it was drawn into doing so by the complexity of the needs of war and the advanced industrial economy. The British people were thus dragged reluctantly into the age of 'big government' at this time of national emergency. The parents of 'the State', the central controlling authority of virtually everything, were not ideology and theory but circumstance and necessity. At the outbreak of war wide-ranging government control was inconceivable to all but radical socialists and neither government nor people was prepared for it. The sacred idols of property and profit were smashed in the name of survival, necessity, and the defence of the realm, and a new era in the development of government was opened up.

The government gradually increased its control of food supplies, too. The need to feed the armed forces was obvious and urgent, but Britain had been unable to feed herself for half a century and feeding the civilian population was a problem also. Food imports were vital, but the war made importing difficult, and as it progressed food became scarce and increasingly expensive. The demand for labour had drasti-cally reduced unemployment, and wages began to rise again, but the working classes were uneasy about rising food prices, and there were stirrings of unrest as some of them began to feel that the rich could buy as much as they wanted while the workers, vital to the war effort, were denied. The links between food supply, prices, and worker unrest led to increasing government concern about food control.

In 1916 a Food Production Department was set up to stimulate the domestic production of food, but the shortages became more severe and a crisis came in 1917 when Germany began a submarine blockade in an attempt to starve Britain into surrender. This crisis forced the government into taking much more far-reaching measures to control civilian food consumption. The Food Controller, one of the many new government control agents, began by fixing the size and price of restaurant meals and guaranteeing high prices for domestically pro-duced corn. The Commission of Enquiry into Industrial Unrest reported that the major cause of disturbance was worker resentment of rising food prices, and it maintained that price control and the priority allocation of scarce supplies were essential. The control of the prices of basic and increasingly scarce commodities, wheat, sugar, and meat, was begun in July 1917. Shortages continued, soon potatoes were added to the list of controlled foods, and by the end of 1917 meat began to disappear altogether from the shops. Early in 1918 a rationing system was finally instituted for certain basic foods, and each person was issued with a ration card which entitled him to his fair share of rationed commodities. Commodities such as sugar, butter, jam, and tea were rationed and a few ounces a week allocated to everyone. Although bread was not rationed, the consumption of meat was regulated by allowing each person to spend only a small, specified sum on it each week.

In the hothouse atmosphere of war, the growth of 'the State' was enormously accelerated. The seedling big government implicit in the Liberal social reforms became a large and many-branched tree which, by the end of the war, had grown enough to shelter and influence activity in almost all segments of national life. The war made non-sense of free trade and the *laissez-faire* economy and in the war years liberal policies and utilitarian, evangelistic, humanitarian social re-forms came to appear thin, faded, old-fashioned cartoons of national and social regulation. By the end of the war, socialistic regulatory ideas and government machinery had been put into operation, and this had been accepted, because it had been justified by practical needs, the national interest, and because the pressures of war left no room for theory. After the war, big government shrivelled and new growth was slow and limited, but the facts and effects of four years of rapidly increasing state intervention could not be denied or forgotten. Im-plicit in the operation and acceptance of the practices of the war years was an acknowledgment, however limited, of the validity of the idea that the government could intervene effectively in many sections of national life.

THE WAR AND SOCIAL CHANGE

Government controls and regulations affected the structure of society in many ways. The allocation of rationed foods was made on a simple *per capita* basis, and wealth and class had no effect on the basic allow-ances, although rich people were able to buy expensive, unrationed foods whose prices were not controlled, and this gave them an advan-tage over the poor who could not afford luxuries. Nevertheless, as regards the basic necessities of life all classes were officially treated equally, and the diet of all sections of the population was more stan-dardized than it had ever been before, which promoted a feeling of increased official equality, even if only in relationship to shortages.

Nutritional studies ensured that individual rations made up a better-balanced diet than the majority of the population had enjoyed in the past, and even the relatively small allowances constituted a larger amount of food than the working classes had had in the past. For example, the average tea allowance of 2 oz. per person per week was four times as much as the average worker had consumed in the 1860s. Once the prices of essential foods were stabilized, the working classes benefited from full employment and rising wages, and this was reflected in a net improvement in their living standards. The wealthy continued to fare better than the poor because they had the means to buy black-market goods and unrationed food, but the regulation of staples meant that they lived at a relatively lower standard than that to which they were accustomed, while the working classes lived at a relatively higher standard.

The overwhelming need for war supplies which led the government to intervene in industry and to do something about the causes of labour discontent also involved it in a more intimate concern for the welfare and productivity of workers. Official concern with working conditions, hours, and wages was heightened and this led to negotiations between the government and union representatives. These negotiations clearly implied that the government recognized the power and influence of the unions, which enhanced the stature and dignity of labour and the unions.

The testing of recruits for the services brought into high relief a variety of social problems hitherto unknown or ignored. Even the perfunctory service medical check revealed that many recruits were below the minimum military standards of physical fitness. Years of inadequate nutrition promoted diseases such as rickets and other bone deformities, while the scars of years of being unable to afford a doctor were even more numerous. The range of deformities and disabilities which could have been avoided with adequate medical care included old smallpox scars, deafness, twisted, deformed, and shortened limbs which had not been set, or which had been clumsily set, after a break, bad and broken teeth, and tuberculosis. The toll taken by preventible diseases and diet deficiency stimulated an interest in medical and nutritional problems and demands for their solution, all of which contributed to the establishment of the Ministry of Health in 1919. The inadequate education of the recruits revealed yet another source of national weakness. Despite the improvements in and expansion of public education in the previous half-century, many recruits performed very badly in elementary reading and arithmetic tests, providing a vivid illustration of the need for new advances in national education.

Government concern for military and industrial efficiency and general morale led it to try to modify drinking habits. In the early stages of the war when patriotic enthusiasm was at its height, men in uniform were heroes and were lavishly 'treated' to rounds of drinks by civilians. Many a soldier and sailor who had been on leave reeled back to report for duty in no condition to defend home and country. In the first year of the war, drinking restrictions were introduced in port towns in an attempt to stop drunkenness and brawling among the troops, but they had little effect. Soon, the licensing authority of any district was empowered to limit the hours during which alcohol could be sold on the recommendation of the local chief of police. By the end of 1914 almost half the licensing districts in England and Wales had restricted hours of sale, and these districts generally had a better record of sobriety and peacefulness than the districts which had not restricted hours. To the self-elected arbiters of public morality, Dora in her most puritanical mood seemed a natural ally, and the increased sobriety which followed the restriction of hours supplied teetotallers with the ammunition to mount a major onslaught against the evils of alcohol. In 1915 'taking the pledge' to forswear alcohol became very popular, especially after the King himself had taken it.

Worker absenteeism in the munitions, shipbuilding, and transport industries affected production, and a government investigation concluded that drinking was the main cause. Official interest in alcohol consumption, therefore, expanded to cover civilian as well as military imbibing, and Dora acquired a sober ally, the Central Control Board for Liquor Traffic. This Board had the power to regulate hours of sale in any area in which vital war work was being done and was later given other powers, such as the special regulation of spirit sales. As more and more hop-growing areas were ploughed under and planted with food crops, hop production declined and beer became less potent, which also helped limit drunkenness. The number of convictions for drunkenness fell from over 3,000 in 1914 to just over 400 in 1918.

In spite of the efforts of the nineteenth-century reformers to reduce drinking, beer remained an important part of the lives of most working men. If a man could afford it, he expected to have a pint at intervals throughout the day, and, whenever possible, a few at the end of it. Some workers did drink to excess, but many of those who considered themselves sober and responsible working men also drank beer regularly, and they resented the official attack on beer as a direct insult and an affront to their respectability. By the end of 1916 hop cultivation had decreased sharply, with the result that the strength of beer fell and its price rose. The new, weaker but more expensive brew, scornfully titled 'government ale' and 'Lloyd George's beer', and the shorter time available for drinking broke long-established links between beer and work and changed some well-worn patterns of life for many people. The regulation of drinking was, however, endured remarkably patiently by the civilian population, although it was an annoying addition to the many trials of wartime and the beginning of 'licensing hours' which have plagued thirsty people in Britain for over half a century. Drinking regulations did show that government regulation could change long-established patterns of civilian life and change them for the better.

During the war it began to seem to many people that no area of national life was safe from government control. In 1916 the government decreed that there would be 'more' hours of daylight, and the days were longer. It had long been argued by 'eccentrics' that useful hours of early morning light were wasted each summer, and these theories combined with the practical wartime need to conserve light and power to produce the Summer Time Act. In the same year, the government also made the nights darker. German air attacks on southern England were irritating and alarming, if not dangerous, and an attempt was made to make life harder for the pilots by depriving them of the lights which helped direct them to their targets. So Dora darkened the night, plunging towns and cities into a gloom they had not known since street lighting was introduced and fining any citizen who dared defy the regulations about covering lights. Under pressure of war, the government controlled what had previously seemed uncontrollable and thereby gave a very effective illustration of just how far and how deeply it could go if the welfare of the nation seemed to warrant drastic action on its part.

The war affected society in many ways, not all of which were directly related to government action. For example, the cause of female emancipation made considerable practical advances in the war years, mainly as a result of the expanded demand for labour. The struggle for national survival ended the long-drawn-out debate about women's abilities and capacity for work by simply making it irrelevant. A national emergency proved no time for the polite discussion of theories; manpower was short and if women worked it would free men for military duty. Lower-class women had always worked—in the fields, the home, as domestics and in cottage industries, factories, and even, for a time, mines. In the two or three decades before the war, even 'ladies' were beginning to work in offices, schools, and all kinds of clerical and administrative work. Hence, the cliché that all women were idle, decorative child-bearers before the war and short-skirted, cigarette-smoking factory hands after it is not totally accurate. The war did, however, change some of the social roles of women by expanding the range of jobs in which they were accepted, by making working women patriots and hence more respectable, by raising rates of pay a little, and, above all, by bringing working women more into the public eye.

In the opening months of the war the suffragettes changed their demands, stressing the 'right to serve' more than the right to vote, and as new employment opportunities appeared women moved into them, proving their capabilities not by rhetoric but by performance. They joined the new women's military corps and the Land Army, drove lorries and ambulances, worked on buses, made guns and ammunition, in addition to working in more traditional 'women's jobs'. The number of women employed in commercial activities almost doubled between 1914 and 1918 as did the number in government and education; the number in industry increased sharply while the largest proportionate increase was in transport.

In spite of the immediate need for more labour, in the early stages of the war there were more women wanting to work than there were jobs for them to do. When the labour shortage became critical late in 1915 and early in 1916, about the same time as conscription was introduced for men, female labour really came to be accepted. The vast increase in the number of working women was, therefore, a feature only of the second part of the war, not of the whole of it, as can be illustrated by the munitions industries. In 1914, 212,000 women were employed in these industries, and in 1915 there were 256,000, only slightly more. In 1916, however, the number almost doubled to 520,000, and by the end of the war there were about 3 million women employed in munitions factories alone.

The mere number of women employed was not the only significant element in the expansion of the female work force. The type of work done and the kind of women employed were also important. Women who had never been inside a factory before, women who were considered to be ladies, engaged in manual work. Many of the newly employed women were enchanted by their new usefulness, impressed by their own ability to perform unfamiliar tasks, and delighted by their new independence and freedom. Others, undoubtedly, only did their duty and resigned themselves rather masochistically to hard work. But all working ladies made a noise about their work, whether it was a shout of joy or a moan of persecution, and thereby drew attention to themselves and, inevitably, to working women of all classes. Some women workers drew attention because they were physically marked out by the yellow skin tone produced by working with the explosive T.N.T., and the patriotic character of their work, and the work of many other women, drew attention to women workers in general. Women were working to help the nation to victory and were patriots, to be accorded all the privileges and respect that go with being a patriot when a nation feels that it is fighting for a just cause or, as in this case, for survival. In 1918 women over 30 were awarded the franchise. There was no militant campaign and no rhetoric. Women had proved themselves in action and earned this as their reward.

Only one area of female employment ran against the general trend and contracted in these years—domestic service. Female domestic employment contracted in the war years by about a quarter of its 1914 labour force. Male domestic employment was also drastically reduced. There was some voluntary cutting down of servants by those who felt that the luxury of having servants in a time of labour shortage was unwarranted and unpatriotic. Some families found their incomes were reduced in the war years and could not afford as many servants, those in which husbands and sons were absent needed fewer servants, and as food controls were imposed there was a decline in formal entertaining of all kinds, which further reduced the need for household staff. Many servant girls, attracted by the extra money and freedom offered by factory and war work, left their old positions of their own volition. The reduction in the number of servants, the employment of which was a major indicator of middle-class status, placed the social standing of some lower-middle-class families in a new and questionable position.

In the emergencies, the increased freedoms, and the heightened emotional atmosphere of war, patterns of social behaviour and standards of what was acceptable were bound to change. There were too few men to go around, and women who had previously led sheltered lives were obliged to appear in public without a male escort. Fewer chaperones were available as maternal friends and maiden aunts found more important work to do or stayed at home to avoid having to cope with the social problems involved in the more vigorous, dynamic, and rougher life of a nation at war. The chaperone and the codes of social behaviour based on her presence began to fade rapidly, and more and more young women began to dine alone or with friends in public restaurants, to order their own meals, make their own travel arrangements, smoke cigarettes, and generally run their own lives with much less supervision or aid than they would have had in the past. Although shorter skirts began to appear before there was a real expansion in female employment, the rigours of working life certainly reinforced their practical appeal. Some young women began to use cosmetics, a practice considered 'fast', certainly not respectable, before the war. Many women now earned their own money and felt entitled to spend it as they pleased; they enjoyed their new freedom and welcomed an opportunity such as this to state their independence of the old ways of doing things. Some probably also began to use cosmetics to emphasize their personal rebellion against the seriousness and the drabness of the war years and to enhance their chances of attracting one of the few men around.

The high casualty rate sharpened the awareness of the fragility and shortness of life. Men knew that each leave might be their last experience of civilian pleasures and were determined to wring the most out of every moment of it. Many women absorbed this feeling, knew that men were in short supply, and felt it almost a patriotic duty to make leaves as memorable as possible. The months and years required to complete established respectable courtship rituals were compressed as acquaintances were more quickly made than in the past, and often friends became lovers and/or marriage partners in the space of a few days or weeks. The marriage rate rose in 1915 from its pre-war rate of about 15 per thousand to 19 per thousand, a rate unequalled in the previous half-century. After this it fell back to something like the normal level until 1920 when it soared again to over 20 per thousand, as marriages arranged in the war years were made when the soldiers and sailors returned home. From 1917 the illegitimate birth rate also rose. There had always been hasty marriages, promiscuity, and illegitimacy, but in the freer, more urgent atmosphere of war they multiplied, to the consternation of the people who worried about the moral structure of the nation and wondered how old standards of respectability could be upheld. When life was short and pleasure rare, many other people found the preservation of old social rituals and forms just for the sake of appearances and reputation a sterile, hollow mockery.

The social and moral codes of the long nineteenth-century peace simply did not fit the conditions and needs of a nation involved in a twentieth-century total war. Adjustments to war conditions were made, the whole moral climate changed, and standards of behaviour, like those of dress, became freer, more casual and relaxed, setting up less rigid patterns which would persist and develop in the postwar years. From the war years came a greater freedom of association between the sexes, an increasing acceptance of casual friendships, and a greater tolerance of emotionally unconventional behaviour. The supplying of contraceptives to men in the armed forces introduced them to people who had previously been unaware of their existence and encouraged their more widespread use. This hastened the downward transmission of what had previously been middle-class patterns of contraceptive use and the increasing acceptability of and desire for smaller families.

Wartime conditions also helped promote a hesitant growth of a new kind of relationship between the classes. The great upheavals of the war flung together members of different social classes who had previously had little or no first-hand knowledge of each other. Under battle conditions class lines came to be overshadowed by the shared experiences of combat and the mutuality of death. The junior officers, drawn from the upper and middle classes in the main, had an appallingly high death rate, while the numerical bulk of the casualties came from the ranks of the common soldiers, the hydra-bodied Tommy Atkins, the human raw material of total war. The conditions of war made contact between upper-class officers and lower-class soldiers inevitable and gave them a set of common experiences which neither group shared with civilians of their own class. Many old stereotyped class images on all sides were eroded by wartime experiences. Many soldiers came to have more respect for and a greater understanding of the upper classes from watching their junior officers in action. For their part, many officers were surprised to find their men to be reasonable, decent, dependable human beings, nothing like the insensitive brutes some of them had imagined. For example, in 1915 Harold Macmillan, then a young officer, wrote to his mother of his growing respect and affection for his men, saying that ' . . . of all the war, I think the most interesting . . . experience is the knowledge one gets of the poorer classes. They have big hearts, these soldiers . . . ' The experience helped change the social attitudes of many men, including this officer, for as Macmillan continued, 'I learnt . . . to be a little ashamed of the intolerance and impudence with which the intellectual classes . . . were apt to sweep on one side as of no account men who had not learnt their particular jargon or been brought up with their prejudices' (*Winds of Change*, 99–100).

At home, too, the classes were thrust together as they had never been before. People from all parts of the country and all classes mixed in canteens, factories, hospitals, and on farms, and many lower-class women were surprised to see some 'ladies' working alongside them in factories and even more surprised that they could get along together. Margarine and custard powder, previously only used in poorer house-holds and, therefore, indicators of lower-class status, began to appear in middle-class homes, and the fixed sum per week meat rationing system forced the prosperous classes to eat fewer socially superior joints and more lower-class sausages. Everyone supported and praised the troops while making no attempt to distinguish classes. These and many similar phenomena weakened class attitudes and preconceptions and began to blur the traditional notions of 'us and them'. After the war class differences opened up again as society returned to something closer to its stratified prewar 'normal', but the return was not complete and the differences, although still heavily marked, were not as deep as they had been. More members of the upper and middle classes were more willing to accord to the lower classes decency, rights, and dignity than they had been, while many of the lower classes were determined that the old cleavages would not be allowed to reappear in such a pronounced form as they had had in the past. Many members of the working classes felt that they had worked and fought as hard as anybody and that they not only were 'as good as everybody else' but had proved themselves to be so.

In the hothouse atmosphere of war, all kinds of social changes grew and blossomed. Overlying everything was patriotism, an impor-tant force for many decades and one which reached new and often absurd heights during the war. In the name of patriotism people were exhorted to refuse service by German or Austrian waiters, mobs broke up shops with Germanic names over the window, German-born residents who had not gone through the formal processes of natural-ization, including many who had for years considered themselves loyal Englishmen, were interned. 'The Hun' came to rival, even to surpass, traditional devils and bogeymen, and no story about the Germans was too bad or absurd to be believed. The lurid pictures of the Germans were coloured by rumours which sprang from such sources as Belgian refugees, whose garbled, only partly understood stories were converted by eager and imaginative listeners into tales of horror involving violated nuns and mutilated babies. The use of mustard gas at the front and the air raids on London and the south coast strengthened the hatred of 'the Huns' and helped whip up anti-

German sentiments. Schoolchildren were urged to write patriotic poems, and the ones which damned the Kaiser and his Huns most vehemently were the most highly praised. The Royal Family, embarrassed by its Germanic name of Hanover, changed its name to Windsor. Residents of southern coastal areas who were careless with lights at night were attacked by patriotic neighbours who claimed they were enemy agents signalling to the Germans.

While imaginary horrors were being invented at home, many real ones at the front were concealed. News from the front constantly announced successes and advances, described the 'happiness' and 'cheeriness' of soldiers in the face of enemy action and general hardship, their love of cleanliness and soap and their 'spirit' and optimism. The churches took advantage of their wartime boom in attendance to announce, in solemnly reassuring tones, that God was on our side and that while war might be unpleasant, it was certainly nothing for a religious man to condemn. Newspapers swung erratically between wild-eyed jingoism and sticky sentiment. For those who cared to look or were forced by personal loss to notice, there was a very different story of the war to be found underneath the colourful versions presented for popular consumption. The soldier in his dug-out, unwashed, ill-fed, cold, wet, and surrounded by the mechanical and human garbage of warfare, was well enough aware of the misery of war, of its frustration, despair, and death. Some civilians also felt the horrors of war keenly in other forms—the hollow despair when a leave was over, the sharp anguish of the stilted letters from a soldier, the cold, grey fear the casualty list brought to families with men at the front.

Nevertheless, there was a brighter side to war where could be found light and gaiety, laughter, alcohol, and a frenzied determination to enjoy life. This provided the foundations for many romanticized pictures of war which presented it as a brightly coloured world in which the sight of the Union Jack brought a lump to all throats, in which cheery, well-scrubbed Tommy Atkins was greeted on his leave by patriotically compliant young ladies and drunken, fun-loving mates; it was a world of munitions factories full of happy, industrious workers, posters of Kitchener's ever-pointing finger, and nutritious margarine.

## THE COST OF THE WAR

Eventually the enemy was defeated, the war was won and the nation survived, but after the jubilation of victory came the counting of the cost. The war proved very expensive and, as well as depleting savings it left many debts which could only be paid in many instalments over many years. The costs of the war, both material and psychological, had a profound effect on society in the interwar years and played an important part in determining the directions social change would take.

The loss of life of the armies of all the nations involved in the war was massive. Casualty lists became so long and the statistics ran into such large numbers that death became de-personalized. Civilians, even soldiers, became incapable of imagining what the loss and maiming of so many men looked like or meant. For example, in just one battle on the Somme between July and November 1916, the British army alone suffered over 400,000 casualties, 60,000 on the first day alone. In total, the British Empire mobilized almost 9,000,000 men, over one-third of whom were casualties. Of the men recruited from the British Isles alone, about three-quarters of a million were killed and almost two million wounded. Counted just as lost manpower, this represented a huge loss, and when all the costs implicit in it were counted, it assumed staggering proportions. The vast majority of the deaths were of men of military age, between about 18 and 35 years old, the age range in which men had the greatest vitality, were most likely to produce children, and were most capable of vigorous work. The cost in life could not be written off in 1918 because the losses echoed on down the years as women not married, children not born, and work not done.

The cost of the deaths had also to be assessed in terms of damaged emotions and disrupted social relationships. Men killed were wounds in the bodies of families which were bound to bleed a little, sometimes for years, and these wounds sometimes crippled a whole family group. In addition to the dead were 'the lucky ones', those who had only been wounded, many of whom were crippled, burned, blind, dis-figured, and shell-shocked. At first, war wounds were honourable badges of service and bravery, and those who wore them were accorded respect, courtesy, pomp, and ceremony. Inevitably, they excited less and less interest as the nation became preoccupied with its peacetime concerns. Slight wounds could be forgotten, remembered only occasionally in a twinge of pain or a story told to workmates, but men with major wounds could not make such easy adjustments to civilian society. Many of the badly wounded could not work, could do only light work, or take charity jobs specially provided for them. Certainly the badly disabled found that civilian society gave them only a limited amount of help which bore little relationship to all the promises, patriotism, and flag-waving with which they were honoured on festival days, all of which tended to make the war-disabled and their families bitter and disillusioned with the social and political systems. The memory of men killed in the war, the awkward gaps their absence left in families, and the presence of the wounded in the postwar world made it impossible for people to forget the war and helped sustain feelings of discontent and disillusion in the interwar years.

After the war the legend of the 'lost generation' began to develop, supported by the fact that about one in ten of the men of military age during the war years were missing. Many men in this age group began to feel that their generation had been decimated for nothing because the prewar world so many of its members had died to save also died in the war, and the brighter, better, postwar world they had been promised was stillborn. This became a generation plagued by a sense of futility, a feeling of having tried to attain some ill-defined goal but having succeeded only in spilling its own blood. The lost generation lost not only a good many of its members, but also lost its way in the maze of trenches, barbed wire, and tangle of deadly orders from incompetent old generals. Some of this sense of loss sprang from the later works of authors in this age group, and much of it was myth, but there is no doubt that many people genuinely, if often only vaguely, shared the feelings of bitterness and disenchantment that the images of the writers conjured up.

It is easy to make too much of the loss of the well-educated young men of the generation which went to war, to attribute the lack of political, business, and industrial leadership in the interwar years to the unusually high casualty rate of the intellectual élite, because this would fit neatly into the pattern of bland, uninspired political leadership and industrial stagnation in the twenties and thirties. It would be easy, but inaccurate, to attribute most of the interwar troubles to this 'loss of leaders', but it must be remembered that many of the men who would become national leaders during and after the Second World War came from this generation and were only working up to high positions in the intervening years. The effects of the heavy losses in the upper and middle ranks of the population cannot, however, be entirely discounted. For example, the decimation of the élite may have helped foster the production of national leaders who came from the lower ranks of society. The experience of the war may well also have affected the attitudes and goals of those who would eventually lead the nation, such as Attlee and Macmillan who were among those who directed the development of the welfare state and the mid-century years of mass prosperity.

The material resources of the nation were drained by the war which depleted both the past savings and future income of the nation. Vast quantities of raw materials of all kinds were devoured by the war and brought no benefit or profit because they could not be reclaimed for peacetime use. Capital and labour were shifted over to war production, resulting in an economic distortion which made industrial reorientation necessary before Britain could cope with peacetime supplies and problems. Taxes were increased to pay for the war, and their revenue met about 30 per cent of the costs (the national debt, which had been £650 million at the beginning of the war, rose to a then-staggering £7,000 million by the end of it), but they had unlooked-for social consequences as well as the anticipated financial effects. For example, the fortunes of the rich were reduced somewhat by the lowering of the income level at which surtax was levied; a heavy Excess Profits Tax was imposed, partly to stop profiteering (at which it was not particularly successful); the standard rate of income tax was increased from 9d to 6s in the pound, and the number of taxpayers was increased. In 1914 less than seven per cent of the population paid income tax, which made it a mark of privilege of the few. In 1918 there were about six times as many taxpayers as there had been at the beginning of the war, and although the payment of income tax was still a sign that the payer made a good income, it was no longer such an exclusive privilege as it had been and, therefore, no longer such a reliable indicator of social rank.

Large quantities of raw materials had to be bought overseas as always, and the price was high. Some of the bills were paid from taxes, some from savings, and some from loans. Throughout the nineteenth century when London was the undisputed financial capital of the world, large investments had been made in foreign loans and securities—in effect, the English had invested their savings and earned interest abroad. Some of these savings were liquidated to help pay for the war, and valuable capital was lost as was the interest it would have earned. In the early stages of the war, the government asked the owners of foreign securities to sell or lend them to the Treasury; by the beginning of 1917 it was no longer limited to polite requests but had the power to requisition certain types of foreign security. During the war about £623 million of private securities were used, and only about half this sum was later paid back to private investors. Some investments were also lost in the wartime destruction of capital

equipment, as in Belgium, and in the confiscation of foreign investments by other governments, as in Russia. The nation's savings of the
prosperous years of the nineteenth century were run down, and the
people and families who had saved found themselves less well-off
than they had expected to be when the war was over. Over all, British
investors lost about 10 per cent of their long-term foreign assets by
liquidation and about 4-5 per cent by confiscation and destruction.
Despite the drain on current income and savings, the government
was forced to borrow from other nations, notably the United States,
and, as a result, Britain, banker to the world in 1914, was in debt by
1918. This was a sudden and drastic shift in the economic role of one
of the major segments of the world economic system, an about-face
which in the long run amounted to the dislocation of the economic
machine built up in the nineteenth century and a disturbance of the
financial equilibrium which contributed to world wide economic
depression and disaster in the postwar years.

Prices rose during the war years, despite the efforts to keep them
stable, and, as always in times of inflation, people living on fixed
incomes found it harder to maintain the standard of life to which
they were accustomed. In the postwar years large sums would have
to be spent on pensions and benefits for the war-wounded, to war-
widows and their children, and on the payments on loans from other
countries. In short, it is impossible to make even an estimate of the
cost of the war. To the loss of life and limb must be added an inde-
finable amount of human anguish and misery, a great weight of
disillusionment which would plague the 1920s and 30s, a loss of confidence and sense of direction and purpose. To the financial costs
must be added at least some of the costs of the consequences of the
dislocation of the machinery of international finance and of the disruption of the national economy.

The First World War marked the close of Britain's golden century
and brought the years of national prosperity, confidence, and world
leadership to a stop with all the finality of the fall of the guillotine.
The age of disillusion and anxiety was opened by the war and, in so
far as these feelings persisted, it may be said that in some respects the
present anxious, disturbed, and cynical generation is still paying some
of the interest on its grandfather's muddy, bloody bills.

*Chapter 6*        The Interwar Years
and Social Readjustments

However desperately people yearned to return to normality after the war, there was no possibility of 'going back' because the shadow of the war continued to hang over most parts of national life in the interwar years. The 'old liberalism' of prewar Britain, already tottering on the brink of senility in 1914, was trampled into the mud of Flanders Field. Patriotic idealism disappeared leaving a gap which would be filled by disillusionment and cynicism. Industrialism, spurred on by the war, entered a new stage of development and the products of assembly lines, numerous and ubiquitous as bacteria, began to spread across the land. The horse and the railway were increasingly challenged for supremacy in transport by the motor car, lorry, and omnibus, and the cinema and radio competed with the popular press for the attention of the people.

For a while the old England of the nineteenth century and the new England of the twentieth existed side by side. The new world was one in which old class divisions were less clearly marked; it was a world of crackling wireless sets, sprawling semi-detached suburbs and modern factories, cigarette coupons, cars and elegant suburban roadhouses, cinemas, flashing fringes and handkerchief skirts in dance halls, 'chara' trips to the seaside for beer, winkles and pottery souvenirs from shooting galleries. It was a world of Woolworth's, greyhound tracks, and 'labour saving devices' bought on hire purchase. In the old world streets were still swept by hand, bootblacks crouched along the pavement, worn old men and battered, bitter soldiers sold matches and shoelaces for a little money and the illusion of work and self-respect. It was a world in which the old-middle class was feeling a serious financial pinch, and workers in the old industries spent a good deal of time on the dole. The work siren sounded all too rarely in old established shipyard, mine, and factory areas, and workers squatted idly on their heels at street corners or sometimes left the dole money for their wives and children and wandered off to look for farm work that offered board and keep and perhaps a joint of meat to take home at the end of the week. There had been upheaval and doubt in the nineteenth century; there had been social cleavage, threats of violence and revolution, but not for at least a century had there been such a general sense of national disturbance, such a strong feeling that the body social, economic, and politic was deeply troubled by new strains and divisions which no one understood.

Symptoms of unease appeared as soon as hostilities ended. The troops wanted to go home and forget the war, but demobilization could not be carried out until a peace had been made. They were impatient of the international negotiations, and their discontent erupted into riots at Folkestone, Dover, Calais, and Luton. The trouble was sparked off by the combination of the troops' impatience with what they considered unnecessary delays in demobilization and their mounting disillusionment with and scorn for national and international leaders whose competence and honesty they questioned. These troops had seen friends and 'Fritzes' fight and die and had been promised a better world for their pains, but when the war was over it seemed as if all the deaths had been for nothing. There was no new world, nothing had improved very much, and the world was still being run by old men like those who had dealt the cards in the four-year game of death. War service had given many of the troops a new confidence in themselves as men and as citizens, while poor high-level leadership, bad conditions, and the high casualty rate had generated a new disrespect for established figures of authority and for the social and political systems they represented. Once the war was over, many soldiers were determined not to be 'messed about' by anybody, and it was soon evident that the prewar forelock-touching and deference of the lower classes would be modified by a new truculence.

The government tried to placate angry troops and restless civilians by attempting to speed up the process of peace-making and by instituting a 'first in, first out' demobilization policy. This replaced the original government plan for demobilizing soldiers according to their occupations in order to get the economy moving again, which may have been sensible but was unappealing to soldiers. Pieces of the promised new world were given to Tommies in the shape of the Franchise Act, which finally brought full manhood suffrage, and the Education Act of 1918. Women received their reward in the shape of suffrage for women over thirty. The first postwar election, the 'Khaki election', was hastily arranged and held in 1918. Most people were still numbed by the war and simply voted for the party which had 'won the war', and, in fact, many soldiers were unable to use their new votes. As an attempt to pour oil on troubled waters it was not very successful, and impatience and irritation soon burst out again. In 1919 the police, some of whom were ex-soldiers, went on strike in London and Liverpool, where riots forced the authorities to call in the army. In the same year the miners threatened to strike, and a railwaymen's strike was prevented only by the use of Dora's powers, which had not yet been removed. Some people feared a revolution and murmured apprehensively about the Russian example, while a few of the more disenchanted began to advocate just such a revolution.

The mood of the nation in the interwar years is more than usually difficult to convey because the nation was dividing along new lines, and at the same time was being subjected to extraordinarily varied and contradictory social developments and expressions of opinion. Even the clichés of the 'roaring twenties' and the 'grim thirties' are inadequate and inaccurate indicators of the extremes of feeling and rapid shifts in mood. For some people, especially the workers in long-established industries such as shipbuilding and textiles, the twenties were simply a dress rehearsal for the Depression, while for many people, such as those employed in new industries like car-making and electronics, the thirties were good years of rising material standards.

After the war some people celebrated their return to civilian life with a whirl of wild-pleasure seeking, energetically affirming that they were glad to be alive. Others were beset by a vague, nagging sense of guilt because they had survived while many good friends and comrades lay dead and on their way to being forgotten. While some people wanted to forget the whole massive trauma of war as quickly as possible and get back to the safe old world they had known, others missed the excitement, the comradeship and sense of purpose of the war years and found the unsatisfactory and disquieting peace an inadequate substitute. No strong, new, absorbing philosophy emerged to replace liberalism; the blandly uninspiring political leaders provided no hero the newly enfranchised could worship with their votes, and while some longed for the satisfactions and the security of the old world, others began to feel that an entirely new one should be founded.

The God of the established churches was one of the casualties of the First World War. Christianity was represented in the war by bishops and chaplains who mouthed the usual platitudes about God's support and exhorted the people to believe and to trust in their leaders. All this seemed cynical and hypocritical in view of the prodigality of commanders with the lives of their soldiers and the obvious failure of goodness, truth and beauty. Many soldiers returned home cynical of 'spiritual' values and with a new respect for the human values which had sustained them in the trenches, loyalty, courage, and concern for the life of comrades. Some of those who had served in the East returned home with a new knowledge of other religious systems which seemed to have as much validity as Christianity. More and more people became aware that there were alternatives to Christianity, and for some people who thought deeply about religion and questioned old certainties there even began to be some doubt, not only about whether or not Christianity was the one true religion, but even about whether or not God was a male Caucasian. The disillusion of the interwar years was thus tinged with irreligion and anti-establishment religion from the start, and although most people were officially religious, that is, they were baptized, married, and buried with the stamp of approval of the church, the churches found they had less and less real popular appeal and influence. The devout and the members of the old-middle class who followed traditional social forms continued to attend church regularly, and some vigorous religious groups, such as the Salvation Army, attracted new recruits, but the social pressures in favour of attending church had almost disappeared, and the number of alternative Sunday occupations was multiplying. Most of the new forces which were shaping the future forms of society, such as the cinema and mass advertising, simply ignored the churches, which found themselves with no new role or function in national life. Their greatest problem was the apathy of the people, but occasionally they were subjected to direct attack. The press, for example the *Daily Herald*, made numerous criticisms of the Church Commissioners for their slum property holdings which they used, not for experiments in Christian solutions to current social problems, but for profit.

Some people sought relief from the problems of the world in amassing possessions and improving their material standard of living, while yet others began to maintain that materialism offered no cures for any ills, personal or social. Government appropriations, high taxes, and inflation showed clearly that small private fortunes were impermanent, not everlasting as prosperous people had supposed in the nineteenth century. This combined with postwar economic problems to break the confidence of the traditional wealth-builders and investors. Few new fortunes were made after the war because economic problems, high taxation, and inflation made the amassing of capital almost impossible and did not give rise to the kind of self-confidence necessary to the accumulation of a small fortune by hard work. The new materialism was, therefore, of a very different character from that which had existed in the previous century. It was more hedonistic, based partly on collector's instinct, partly on responses to mass production and advertising, and partly on a desire to get the most out of life while the going was good.

Intellectual pursuits offered little comfort or security because the questioning and confusion of the prewar years continued. Mathematics, physics, and philosophy seemed joined in a conspiracy to dazzle and bewilder and to produce new discoveries and theories which destroyed the already battered framework of the intelligible universe. Man was left, lost and bewildered in limbo between the vast universe of Einstein, where old constants became variables, and the tiny universe of the Curies, where invisible things produced mysterious glows on photographic plates and strange rays penetrated flesh and bone. In the interwar years scientists and philosophers continued the destruction of the old, predictable universe which had helped sustain the Victorians in their solid self-confidence. The notion that the universe was the setting for the drama in which man had the leading role became absurd in the light of scientific discoveries. The evidence now suggested that man was an insignificant accident on an unremarkable planet populated primarily by microscopic organisms—an idea hardly likely to support a self-confident philosophy of life.

The mourning for youth lost in the war developed into an unprecedented indulgence and adulation of the young which was, perhaps, compounded by guilt and/or gratitude. Young people were admired less for their achievements and virtues than for the simple fact that they were young. Because they were admired and indulged and because they were more in tune with many of the new forces of change, young people became important social pace-setters at this time and were on their way to forming what would come to be called a youth sub-culture in the middle years of the century. The greater emphasis on freedom and the adjustments of the old social code brought, among other things, more freedom of discussion about sex while the more widespread use of contraceptives permitted more freedom of action. The blending of these and many other ingredients, including dashes of short skirts, cosmetics and frantic new dances as seasoning, made a potent new social mixture. This produced new codes of behaviour and new amusements, a whole new way of looking at things which was as different from the old as the martini was from a pint of porter.

The interwar years were years of social fracturing and readjustments.

The old, the young, the prosperous, the unemployed, southerners, northerners, pacifists, fascists, middle classes, working classes, and a whole range of other overlapping and interlocking groups had their own special feelings, sorrows, joys, and opinions, many of which underwent rapid changes from time to time. These years brought no solutions to the problems of life in an increasingly unstable, unpredictable, and swiftly changing world. There were no certainties, nothing seemed to last very long any more, and many people simply resigned themselves to surviving, coping with life as best they could from day to day, and wringing out of it as much pleasure and happiness as they could when the opportunity was offered. For all the surface frivolity, the hysteria, the passions, loud music, and fast living, the nation was, in many ways, less dynamic than it had been before the war. Perhaps the failure of the dream of a quick victory and a better world was responsible for the loss of the old confidence and vitality; perhaps it was a weary resignation to carrying the many burdens left by the war; perhaps it was the numbness produced by the horror of so much death for so little reason or reward. Whatever the cause, the product was a loss of dynamism in the often drab and bitter interwar years. The spirit of the lost generation haunted many of the people who spent their young adulthood in these two decades when nothing was right and when there was no sure peace and security for men by their firesides, in their minds, or with their gods.

TRANSPORT AND COMMUNICATIONS

The wartime demand for rapid land transport stimulated the production and development of motor vehicles, which became one of the important 'new' postwar industries. The motor car, merely a rich man's toy before the war, became a more common possession in the interwar years, mainly because mass production lowered prices. In 1922 Austin brought the car within reach of the merely prosperous, as opposed to rich, when it put its first 7 h.p. car on the market. The number of cars on the road increased from 200,000 in the early twenties to almost two million by 1938. Despite this boom, the horse continued to provide a substantial proportion of the power for road transport. As late as the second half of the thirties, outside prosperous districts of the midlands and south, the car was still something of a novelty, the prized possession of the local doctors, lawyers, and businessmen and nothing but a dream for most other people.

Even in the days when the horse was undisputed king of the road, traffic accidents had been a commonplace. The railway also had claimed many lives since Huskisson, President of the Board of Trade, had been killed by Stephenson's *Rocket*, but, from the first, motor-car accidents aroused more public concern, probably partly because of the apparently excessive speed of cars, partly because accidents began to occur in significant numbers at a time when statistical compilation was becoming more sophisticated, and partly because the car was dramatic and excited the popular imagination. Press agitation about car accidents increased, especially after the 20 m.p.h. speed limit was removed in 1930. The 1934 Road Traffic Act imposed government regulations on both public and private vehicles. A 30 m.p.h. limit in built-up areas, new road signs, one-way streets and roundabouts were introduced along with safety regulations requiring, for example, that cars have non-splinter windscreen glass, better lights, and windscreen wipers. Driving tests were introduced for all new drivers, although current drivers were not required to take a test, a provision which was either an anachronistic echo of the ancient idea of endurance being the equivalent of legality, or one which was based on the assumption that anyone who had managed the early temperamental cars was, by definition, a good driver.

Although by the early thirties there were enough cars on the road to warrant government regulation, they remained the prestige possessions of the comfortably off. Having been born a rich man's gadget, the car seemed destined from the first to be a great and enduring status symbol. The downward transmission of status symbols which had been evident in Victorian England persisted into the twentieth century, and even when cars were mass produced and within reach of the new-middle and upper working classes, they remained status symbols. At lower social levels the siren song of the motor car was sung less expensively if more noisily by its cheaper little brother, the motor cycle, whose numbers also increased throughout the 1920s. The motor bike was beyond the financial reach of most people, but within the reach of many who were not quite rich enough to afford a car. It appealed to the young but, except as personal transport to and from work, it had little appeal for the family man because it could carry only one or two extra people when equipped with a sidecar. The prosperous young tended to abandon a bike for a car on entering marriage or a profession, and few working-class men could afford to keep their luxuries when faced with such financial strains as marriage and the cost of setting up a home. The motor bike was, in the main, the vehicle of the marginally prosperous elements in society, and as soon as their margins were cut, the bike had to go. The number of motor cycles, which reached its peak of 720,000 in 1930, dropped, as unemployment rose, to under 520,000 in 1935. By contrast, although the rate of growth of the number of cars slowed down in the depression, there was no absolute fall in their number because they were not within the range of the people who were hardest hit by unemployment.

More important than either the car or the motor cycle in the development of public transport was the motor bus. Trams and trolley buses, the established public road carriers, continued to increase in number and in importance to the cities and towns they served. The bus, while performing the same functions as the tram and the trolley, had the advantages of being more flexible since it was able to go anywhere there was a road and needed no fixed equipment like cables or tracks. In and around towns the effects of the bus service were much like those of past carriers in establishing new suburban areas. The long-range capabilities of the bus, however, introduced new elements into public road transport. Buses were used on long-distance routes which strung together hitherto isolated villages and towns and made a vital contribution to the increased mobility of the rural population. The weekly, bi-weekly, daily, or even hourly appearance of the bus became a regular feature of village life in the interwar years. The bus service made it possible for even quite poor people to go to town or to visit friends in the next village on occasions; it allowed the people of small towns and villages to shop at the big glossy stores and to see new items the village shopkeeper had not even considered stocking; it allowed the people of isolated areas to go to the cinema every now and then. In short, it helped bring towns, and their social forces and forms, into much more direct contact with the lives of rural people and in so doing made a great contribution to increasing national social uniformity and to the widening of the pool of common experience. The bus service also helped drain life out of the countryside by encouraging the movement of young people from rural to urban areas, helping push many of the villages it served to the edge of extinction by draining off their young people.

The bus added an important new element to the mobility of the urban masses. The traffic between town and country was two-way, and the long-distance bus route allowed the townsman to go to the country on his day off. Trains had long provided a similar service, but there were important differences between buses and trains. The bus proceeded at a more leisurely pace and was better for sightseeing; it stopped more often, frequently at the driver's discretion, and the traveller could often get off precisely at his favourite picnicking place or the start of his walk. The bus was cheaper than the train and went to places which had no railway, especially to rural areas in the midlands, East Anglia, Cornwall, Devon, and Wales, all important recreation areas for the rapidly growing towns and cities of the midlands and south.

The bus provided a new kind of inexpensive travel service. It could be hired cheaply by a small group to take the group almost anywhere it wanted to go; trains could go only where there were lines and were too expensive for anyone except the most prosperous people to hire. The only forerunner of the chartered bus service was the horse-drawn charabanc, a conveyance whose occasional appearance had delighted and terrified schoolchildren and club members since the turn of the century. The motor-powered successor to the charabanc was faster and had a wider range. Its hiring for the annual school trip allowed many children to experience the delights of the countryside or gave them their awesome first sight of the sea. Clubs, societies, works organizations, and groups of all kinds quickly grew accustomed to hiring a bus for an annual outing for their members. Some groups made educational visits to museums and historic sites; some went to London, Birmingham, or Manchester to see the big city and perhaps a play or Christmas pantomime; many went to the sea, to paddle, to walk on the pier, or just to wonder at the waves. These trips were big occasions for their participants, many of whom had never been more than a mile or two away from home before the bus came. They were highlights of life to be stored away in the memory; they were spending sprees and times for doing and seeing new things. In many ways they were the forerunners of the modern, group-excursion, package holiday away from home.

Unlike motor vehicles, aeroplanes did not come of age in the war, but their early stages of development were accelerated. By the end of the war, planes were showing promise for the future and were being treated more as serious transport machines and less as the impractical fantasies of fevered imaginations. The first serious air service, between London and Paris, was established in 1919. Other regular services followed, and by 1922 air transport was a serious enough proposition for the government to begin granting subsidies to air transport companies. Government interest in air transport continued, and in 1924 it merged four companies to form British Imperial Airways. In 1935 a second amalgamation produced British Airways, and in 1939 the two companies were themselves merged to form the nationalized company, the British Overseas Airways Corporation. Few people travelled by air in the twenties and thirties, but air travel, by its very novelty, attracted attention and helped popularize the idea that distant places could be reached in very little time. Air travel had little real social significance until the 1960s when the plane would become a more expensive, longer-range bus, whose services would enable many working people to catch their first glimpse of foreign lands, just as the bus had enabled their parents to catch their first glimpse of the sea.

The press progressed along lines already well established by the turn of the century. The large circulation newspapers of the prewar years developed into big business to which advertising revenue, rather than sales revenue, contributed an increasingly large proportion of the profits. Circulation continued to grow, and by 1939 the *Daily Express* and the *Daily Herald* each sold around two million copies a day. The continued stress on enormous sales and the saturation of the market by national newspapers undermined the regional press and relegated most local papers to the weekly publication of purely local news. A few regional papers survived as dailies, notably the *Manchester Guardian*, but most found survival difficult and managed to continue only by cutting costs and limiting the number of editions. The growing importance of the volume of sales resulted in a 'sales war' between the national papers which became quite bitter in the 1930s. The papers invented a variety of schemes to attract readers, the most important of which was the offer of free health and life insurance to regular readers. This ingenious exploitation of the widespread insecurity of the early thirties proved very expensive, and the competition was slowed down in 1932 when the major papers, to ensure their own survival, reached an agreement to offer more or less equal insurance coverage and to compete in other, less expensive ways. Thereafter, they concentrated on competitions of all kinds, prizes and free offers and gifts.

The popular press doubled the rations of traditional items of diet for its readers and strove to give them as much sensation, death, scandal, and gossip as possible, although it dealt with the scandal of the century with the greatest restraint. For some time the press had accepted that the royal family was not a fair target for mud-slinging because it exercised no right of reply, and this self-imposed censorship continued to apply to reports of the affair of Edward VIII and Mrs Simpson. Few other holds were barred, however, and the press busied itself with one popular whimsy, fashion, and scandal after another. Some newspapers even created their own crusades. For example, in the 1930s, Beaverbrook of the *Express* took up the cause of the Empire and seemed determined to out-jingo Kipling. He launched an embryo political party in co-operation with the *Mail* and collected £100,000 in party funds from readers before abandoning the enterprise and contenting himself with patriotic rhetoric.

The number of human-interest items was increased to include 'advice by experts' articles. The popular press of the late nineteenth century had included a few special-interest items, notably ladies' columns, but the 'expert' columns of the interwar years were more varied and sophisticated than these early items. Many columns appeared which were at least said to have been written by professionals, including some who, for real or imaginary ethical reasons, could only sign themselves 'Doctor', 'Lawyer' or 'Nurse'. Columns dealing with advice to the lovelorn, etiquette, and practical skills such as gardening and home repair were also popular. The proliferation of these items both reflected and stimulated a widening public interest in all manner of topics and an increasing concern with the advice of 'experts' in all fields. Their popularity may also have drawn something from a vague general awareness of increasing specialization in all walks of life and from the insecurity which prompted some people to seek the support of others to justify their own actions.

A good deal of criticism has been levelled at the popular press for vulgarizing, distorting, sensationalizing, and generally abusing the news. Much of this criticism was and is valid, but beneath the often dramatic failures of the press lie its less-publicized successes. However simplified or unreliable its information might be, the newspaper-reading public of these years was generally better informed than any really large segment of the population had ever been because, along with the sensations, trivia, and nonsense, the press provided information and education in massive doses for its readers. All this helped propagate the growth of a more standardized national culture and of an increasingly common set of ideas, prejudices, and aspirations. Because some of the ideas popularized were outdated or impractical and many of the emotions newspapers generated were neither noble nor productive, it is easy in retrospect to condemn the popular papers for not being more informative, more educational, and a more positive force for good in national life. Nevertheless, they helped produce a better-informed 'general public' than there had ever been in the past.

Technological advances produced new communications media

whose widespread use was made possible by mass production in the electronics industry and more efficient retail distribution of consumer goods. One of the first to benefit from these conditions was the motion picture industry. The rapid rise in the popularity of the cinema in the interwar years sapped the strength of older forms of entertainment such as the music hall and provincial theatre, many of which closed or submitted to the final indignity of being converted into cinemas. The cinema has been praised and damned, over- and under-estimated as an agent of social change to a greater extent than any communications medium except television. There can, however, be no debate about the fact that in the interwar years the cinema became enormously popular and wove itself into the fabric of social life at all levels. Cinemagoing quickly became a habit among the prosperous working and lower middle classes, many of whom went once a week and sometimes more often. It became a longed-for treat for the poor, who could afford to go only occasionally, and in the 1930s it began to become respectable among the upper classes when the royal family had equipment installed at Sandringham.

The cinema was the magic carpet of the masses. It required, and was willingly given, a suspension of disbelief more absolute than the theatre demanded, and in return it offered an escape from reality more complete than anything except drunken stupor. In wide-eyed semi-hypnosis under the flickering screen, audiences forgot the Depression and personal problems and lived in a celluloid world where heroes were handsome, brave, and successful and heroines beautiful, romantic, and eventually rescued. The importance of the cinema to social development lay in its national coverage and the enormous size of its audience. In 1931 it was estimated, on the basis of total weekly cinema attendance, that one-third of the population of London went to the cinema (Smith (ed.), *New Survey of London Life and Labour*, vol. IX, 47). A similar proportion of the population probably went to the cinema in other parts of the country too, and the number of 'picture palaces' everywhere increased rapidly. The audience was not made up of exactly the same people each week, and so it can be said that, over an extended period, most people went to the cinema. Because its coverage of the population was so complete, the cinema was a great standardizing agent which brought huge numbers of people together through vicariously shared experiences and promoted a general worship of the same heroes and the formation of similar dreams. It was a powerful advertiser for the 'good life', although its interpretation was American because most films were made there.

Because cinemagoing was a cross-class, inter-regional phenomenon, it helped create increasingly common standards of expectation and aspiration for all sections of society. Even the rich wanted the world of youth and glamour it portrayed; the poor wanted its material benefits also.

The establishment of the nationwide habit of cinemagoing was bound to affect old leisure-time habits because people who spent their limited margin of time or money on it could not pursue their old leisure-time occupations. Churchgoing, game-playing, even drinking, paled beside its ever-growing popularity. The precise relationship between one form of escape and another is impossible to assess, but it is possible that there was some connection between the popularity of the cinema and the low level of drunkenness after the First World War. The working classes did not resume their traditional drinking habits after the war, partly because restrictions on sales continued, partly because standards of living and aspirations changed, and possibly partly because the cinema offered an attractive alternative form of escape. It offered, like drunkenness, a period of total escape from reality, but it was cheaper and its after-effects, both physical and social, were not unpleasant. It also had the advantage of providing the raw material for daydreams, which extended its escape potential far beyond the time actually spent in the cinema. Other effects of the cinema on social life are also difficult to measure precisely. It undoubtedly changed the appearance of the people by influencing popular fashions. Like fashion magazines, films conditioned the audience to accept certain styles as attractive and desirable and others as ugly or unfashionable. The fact that Garbo or Shearer, after a variety of glamorous escapades, got her man, encouraged women to copy significant details of her style in the hope of achieving similar results. Although the audience was largely unaffected by the stories of the private lives of its Hollywood heroes, the manners and *mores* presented by the films themselves had an impact which occasionally went deeper than selfconscious mimicry. The adoption of American words, phrases, and slang was encouraged by the massive import of films from the U.S.A., as was the idea that the material surroundings of the phantom people of Hollywood's make-believe land were necessary basic equipment for the leading of the good life.

The political and social potential of the new medium of radio was quickly recognized, as was the fact that the control of the medium was of paramount importance in Britain because its limited area could be covered by relatively few transmitters. The chaos produced in

America by the operation of free enterprise in broadcasting could be avoided if British radio were placed under public control. Consequently, the British Broadcasting Company was the only company allowed to broadcast and was made responsible to Parliament through the Postmaster General. The Company was established in 1922 and became a Corporation, operating under a charter renewable every ten years, in 1927. The popularity of radio, and the number of receiving sets, grew steadily in the 1920s, and 'the wireless' came into its own in the 1930s in which decade it became an important part of national life.

At first, the thrill of radio lay simply in getting a noise out of a strange machine, but this soon wore off and interest became centred on the content of the programmes, which in the early days of the BBC were characterized by their solemnity, high purpose, and conscious educational intent. The early debates about the great potential of radio had something to do with this, but the BBC owed a great deal of its early earnest and selfconscious respectability and dedication to its first Director General. Sir John (later Lord) Reith was head of the Corporation until 1938, but his influence lingered on for many years and is still acknowledged in the stately verbal gavottes of the annual Reith lectures. Reith's BBC provided serious musical programmes, news, weather forecasts, talks on serious subjects, and religious services on Sunday, interspersed with lighter items such as dance music programmes. In the later 1930s serialization of such works as *The Count of Monte Cristo* were presented and 'Band Wagon', a forerunner of the wartime and postwar comedy shows, was introduced. In these early, solemn years the image of 'aunty' BBC, a straight-laced second cousin of Dora, was created, but, despite this, 'listening in' became a national pastime in the thirties. Families collected around their wireless sets and gave their favourite programmes their undivided attention. In the thirties the radio set was not the half-heard provider of background noise it would become after the Second World War but the focus of attention, as the television set would be in the 1960s. Children sometimes complained that they could not do homework because the radio was too distracting; some families squabbled about who should listen to what and when, but on the whole, radio probably strengthened family life by giving the family group a new common interest.

The new ideas and standards promoted by the mass communications media were more widely diffused throughout society and across all parts of the country than new ideas had ever been before, simply because the coverage of the new media was so wide. This widespread dissemination of ideas and information promoted an increasing degree of standardization and uniformity throughout society and helped close old gaps and set up new social patterns. For example, films played a large part in the 'Americanization' of England with their promotion of American ideas, phrases, and products. By popularizing music, literature, and serious debate, radio helped narrow the knowledge gap between the 'educated' and 'uneducated' segments of society. The monopoly and central control of the BBC promoted a drift towards standardization of accents and speech patterns. The voice of the BBC was heard by people of all classes and regions, and the rounded tones of 'BBC English' became the recognized, respectable standard accent of the nation as a whole against which all others were measured. Although radio did not abolish regional and class accents, it did help smooth off some of the more extreme edges, and it provided something the nation had never had before, a standard pattern of pronunciation which was readily available to anyone who sought to replace his incriminating vowel sounds with something more socially acceptable. Accent was still an important element in social classification, and anything which helped erode accents made an important contribution to increasing social uniformity.

EMPLOYMENT AND THE DEPRESSION

Fundamental economic changes took place during and after the war which profoundly affected the living standards of the people and which brought about changes in the social structure. Many important markets of the prewar years were restricted after the war because nations which Britain had previously supplied had either established the habit of buying elsewhere in the war years when British exports were restricted or had established industries of their own which they protected with high tariffs. The contraction of markets which had begun during the war continued into the peace partly as a result of the fragmentation of the international economy. Economic muscle passed to the United States, while economic control, exercised by the central institutions of the international finance system, remained in Europe in the hands of the nations who now lacked the economic power to carry their traditional burden. The structure of the world economy which had been built up slowly in the nineteenth century cracked and crumbled as power was rapidly shifted away from the centre of responsibility, and the whole edifice finally came crashing down in the Great Depression.

Industry separated out into two major parts, the old industries, the pace-setters and prosperity-makers of the nineteenth century, settling into decline, and the new industries, the pace-setters and prosperity-makers of the twentieth century, making great strides forward. This economic division of the nation gave birth to a new kind of social division because local prosperity, or the lack of it, increasingly determined the living standards of the people. Those in prospering districts enjoyed higher living standards, while those in stagnating areas struggled along with only very slowly improving conditions. The basic industries, iron and steel, coal, shipbuilding, and textiles, were given a great boost by the war's demand for their products, but this provided no foundation for long-term prosperity and simply distorted the appearance of the condition and importance of these industries. Wartime prosperity was extended for a short time by the release of pent-up domestic demand, but after this was satisfied the old industries began to decline. There was less work available, wages began to fall, and a pool of worker resentment began to accumulate which would eventually contribute to the General Strike, the most obvious symptom of industrial *malaise* to appear before the Depression.

After the war, fuel demands fell as world trade declined, coal-powered industries reduced their production, competition from oil and electricity increased, and other nations poured cheap coal onto the world market. Mine owners responded to their increasing economic problems by cutting both production and costs, both expedients which hit the miners hard, and the blows fell all the harder because the miners had enjoyed an unprecedented degree of prosperity and security in the war years. During the war they had been treated less like grimy trolls to be sneered at by other workers and by the wearers of white collars, and more like specialists, so necessary to the nation that they were not allowed to go to the front. As soon as the war was over, their new status was lost, their wages and living standards began to fall, and many miners feared a reversion to nineteenth-century attitudes on the part of the nation and their employers. In 1925 the mine owners announced that in July wage rates would be cut by 10–25 per cent, although they said that the rates might be a little better if the miners would agree to a shorter, eight-hour, working day. The owners also suggested that the retail cost of coal could be cut if railwaymen's wages were cut to reduce transport costs. The unions in the long-established industries saw this threat to cut wages as the thin end of the wedge and felt that a victory for the mine owners would encourage the owners of all other industries in economic difficulties to follow suit. Thus when a royal commission, while criticizing the mine owners for the neglect of their industry, endorsed the demand for a wage cut, there was strong union support for the miners, and when further negotiations failed to produce a settlement, the General Strike began on 4 May 1926. The Strike was a milestone marking both the strength and the weakness of organized labour in postwar society. Although the miners were supported by sympathetic strikes by unions in the older industries and a few of the new ones, there was little public sympathy for their cause. Troops were called in to perform essential services, and other sections of society drew together to cope with the emergency while the striking unions began to split apart. After fresh negotiations with the government, the Strike was called off on 13 May, although the miners remained out until the end of the year.

The Strike brought no immediate benefit and much individual hardship to mining communities. Indeed, the entire trade union movement was temporarily weakened by the passing of the Trade Union Act of 1927, which not only forbade sympathetic strikes calculated to put pressure on the government, but also crippled union finances by making members' subscriptions to the Labour Party a matter of individual choice rather than routine practice. The Strike did however alert trade union leaders to the need of forging a better machine for both negotiations and strike action in a sophisticated industrial society. Despite its failure, the Strike had shown that unions were no longer lame dogs in need of assistance and sympathy in their struggle for liberty but a powerful force and potential threat to the profits of capitalists, whose strength and activities foreshadowed future changes in the balance of society.

The prospering new industries were founded, in the main, on technological advance, mass production, advertising, mass markets, and the provision of services. Although very varied, they shared common elements including their freedom from the industrial determinants of the nineteenth century and their high levels of flexibility, mechanization, mass production, and profitability. Most of them were powered by electricity or oil, not coal, and were thus unaffected by the old siting tyranny of the coalfields. They were generally cleaner than the old industries, and working conditions were more pleasant. They produced not boilers, railway lines, rolling stock or huge quantities of bulky textiles, but radio sets, motor cars, light bulbs, vacuum cleaners, and the man-made fibres for brighter, lighter textiles. The conditions of work helped accentuate the social differences between the new and the old industries. For example, workers in the new industries often did little physically exhausting work and wore clean overalls or antiseptic white coats, while those in the old industries continued to do tiring work and to wear the battered and grimy work clothes which had been characteristic of nineteenth-century workers.

Just as agrarian society had shifted and resettled along new geographical and social lines in England's transition into a heavy industrial society, her heavy industrial society underwent a series of geographical and social shifts in the process of becoming a light industrial society. The population's centre of gravity, which had moved from the agrarian south and east to the coalfields of the north and west, began to shift again as the coal-fed industries declined, moving to the developing light-industrial areas in the midlands and the south-east. There was a gradually accelerating drain of people away from the low wages and poor working conditions of the coalfields to the better pay and conditions around Birmingham and London.

This simplified picture of the broad outline of change suggests an ease of transition, a degree of inevitability, and an orderliness that were not apparent to contemporaries. The new industries produced consumer goods and depended on mass production, advertising, and the creation of a large market. They produced, in the main, non-essential commodities for relatively large numbers of modestly prosperous people, but England was not very prosperous in these years and export markets were restricted. Once the new industries were established, they themselves built up a pool of modestly prosperous manual and white-collar workers who could, and would, buy consumer goods and generate a continuing expansion of the market. The problem was to get this process started. In addition, the attraction of the new industrial areas for workers was not as immediately evident as the simple outline might suggest. While wages and conditions of work were generally better in the new industries, there was no guarantee that these industries would prosper and offer permanent employment, and while the housing in the developing districts was newer, demand was high and there was a good deal of overcrowding. The developing industrial areas were initially something of a new frontier. An air of rawness and impermanence hung over them, and newcomers had to learn to adjust to new accents, habits, and social structures. A few of the migrants could not adjust and returned, disillusioned, to their home districts.

Migration, both temporary and permanent, tended to deepen the new geographical social dividing lines. Those who returned to the coalfields brought home stories of the abrasive newness and absence of traditional social forms and observances in the south and midlands. Those who did not attempt to move but stayed on in the established industrial areas to face unemployment or short-time felt that they possessed a tenacity and reliability the migrants lacked. In their poverty and dim awareness of the widening gap between the poor north and the rich south, they strengthened, partly in self-defence, the myth of the soft, spineless southerners who were not as honest, hardworking, and loyal as they. On the other hand, the migrants who settled in the new areas strengthened the obverse myth of the intelligent, progressive, and polite southerners who provided a sharp contrast with the gruffly behaved, roughly-accented, hard-headed, stubborn, backward northerners.

The broad lines of national division into old and new industries, stagnating and developing areas, and backward and progressive societies had been pretty well established by the time the 'Great Depression' struck at the end of the twenties. In 1929 the American stock-market boom ended with the Wall Street Crash; the effects spread to Europe as impoverished and nervous investors called in short-term loans, foreign credit dried up, exports fell, production was cut, and unemployment increased, soaring in Britain to its peak of over three million people out of work in 1932. In the new industries the Depression was a relatively brief check to expansion; in the old industries it was an intensification of an economic decline which had already been evident for a decade.

Although some contemporary commentators maintained that the unemployed were too idle to seek work and liked living on unemployment allowance, the vast majority of the unemployed hated their idleness and longed for work. Their aversion for the dole was suggested by the hostility aroused by the new means test introduced by the National Government. Infuriated unionists accused the ex-Labour Party members of the new government of betraying their party and class, and an estimated 2,500 people formed a hunger march and advanced on London to present a petition with a million signatures to Parliament demanding the end of the means test. The means test was designed to make people use their savings and any other resources available to them before they were allowed any public money, which seemed to penalize people who had managed to save a little and to reward people who had prodigally squandered all they earned. Allowances were assessed on the basis of household, not personal, income, and when anyone applied for relief, the earnings of all the people living in the same household were investigated. Adults were to contribute everything over the first 5s earned or over half their earnings, whichever was the least, to the income of the household, while young people had to contribute two-thirds of the first £1 earned and three-quarters of all earnings over £1. The embarrassment of having some strange official questioning all the members of a household about their income was enough to ensure resentment of the means test, especially among the aristocrats of labour in the old industries such as skilled shipyard and textile workers. The pride in their craft, their union, and themselves which workers had slowly and often painfully built up over years of struggle was badly beaten and bruised by official forms and bureaucratic pencils. The few jobs that were available in areas of high unemployment were generally given to women and young people because their wages were lower than those of adult male workers, and the young also found it easier to move in search of a job. This meant that in many households the father, and perhaps some other older males, able and willing to work, were kept by their wives and children. Many men found this shameful, a few found it intolerable, and most families found it a strain.

Life on the dole was lived in bad or inadequate housing, such as that described by Orwell in *The Road to Wigan Pier*, in the mid-1930s. At the lower extreme was utter misery—'What chiefly struck me was the expression on some of the women's faces, especially those in the more crowded caravans. One woman had a face like a death's head. She had a look of absolutely intolerable misery and degradation. I gathered that she felt as I would feel if I were coated all over with dung' (from 'Road to Wigan Pier Diary' in Orwell and Angus (eds), *Collected Essays, Journalism and Letters of George Orwell*, vol. 1, 177). Most unemployed people, however, continued to occupy the worker housing left over from the nineteenth century, which long remained 'typical' worker housing in old-established industrial areas. Most of these terrace houses had two rooms downstairs, two upstairs, and sometimes an attic or cellar. Heat came from the old-fashioned, cast-iron, 'black-leaded' stoves, which were also used for cooking, in the living room. A sink and a 'copper' (a large cauldron over a coal fire in a brick framework for heating large quantities of water) were the basic kitchen equipment in the back room, and the complement of sanitary facilities was made up by an outdoor lavatory, often shared with neighbours, and a tin bath which was filled from the copper for weekly family ablutions. In these small houses, whose main rooms were generally not much larger than 10 or 12 feet by 14 feet, overcrowding was common. Orwell felt that the most striking difference between lower-class and middle-class housing was the degree of overcrowding. In even lower-middle-class housing, ' . . . if you definitely want to be alone you can be so— in a working-class house *never*, either by night or day' (*Collected Essays . . . of George Orwell*, vol. 1, 196).

Life on the dole also meant dull and inadequate food, patched clothes, sparse furnishings, 'making-do', and trying to find some way to retain self-respect in idleness. Many women wore away their active lives in the never-ending, soul-destroying round of the necessities of making-do, whereas for men sheer idleness was generally the greatest burden. There was little enough money to feed the family, let alone buy entertainment, and prolonged idleness had few pleasures. Traditional worker hobbies, such as whippet- and pigeon-keeping, declined when there was little or no food for the dog, and the birds had made their last contribution to family welfare at the dinner table. Staying at home only reminded a man of his failure to provide for his family, and many men went out a great deal, only to collect with others at street corners in the dingy groups pictured by contemporary photographers which seem to epitomize the Depression and the misery of unemployment. With chronic unemployment, skills decayed, hands became less deft, eyes less quick, muscles softened, and self-respect withered.

As the months and years passed and the nation began to ease slowly out of the Depression, the gap between the new and old industries, and rich and poor people, opened wider as the new industries recovered quickly and began to expand while the old ones lagged even further behind. By the mid-1930s it was fairly clear that the future lay with the new industries, but long-term national trends could not always alter human realities. For example, a middle-aged, unemployed shipyard worker knew that he was not trained to make electric light bulbs or to pack food, that he was probably too old to make re-training either possible or worthwhile, that he had a wife, children, and home he was reluctant to leave, and that, in any event, he had no money to gamble on a long journey to look for new work. Recovery was first felt in the new industrial areas which needed residential development to provide homes for the expanding labour force, and a building boom, generated by both government and private investment, began to ease the unemployment problem. Construction alone involved bricklayers, plumbers, labourers, electricians, and the makers of mass-produced components like doors and window frames. The new buildings needed decorating and furniture, electrical equipment, soft furnishings, and so on. By 1936 unemployment had fallen to below 2,000,000, but, in spite of the efforts of government and industry, it persisted in many districts, and it was not until war production began in 1939–40 that it again fell to the levels of the pre-Depression period.

## THE STANDARD OF LIVING

Generalizations about living standards in this period are difficult to make because, to an ever-increasing extent, conditons of life depended on areas of residence. Disaster is always more newsworthy than normality, and unemployment and poverty more likely to leave a lasting impression than slowly increasing prosperity. Poor conditions and unemployment attracted official and national interest during the twenties and thirties, while prosperous contentment went largely unnoticed and unrecorded. This imbalance of contemporary interest helps obscure the nature of changes in the standard of living in the interwar years when in fact average living standards improved despite obvious economic problems.

For people who were able to remain in regular employment, the twenties and thirties were good decades, especially after 1929 when prices began to fall. Between 1914 and 1937 average working hours were reduced slightly, while the average earnings of employed workers nearly doubled and prices rose only by about 50 per cent, producing a considerable improvement in real wages. While all this was taking place, the general level of mass expectations was rising. The war had given the working classes a greater self-confidence and feeling of personal worth in society, as well as a determination to obtain their fair share of the good things of life. Many of the changes of the inter-war years, such as mass production, advertising and cinemagoing, built upon this foundation and kept standards of expectation rising. More and more people came to expect hot-water systems in ordinary homes, with either a boiler behind the fire or a gas-geyser over the sink; more and more people began to entertain realistic hopes of having electricity, a wireless set, a gas cooker and perhaps even a vacuum cleaner. Nineteenth-century investigators into the living conditions of the masses had classified such items as sugar and tea as luxuries, but by this time most people expected a far better diet than their ancestors had had, and few, even among the poorest sections of society, considered that sugar and tea were luxuries any more. In popular terms, 'luxury' now meant meat twice or more a week, a joint on Sundays, and treats such as tinned salmon, fruit, and condensed milk when visitors were being entertained. The fact that a growing number of people were occasionally able to enjoy these luxuries helped sustain the rise in the level of expectations while it added to the poignancy of the plight of the unemployed.

The increasing number, variety, and availability of mass-produced consumer goods played an important part in raising average living standards while helping to minimize old social differences and accentuate new ones. For those who could afford them, domestic appliances such as washing machines, electric irons, and vacuum cleaners took much of the drudgery out of housework, and as domestic servants became harder to find and old-middle-class incomes dwindled, middle-class people began to buy household appliances. Price thus combined with old social prestige to make consumer goods desirable new status symbols. Mass production methods were applied in food processing industries which became 'big business' in these years and produced a wide variety of convenience foods—bottled and tinned sauces, spices, relishes, jams, potted meats and tinned fish, canned fruits and vegetables. The small independent local grocer became less and less a skilled tradesman who blended his own tea and chose his own cheeses, and more a retail outlet for the pre-packed products of large food packers and wholesalers with a nationwide distribution. More and more foods were processed, standardized by size and quality, and packaged under brand names, reaching the consumer at higher prices but in more convenient forms which helped to reduce the preparation time of meals, and also helped standardize the diet of people of all areas and classes.

The success of convenience foods and labour-saving products was made possible by the growing wholesaling industry coupled with the advertising campaigns of manufacturers who took great pains to ensure that their brands were widely known and in general demand. Chain and department stores had existed for many years, but in the twenties and thirties they became more numerous, far-reaching, and of much greater significance in the shopping habits of the nation. In these years Woolworth's became almost as ubiquitous, certainly as common a part of life, as the local Post Office. The mass producers realized that their business depended on small profit margins and volume sales, and that it was therefore essential to create as broad a market as possible for their products. Merchants and manufacturers proclaimed their wares on billboards, posters, and signs, told of their delights in song and story, animated and glamorized them on film, and generally sloganized, popularized and standardized on a vast new scale.

The development of hire purchase arrangements in the 1930s provided people with small incomes with a new way of buying relatively large and expensive goods. Hire purchase was not, however, considered respectable at this time, possibly because working- and lower-middle-class people, who were most likely to use it, associated it with the 'buying on tick' at the corner shop which the very poor or careless were forced to do when their money ran out. Although socially questionable, hire purchase was certainly convenient, and more people began to use it to buy things which would otherwise have been beyond their reach except after years of saving. Many people found weekly payments more attractive than weekly savings because with hire purchase they could enjoy the desired object almost at once instead of having to wait for it and also because hire purchase contained an element of compulsion and put less strain on will power than voluntary saving. Hire purchase salesmen were aware that their arrangements carried social risks for their customers, and they made much of their tact, discretion, and unmarked delivery vans. Some people were cheated by hire purchase schemes, others charmed into ruin by them and revisited by the plain van which took away the furniture and appliances and left social disgrace, but the system benefited many people and helped raise living standards.

In 'building boom' districts where the local authorities used the government housing subsidies of the 1930s, housing standards improved. To qualify for building grants, local councils had to conform to government standards and specifications, a requirement which produced a rather monotonous 'council house look', but which also ensured that fairly high minimum standards of size, lighting, ventilation, and sound construction were met. Houses on the new council 'estates' were also equipped with basic household conveniences such as indoor lavatories, gas and electricity, and even bathrooms. Council standards came to be regarded as the prosperous working- and lower-middle-class 'normal', the standards which the majority of the people hoped for and tried to achieve, and council building helped in a very practical way to lift the level of expectation of the mass of the people. A council house carried with it the implication of lower-class status, but the difference between the new council houses and cheaper middle-class homes was minimal, and in reality the gap in living conditions which divided the lower-middle class from the council-housed classes was very narrow and in some cases non-existent.

State social services, limited as they were in these years, helped many people and were of at least marginal assistance in raising lower-class living standards and expectations. For example, a few working-class children were able to take advantage of the slightly better educational opportunities and to rise both economically and socially. Old age pensions, health and unemployment benefits were small but they did help sustain the least fortunate elements of society at a higher standard of living than they could have hoped for in the past. Relief payments represented a system of social salvage which operated on an unprecedented scale. Life on the dole may have been miserable, but life without it could well have been impossible, and the fact that so many people lived when they might previously have died represented a buoying up of living standards at the most critical level. The living standard of the unemployed was miserably low compared to the rising standard of employed workers, but they did not have to sleep in the street, see their families split up according to the administrative needs of the workhouse, or endure oakum-picking and gruel in the Poor Law Bastilles. They could live at home with their families and hope for future improvement because the dole kept them alive and did not remove them from the labour market.

The gradual decrease of family size in these decades contributed significantly to the higher living standards. The use of contraceptives became more common, even among the lowest classes, as they became cheaper and more readily available. The economic situation also favoured family limitation. More and more working-class families were beginning to face a choice similar to that which had confronted the middle classes at the end of the nineteenth century: either to improve their living standards by having fewer children, or to have large families and face the consequences of this on their material standard of life. The middle classes had chosen higher living standards, and the working classes followed their lead. Fewer children, labour-saving devices, smaller homes, convenience foods, and extra-domestic services such as laundries, meant more freedom for women and allowed them more time for both paid employment and leisure.

With the return of the soldiers and the ending of wartime production, female employment contracted and many of the trends of the war years were reversed as women moved back into domestic service and other traditional female occupations, although there was not a complete reversal to the old situation. Wartime developments had made permanent changes in the attitudes of respectable people to female employment. The acceptability of war work gave female employment a new seriousness which after the war promoted a more general expectation that some women could do more with their lives than bear children, be decorative, and keep house. Charity work became a more serious matter, and some charity workers began to see themselves as social workers rather than Christian ladies. The interwar years provided many new fields for dilettantism, and women became amateur poets, painters, potters, singers, folk-dancers, fortune-tellers, psychologists, pacifists, political workers, and followers of the multiplicity of fashions which helped give these two decades their particular flavour of fad and frenzy. On the more serious side of life, many respectable women now needed to work, either to support themselves or to bolster up declining family incomes. The fortunes of many previously prosperous families were destroyed by the war or the Depression. Some lost overseas investments, others found business profits smaller after the war, and some lost the sons essential to a prosperous family firm. The disproportionate number of adult females meant that fewer women could expect to marry or to return entirely to their previously male-sheltered lives. Some women also simply took advantage of the increased acceptance of working women to seek the interesting careers they preferred to marriage, and technological change and shifting economic patterns provided them with more job opportunities. As industry became more sophisticated it was increasingly dependent on the people who did paper work, and many of these were women. The new light industries also provided many clean, physically undemanding jobs which were ideal for women workers. Wherever the sex of the worker had little to do with the requirements of the job, women were preferred by employers because their wages were lower than those of adult male workers.

The expansion of the legal rights and responsibilities of women continued in the twenties and thirties. In 1919 the Sex Disqualification Removal Act abolished many of the legal barriers which had previously prevented women from entering certain occupations; the Matrimonial Causes Act of 1923 allowed women as well as men to claim adultery as grounds for divorce; the Criminal Justice Act of 1925 did away with the presumption that any woman who committed a crime in her husband's presence had been forced to do so by him; a further extension of the franchise in 1928 gave women the vote on equal terms with men. Society was accepting that females were fully competent human beings, deserving neither patronage, special protection, nor inferior legal status. While gains were being legally consolidated, some women were breaking ground in highly visible occupations such as politics. After 1918 women were allowed to stand for Parliament, but few did because no party was willing to waste a safe seat on a woman unless she had some strong family connection in the constituency. In 1919 the first female MP, Lady Astor, was returned for Plymouth after her husband's elevation to the peerage. In the twenties a sprinkling of other female MPs appeared, generally taking over the seats of dead husbands. Women had achieved a higher degree of social and legal equality than ever before, but their acceptance in professional positions was limited, and only a few determined individuals succeeded in making full use of their legal freedom. However, some major battles were won, and a few hardy pioneers went out to explore the land of 'equality', to chart its terrain, and to work out the rules of the game of survival for those who would follow.

The 'roaring twenties' saw the social pace-setters radically change appearance and behaviour as the flappers and flaming youths, without whom no fashionable dance, cocktail party, or younger set gathering of any kind would be complete, set entirely new standards. Although the flappers have been seized upon by later generations as the archetypical characters of the twenties, it must be remembered that they were a colourful and occasionally shocking minority and that by no means all young women were flappers. The term 'flapper' first appeared in the later nineteenth century when it was applied to young women of easy virtue. By the early twentieth century it was being applied to eccentric, 'bohemian', young women who wore bobbed hair and, later, short dresses. In the 1920s it came to be applied to the bright, gay, cigarette-smoking, energetic young women who were the convention-breakers of their generation. By breaking conventional standards of dress, behaviour, and sometimes morality, so outrageously, they made the far less extreme but more widespread contraventions of the old rules by other women seem less dramatic, even innocuous, and thus helped moderate departures from the old ways become more socially acceptable.

Mass transport, rising living standards, and shorter working hours combined to change patterns of leisure. The new leisure patterns reflected the new social patterns in many ways, including the standardizing effects of mass production and the rise of working-class standards to a level closer to that of the middle classes. The annual holiday, enjoyed only by the upper and middle classes before the First World War, came within the reach of many working-class people in the interwar years as more and more workers got holidays with pay. By 1939 about eleven million workers, the majority of the labour force, had holidays with pay although most of them seem to have spent their time at home, (Pollard, *Economy*, 293.)

By the 1930s enough people were taking holidays to attract the attention of businessmen, who began to introduce mass-produced, assembly-line holidays in holiday camps. Early holiday camps were small, specialist establishments, catering for people who wanted to combine a holiday with education or a hobby like painting or acting, but these were soon overwhelmed by the large, commercial camps which tried to provide something for everybody. The large camps offered all kinds of entertainment facilities, rows of chalets, gargantuan dining halls, and the security of knowing that the staff would not allow a dull moment. Holiday camps were typically working-class institutions, rarely patronized by the middle class, and a rough class demarcation developed even in seaside resorts. Brighton and Hastings were generally regarded as middle-class resorts, Blackpool and Clee-thorpes as working class, and resort managers tailored their recreational facilities accordingly. Class differences in recreation were further emphasized by the increasing middle-class practice of taking their holidays abroad on cut-rate holiday cruises offered by shipping companies whose business was stagnating as a result of the decline in world trade.

Rambling and cycling continued to be popular among the young, and in 1930 the Youth Hostels Association was founded to provide cheap accommodation for the wanderers in appropriate locations. Tours and excursions by train, bus, motor-bike, and car offered endless entertainments for the restless with money to spend. For the less prosperous and more sedentary there were many activities which could be enjoyed at home. A radio set offered hours of diversion, and large numbers of people continued to enjoy reading. The press was producing a wide variety of publications for all ages and interests, and the established cheap editions were joined by an important newcomer, the paperbacked Penguin book. The interwar years were vintage years for thrillers—adventure and detective stories—and Dornford Yates, Sapper, Sexton Blake, and Agatha Christie became names as well known as the names of cinema stars.

Spectator and participant sports provided recreation for large numbers of people. Cricket and tennis were popular at the upper levels of society, as was horse racing, while greyhound racing attracted an increasing number of working-class spectators in the 1920s. The sport which attracted the largest number of spectators in these years was football. Many men and boys played soccer, and this amateur participation created a widespread acquaintance with and interest in the game. Football pools also helped stimulate an interest in professional games, especially in the 1930s, by giving coupon-fillers the chance of winning anything from a few shillings to a small fortune for the investment of a few pennies. In many parts of the country, the Saturday match of the local football team became *the* social event of the week for many men, and many offices and factories set up their own teams and schedule of amateur matches. Simple football, however, needed nothing more expensive than a ball, goal markers, and the agreement of the players about the size of the playing area. It was a cheap, simple, group sport which could be enjoyed in a variety of ways in a variety of settings—it was mass sport *par excellence*.

Many of the new agents of social change were international forces, cutting across national as well as class lines. Because the economic and technical leadership of the western world passed to the USA after the First World War, it was inevitable that the introduction of new technical forces, and the social changes they helped produce, would appear as 'Americanization'. Anti-Americanism in England in the interwar years was engendered by a feeling that Americans claimed too much credit for their efforts in the war and had taken advantage of an impoverished Europe by buying up its treasures and taking them across the Atlantic. Gainsborough's *Blue Boy* and Agecroft Hall, an old Lancashire house, were just two of the pieces of 'old England' which changed hands and countries in these years. Anti-Americanism did not, however, stop American products, inventions, and fads becoming an increasingly significant part of English life. Jazz, the Charleston, cocktails, and slang were all imported from America, as were most of the films shown in English cinemas. As the techniques of mass production were of American origin, the products of Britain's new industries inevitably echoed the American style, just as the products of nineteenth-century industry all over the world had reflected the British style.

## THE SOCIAL CLASSES

Few of the very rich suffered overwhelming financial setbacks in the interwar years, but the less wealthy upper and middle classes generally became poorer. Signs of lower-aristocrat and old-middle-class distress were numerous. Many town houses around what had been exclusive London squares were sold and converted into flats for white-collar workers; society magazines published pieces on new residential areas like Putney, where no one of any social note had lived before; as paying adequate wages to servants became more difficult, serious consideration was given to labour-saving devices. The decline in the political influence of the aristocracy and old-middle class continued. The Lords had lost the veto power, fewer aristocrats had the time or money to devote to a life of full-time public service, and the old-middle class was poorer, smaller, and formed only a tiny proportion of the mass electorate. The popular papers continued to find in the aristocracy a source of interesting stories which would help to satisfy their readers' eternal curiosity about the lives of the famous, but the social leadership of the aristocracy faced overwhelming challenges. The wartime increase in the confidence of the lower classes persisted and created a less deferential social climate in which the significance of a title and established family background began to fade. New social pace-setters and status-symbol-makers emerged in these years, and the people abandoned the leadership of the aristocracy and followed styles and standards set by advertisers, films, and radio.

The new-middle classes, the white-collar workers, began to enjoy a new degree of influence and importance. The growth of professionally managed, highly sophisticated industry was a stimulus to the growth of this group because as the new industries grew in size and importance, so did the social class which operated them. The middle-class entrepreneurs who had owned and run nineteenth-century industries became less important and less prosperous as old-established industries declined. The new industries were corporate concerns, their capital contributed by faceless shareholders interested only in profit from their investments and more than willing to leave the running of the firm in the hands of salaried professional managers. The new-middle class began to set the new social ideals for the masses at this time by moving to suburbia and buying the cars and appliances which were being turned out by the new industries. It closely resembled the old-middle class in its desire for respectability and success and in its emphasis on privacy and hard work. Its members spent money on a good education for their children and comfortable surroundings, but differed from the old-middle classes in many respects, too. The new-middle class ran industry, whereas the old-middle class had owned industry. The new-middle class was less prosperous than the old-middle class and more closely related by birth and family ties to the working class. It was less self-confident and sure of itself than the old-middle class had been.

Social changes among the working classes reflected the division of the nation into developing and stagnating areas. The workers who remained in the old industries of the north and west suffered all the worst effects of the chronic interwar depression while life for workers who moved to developing areas improved greatly. Those who performed some small and specialized task in an assembly-line process experienced increasing prosperity and rising material standards as business expanded. Many of them lived in houses which looked very much like those of the office workers, the new-middle class, and they showed a similar desire for respectability and comfortable homes. The lines which divided the new-middle class and the workers in prospering industries were much more subtle and difficult to draw than those which had divided the old-middle and established working classes. The worker probably had a smaller house than the middle-class manager; he arrived at work earlier and did not own a car; workers wore overalls at work while managers wore suits. Even in the prospering districts which were setting the social patterns of the future there were class differences, but they were not the class gulfs of the past.

The educational system, the great avenue of social mobility, continued its traditional class orientation between the wars. Plans were made in 1918 and 1926, first to provide compulsory part-time education to the age of 18, then to raise the school-leaving age and to reorganize the primary and secondary schools system, but these plans, the practical extensions of wartime promises, were cut back by economic crises and the Depression. The only long-term gains were the raising of the school-leaving age to 14 and the opening of some free scholarship places to poor but able children. Few primary schools had the facilities for advanced instruction, and for their pupils extended secondary 'education' consisted of no more than marking time until the raised school-leaving age had been reached. Only a small number of children reached the grant-aided secondary schools by passing the 'free place examination'. Many of those who did pass could not complete a secondary education because they had no respectable clothing, their parents could not afford to buy uniforms, they were discouraged by taunts about their 'charity' status, or because they had to leave school as soon as possible to help support themselves and their families. But despite these enormous disadvantages and limitations, some working-class children did manage to get a secondary education and go on to become white-collar workers. Some others found the road to new-middle-class status through hard work, luck, and training on the job or after work.

Although class distinctions were made with less precision than in the past, they were still made, and there were even some developments which ran counter to the general trends and reinforced social stratification. Even in the new residential areas, old class distinctions in housing were honoured—manual workers living on 'streets' while white-collar workers lived on 'avenues' and 'crescents'. Distinctions were created in blocks of flats between the working-class 'building' and the middle-class 'house' and 'court'. A multitude of class distinctions existed in various scales and degrees, in the time of arrival at work, between wages and salaries, between working-class Blackpool and middle-class Brighton. The distinctions were still great scars on the face of society, but beneath them a slow healing, a closing of long-established and deep lesions, was taking place.

# Chapter 7

# War and
# Welfare State

Revulsion against the bloodbath of the First World War showed itself in pacificism and anti-militarism in the 1920s and 1930s. In 1929 the Labour Government ordered Armistice Day celebrations de-militarized; in 1933 the Oxford Union declared that it would not fight for King and Country; in 1935 the Peace Pledge Union was founded and gathered 80,000 supporters for its renunciation of war. Loss of confidence in old-established ways of doing things led many people to respect the European dictators, even to envy their people the discipline and sense of purpose the dictators seemed to provide. Mussolini was much admired for making trains run on time, and many people found the revitalization of the German economy under Hitler impressive and dismissed reports of brutal treatment of Jews as probably untrue and in any event a German domestic issue which was no concern of Englishmen, who had enough problems of their own. Sir Oswald Mosley founded a domestic Fascist party, the British Union of Fascists, in 1934, after he had failed to get his economic reform programme put into practice through the operation of the established party system. The Communist and Fascist parties attacked each other and the parliamentary system with such vigour and violence that special measures, such as the Public Order Act of 1936, were taken to restrain them. As these examples suggest, there were many shades of political opinion in the interwar years, but few people were inclined to take action against Fascism in Europe. The confidence which had supported nineteenth-century Englishmen in their determination to put the world to rights had disappeared. What had not been burned up in the First World War was shrivelled by the chill winds of the Depression, and when Chamberlain returned from Munich with the news that he had bought 'peace in our time' with the life-blood of Czechoslovakia he was hailed as a hero, a strong man who had the courage to work for a compromise instead of accepting a conflict.

The peace which followed the first 'war to end wars' had never been an easy one. The peace pacts and the League of Nations were just thin sugar coatings on the bitter pill of political instability and worsening international relations. In the twenties people hoped that the peace would be permanent and that the forces which threatened it would dissipate. By the mid-thirties, however, it was becoming clear that the threats were mounting. The peace-pledgers continued their worthy but hopeless campaign for peace, while the BUF yearned to import the discipline and order Fascism had brought to Europe, but more and more people began to discuss 'the next war'. By the mid- and later thirties the phrase was in common currency, although few people bothered to define precisely who the combatants might be or when it would come. It was the eventual failure of the policy of appeasement to restrain German expansion that brought the troubled peace to an end. When war was finally declared on 3 September 1939, Germany having made no reply to Britain's ultimatum demanding that she vacate Polish territory, there was no outburst of joy, simply a resigned acceptance that the peace had failed and that a further effort would be needed to win another chance to settle the troubled world.

THE NATION AT WAR

The people again tensed themselves for war and the feeling of national solidarity increased as all sections of society came under the pressure of the unifying forces of mutual danger. The experiences of the First World War and of interwar government controls provided organizational experience which proved invaluable. In 1939 many preparations had already been made for war, including the printing of ration books and the drawing up of plans for new ministries and propaganda programmes, but the country was prepared only on paper and much of the material necessary to implement the plans did not exist. For example, call-up proceeded very slowly because there were far more men available than there were supplies with which to equip them. The period between the declaration of war and the Battle of Britain in July 1940 developed into a war of nerves when the nation braced itself for a German attack which did not come while it continued to prepare for actual hostilities. The very real dangers this war presented to civilian society were signalled by the issuing of gasmasks to all civilians. These grotesque masks became part of civilian life for some time although, after the first novelty wore off, people became careless about carrying them everywhere in their cardboard cases as regulations required. Public lighting was again banned, the showing of lights made an offence, and 'blackout' descended. The dimming of car headlights was immediately followed by a considerable increase in the number of road casualties, which proved, in the first few months of the war, to be much more dangerous to civilian life than enemy action. Plans were set in motion for the evacuation of mothers and young children from areas which were likely to be bombed. By no means all the people who were supposed to move did so, but this government-sponsored urban-rural migration was a considerable operation which involved about three million people. There were no enemy attacks in 1939; the operation seemed rather foolish, and about a third of the migrants returned home by the end of the year.

Few of the lessons of the First World War with regard to the regulation of scarce resources had been forgotten. The National Registration of Citizens of 1939 provided the government with information about labour resources and issued every citizen with an identity card that he was supposed to carry at all times. Food subsidies, which were also introduced in the first year of the war, proved to be enormously expensive, but paid enormous dividends in industrial peace and in a high level of national morale, both essential to a nation engaged in total war. An equal distribution of food and other supplies was ensured by the ration book system. By mid-1940 the civilian Englishman, whatever his social status, was deemed ready to face the rigours of war only when caparisoned in his gasmask, faintly reminiscent of the headdress of a medieval war-horse, and carrying his official certificate of identity and the buff booklet which guaranteed him a fair share of national food and supplies.

The war of nerves ended in July 1940 with the German attack on British air bases. The Battle of Britain lasted until September when the Luftwaffe turned to civilian targets, especially London, and, as far as civilians were concerned, the war began in earnest. By the end of 1940 'blitz' was one foreign term which needed no definition. In addition, German attacks on Atlantic shipping were becoming a serious threat to lend-lease supply lines from America. In 1941 under pressure of the Battle of the Atlantic, increasing shortage of labour and materials, bombing raids, and an empty treasury, the coalition war government took over direction of virtually all aspects of national life along the collectivist lines first outlined during the First World War.

Again resources were scarce and the nation could afford few luxuries. In an attempt to conserve resources, in 1941 the Board of Trade introduced 'utility' schemes, the effect of which was to standardize the quality and design of many goods available on the domestic market. Furniture, clothing, and other consumer goods were produced which made the minimum use of resources while adhering to reasonable standards of quality in materials and construction. Utility goods were rarely beautiful but were usually serviceable and their identifying stamp of stylized twin half-moons entered the lives of people in all sections of society on everything from furniture to underwear. In the 1941 Budget an attempt was made to keep pace with soaring war costs by reducing income tax allowances and increasing the standard rate to 10s in the pound. Many more members of the working classes were drawn into the tax system for the first time in the war years, making this a 'people's war' in the sense that the working classes not only suffered, worked, and died for it, but also helped pay for it. By the summer of 1941 labour shortages were beginning to become a problem, and the government tightened central control of labour resources and at the end of the year instituted a system of female conscription for the first time.

Food subsidy and rationing schemes were put into operation before increasing scarcity caused much distress or disruption. Thanks to a combination of efficient rationing, intensive dietary research, effective persuasion, and general co-operation, rationed food supplies never ran out. There were black-market operations and some hoarding, but these were never sufficiently widespread to cause social unrest. The majority of the people expected equal treatment for all social classes and income groups and, on the whole, that was what they got. The basic rationed diet was well below the standards well-to-do people normally enjoyed, but it was nutritionally sound, more than adequate for a healthy life, and much better than the poorer majority of the population had had in the past. The government required, in the interests of public health, that calcium, iron, minerals, and vitamins be added to all kinds of food, and by 1944 the protein content of the average diet was 6 per cent higher than it had been before the war. This upgrading of the diet of the majority of the people undoubtedly played a great part in the improvement of the nation's health during the war, an improvement which was illustrated, for example, by a drop of almost half in the number of cases of maternal mortality between 1939 and 1946.

The rationing system was socially acceptable because it was generally understood to be necessary and because it was egalitarian. Allowances were made on a *per capita* basis with extra supplies allocated on the basis of special needs. The prices of basic foods were kept low by subsidies and no social class received preferential treatment. The general character of food allocation schemes can be illustrated by the example of the Emergency Milk and Meals Scheme of 1941. This was instituted to provide supplements to the basic allowances for people with special needs—children and expectant mothers—regardless of class or income. The scheme allowed mothers and children extra cheap milk and provided for the improvement of school meals. Not everyone who was entitled to the extra benefits claimed them but an important egalitarian principle was stated in the scheme, and, thanks to the inevitable popularity and inviolable morality of mother-and-child causes, was generally established as unassailable.

Almost everybody grumbled about food allowances, and even those whose diet improved joined in, either because they were unaware of the improvement or because they were unwilling to admit their previous deprivation. People felt that rationing did constitute a hardship, but they were determined to overcome this with as much ingenuity as they could muster because this was a time of emergency and even civilians were expected to be courageous in their making of sacrifices. Complaints about the inadequacy of the allowances were heard from all sections of society, which strengthened feelings of national unity and heightened personal pride in the achievement of overcoming adversity. A good deal of official and commercial advice was given about ways of making the best of the supplies available, and many people bent their talents to making a decent family meal out of a few slices of bread, fractions of an ounce of margarine, a few potatoes, and a couple of fatty, highly flavoured but almost meatless sausages. In this atmosphere of pride in invention, in the gastronomic equivalent of pulling white rabbits out of hats, it would have seemed ill-mannered to observe that one had never eaten so well for so long ever before. Many grumbles were simply preludes to prideful descriptions of such ingenious projects as cutting down old clothes to make things for the children, and 'making a home' out of one utility table, some broken chairs from a junkshop, and Aunt Ada's old curtains. Favourable comments about good food and the relatively high quality and low prices of utility goods would have seemed unpatriotic and indicated a deplorable ignorance of the new game of rationing which the nation was playing. The persistent rumble of national grumbling, which was a major feature of the forties, was not a symptom of distress and unrest but a by-product of necessity which had turned into a national hobby. It was a symptom of unity rather than a sign of discontent—'everybody' played the game, 'everybody' grumbled.

Enormous manpower demands again made government control of labour necessary and rapidly brought an end to high unemployment. By 1940 unemployment was lower than at any time since the end of the First World War, and it continued to fall to the lowest level in at least half a century in 1944. As was the case with rationing, those who benefited most were those who had been worst-off before the war, those who had endured the long idleness of the Depression. The pattern of the First World War more or less repeated itself in the field of female employment, with a very slow start, rapid advance in the later stages of the war, and considerable achievement by the end of it. Female employment attracted much less attention than it had in the First World War, but it rendered more real service. In areas in which women had long been employed, such as commerce and the civil service, women took over in large numbers and made up about half their labour force by the end of the war. Women were again employed in agriculture, medicine, and the clerical branches of the armed services, while a great number, with surprisingly little fuss, took jobs in such 'unfeminine' industries as metal-working, engineering and vehicle-building. Female conscription was neither all-embracing, nor tightly enforced and was never applied to women keeping house for husbands or children. In practice, only unmarried females in their early twenties were called up, and most women who wished to stay close to their homes were able to do so by opting for some special local duty such as serving in the Civil Defence force or in nearby factories.

To food and labour problems were added bombing raids, which made up the trilogy of civilian woes in this war. With the dropping of death and destruction from the sky, the phrase 'the home front' came to mean not just war production and supply, but something more bloody and literal. The Luftwaffe began its 'blitz' in 1940 with the attack on London which, it was hoped, would break civilian morale and weaken Britain's resistance. In addition to the physical damage it wrought, the Blitz had a great psychological effect on the population. The drone of the bombers and the wail of sirens signified that the Channel was no longer a defence against attack and that Britain, like other nations, had to face the prospect of a conflict if not on, very much over her own soil. The raids produced another wave of evacuation; many Londoners took up temporary and even semi-permanent shelter in tube stations. In London and other cities people set up second homes in cellars and basements, and some even managed to make their cramped official air-raid shelters into tolerable living quarters. The majority of people in target areas, however, stayed at home or went about their business with only brief interruptions even in the worst raids. Provincial cities of strategic significance, such as Sheffield, Coventry, and Plymouth, were bombed, but the effect on production was not overwhelming, and factories were generally back in production a few days after a raid. The Blitz caused many casualties and much destruction, but although there were probably some areas in which morale did falter for a while, the raids did not have the intended effect. Paradoxically, the bombing raids boosted general civilian morale by promoting unity, co-operation, a sense of moral outrage, and a determination to succeed despite the odds. They reinforced national solidarity by providing a series of focal points around which sentiment and emotion could gather. Pictures such as those of St Paul's, standing alone in the middle of an inferno, of the damage to Westminster, of King George and his family visiting Blitz victims, had a tremendous emotional impact, as did the most famous speeches of Prime Minister Churchill. Instead of bringing despair and surrender, the Blitz brought a great upwelling of patriotism and determination. The attack of the foreigner on the icons of Englishness simply united the nation and hardened resistance while promoting a sense of mutual endeavour which would help sustain the drive for social change after the war.

New facts about the conditions of the poorer section of the population emerged from wartime inventories of national resources and the evacuations which placed the condition of the urban poor very much in the limelight. The evacuation of mothers and children from cities brought large numbers of the urban poor into contact with people in the country, suburbs, and small towns. The relatively poor provided a great number of the billets for the evacuees, but many comfortably off and prosperous families also took in the migrants. Many of the better-off hosts were horrified by the condition of the people, especially the children, who came from the poorest urban homes. Many of them were verminous, undernourished, miserably clad, dirty, and obviously used to every degradation urban poverty had to offer. Some of the children provided irrefutable evidence that urban overcrowding still existed by being unable to sleep in the beds provided for them and sleeping instead under them as they always had, of necessity, at home. The evacuees' inevitable ignorance of country ways caused some amusement, but their obvious ignorance of the functions of baths and water closets and their bewildered barbarism on being presented with a full table of good food also generated serious concern. The majority of the evacuees came from decent homes and behaved well, but there were enough among them whose behaviour unconsciously spoke of their chronic deprivation to provide stories which caught the popular imagination. By no means every host was horrified by his guests, but those who met the extremely poor drew attention to their condition. Among the ranks of the comfortably-off, stories of one verminous, ragged child who did not know how to use a lavatory or a knife and fork travelled great distances and plagued many consciences. On the national scale, thousands of such poor children went a long way to stimulate an enduring interest in poverty and a renewed determination to do something about it as soon as possible.

The bombs were no respecters of persons, class, prosperity, or poverty, and the Blitz was a shared horror which, by simply overriding old class and other social differences, helped accelerate the development of a more uniform society. Civilians accounted for about one-sixth of the war deaths, and almost all of these were produced by bombing raids. (Total deaths were almost 400,000; 300,000 armed services, 60,000 civilians, 35,000 merchant marine.) Some people paid a high price in destroyed homes, scattered families, and dead relatives of both sexes and all ages. Over $3\frac{1}{2}$ million houses were damaged or destroyed in air raids, the most severe of which reduced entire sections of cities to heaps of rubble and left only the bare discernible lines of roadways to guide rescuers and residents to where the houses had been. 'Regular features of the time: neatly swept-up piles of glass, litter of stones and splinters of flint, smell of escaping gas, knots of sight-seers waiting at the cordons' (from 'War-Time Diary 1940' in Orwell and Angus (eds.), *Collected Essays . . . of George Orwell*, vol. 4, 371). Among the less obvious effects of the raids were the nights of lost or disrupted sleep when air-raid sirens wailed, bombers rumbled overhead, bombs exploded and fires broke out, anti-aircraft guns pounded, and the Home Guard cursed during lulls in the firing, adding to the distress of old ladies with sharp ears. It was often difficult to make a telephone call, to travel, or to visit people as there were frequent disruptions of all kinds, and people and goods might arrive early, late, in the wrong place, or not at all. The fear that the Luftwaffe might begin to drop paratroops instead of bombs led to the introduction of all kinds of anti-invasion measures including the removal of signposts, which effectively confused native travellers. Despite death, destruction, shortages, and annoyances, civilian morale remained at a remarkably high level, and the war years remained in some people's memories as a good time to be alive, a time of co-operation and friendliness when help was given and accepted from both friends and strangers and old social differences simply did not matter, a time of incredible generosity and selflessness and of great good humour.

The bombing raids reached a peak in 1941, after which they came less frequently. With the easing of this pressure, evacuees again began to return to the cities until 1944, when the flying-bomb attacks sparked off a third wave of evacuation. Unmanned flying bombs, popularly called 'buzz bombs', moved at aeroplane speeds and could be destroyed by adaptations of anti-aircraft techniques and armaments. Rockets came into use in the very last stages of the war. They were fast, came without warning, and could not be countered by conventional defensive weapons. Fortunately, they were expensive to produce, and in any event the Allied armies in Europe soon overran their launch sites. Flying bombs and rockets came too late to do much damage, but they were frightening and as prophetic of the future as the air raids of the First World War had been. They promised a horrifying future in which warfare would mean fast, mass civilian deaths produced by attacks which came with little or no warning and no hope of defence. The dropping of American atomic bombs on Japan in 1945 punctuated the prophecy with a mushroom-shaped cloud.

The Second World War, like the First, produced a whole range of socially cohesive by-products. The camaraderie of soldiers and civilians of all classes under fire, the standardization of diet, the sense of national unity and purpose, all reappeared in stronger forms than they had taken in the First World War. Radio reached new heights as a unifying force during the war. Interest in the conflict and concern about bombing raids gave news a new urgency, and people who had never heard or owned a radio set before bought one. Certain programmes became national rallying points around which vast numbers of people of all classes gathered to assure themselves that they and the nation were still intact. Churchill's skilful use of the radio was an important feature of the war years, for few people could resist the appeal of the emotional, inspiring, compelling words which came rumbling into their workplaces, living rooms, and lives. The chimes of Big Ben which preceded the news were another major rallying point and millions of people waited around their radio sets every evening for their reassurance that Parliament still stood and that the nation had survived another day. Next to the Prime Minister and the News in popularity was a comedy programme, ITMA ('It's That Man Again'), which starred Tommy Handley. This piece of nonsense was heard by a vast audience, and its characters, such as Mrs Mopp and Colonel Chinstrap, passed into the popular mythology of the decade. In its univer-
its wide appeal, its ability to pass new catchphrases into popular
, and its dissociation from reality, it foreshadowed the  popular
inment of the 1950s and 1960s.

## BUILDING THE WELFARE STATE

The war drew together all the prewar trends towards collectivism and concentrated them until, by the end of it, British society was subjected to tighter and more efficient government controls than that of any other combatant nation except Russia. Interest in social welfare had mounted in the 1930s as many people, including some of the better-off, better-educated classes, became disturbed by the Depression and its effects. Interest in social conditions and in the setting of acceptable standards for the future was stirred by such things as the complaints about the means test, the hunger marches of the early thirties, and the works of realistic, journalistic writers like George Orwell in *Down and Out in Paris and London* (1933) and *The Road to Wigan Pier* (1937). Social surveyors and other collectors of statistics established factual foundations for the more highly coloured reports of social evils. Work by Crawford and Boyd Orr, for example, indicated that a large segment of the population, including a disproportionate number of children, was undernourished. The Army again made its contribution with an announcement in 1935 that over half its recruits were still below its minimum physical standards. While all this material was being produced and assimilated, more government social and economic controls were being applied, apparently fairly effectively, in an attempt to reduce distress and bring the nation out of the Depression. Meanwhile, the presence of Labour Party leaders in the National Government was adding to the respectability and acceptability of that party. Thus by the time the war broke out there were many signs that the nation was due for another bout of social reform legislation and many suggestions that the legislation would involve a great deal of governmental organization.

During the war more sophisticated and far-reaching government social control gave practical evidence that the mechanism for extensive government-directed social reform now existed. Social issues and problems became clearer during the war, and by the end of it the people, still with a sense of unity and mutual purpose developed during the war, seemed ready to work for the establishment of a more equitable social order. By this time, too, many people had realized that Britain faced a variety of major problems, including adjustment to a world ruled by two giant powers too big for her to challenge, the repayment of tremendous war debts, and the rebuilding of a severely damaged nation. The problems could only be solved by major rebuilding and readjustment, and while such massive changes were taking place, it seemed reasonable that social problems should be dealt with too. Few people wanted to 'return to normal' after this war as so many had after the First because few saw anything overwhelmingly attractive in the prospect of a return to the conditions of the thirties, and most preferred to take the opportunity to try to build a better way of life for the future. The war years, for all their hardships, rationing, and near-disasters, gave the nation a new feeling of social solidarity. This combined with an appreciation of the practical virtues of wartime egalitarianism to produce the feeling that it would perhaps be best to continue wartime procedures into the postwar years in the interests of national and social improvement.

The cresting of the new wave of social legislation which had been building for a decade was heralded by an important document published during the war, the Beveridge Report. This was a vital document in the social planning of the forties, not because it proposed new and innovative schemes, but because it organized most of the current practical schemes for social welfare legislation into a wide-ranging plan which was relatively simple and which sounded reasonable and practical to most people, and because it laid the foundations on which social legislation was based. The Beveridge Plan was based on six principles for social welfare. First, there was to be unified administrative responsibility for services. Second, social welfare provisions were to be comprehensive and care for the individual from birth to death through such contingencies as illness, unemployment, widowhood, pregnancy, and old age. Third, for welfare purposes, people were to be classified only by categories which related to probable need, such as age and occupation, and not by birth, ancestry, possessions, or class. Clearly this was closely related to the wartime principles of allocation according to need. Fourth, the payment of adequate benefits was to be guaranteed by the establishment of a scale which was the result of careful investigations. Beveridge was no radical and his personal definition of adequate was probably fairly close to the current subsistence level, but there is little doubt that he had in mind more than the grudging, niggardly, means-test-apportioned 'adequate' of the past. Fifth, benefits were to be given according to flat rates based on need factors such as family size. Last, contributions were to be paid as a flat rate, not on a sliding scale or as a percentage of income. The plan embodied a guaranteed minimum income policy, a policy of full employment, and a national health service. This was not the testament of a fire-breathing revolutionary but simply a plan designed to provide a basic minimum of social security for all citizens on all occasions.

In the election of 1945 the people displayed relatively little interest in international issues. There was little or no desire to punish Germany this time; the war was over and most people wanted to put it and its issue behind them and get on with the domestic peace. They were well aware of the economic and social questions involved in making a better nation for themselves, and most of them were looking for government plans which would solve peacetime problems as efficiently as wartime problems had been solved. The major issues were reform, social welfare, jobs, and housing. Both Conservative and Labour parties offered similar programmes, but Labour seemed a more 'natural' planning party, and its rather drab solemnity and determination to get on with the job fitted well with the national mood. The Conservatives brandished the recent victory, Churchill, and well-modulated rhetoric, but few people were inclined to rest on their laurels when so many domestic problems still remained to be solved. Churchill's rhetoric, so effective in the war, seemed too harsh for the peace, and some of his remarks, such as those which characterized bland Labour leaders as potential heads of an English Gestapo, were patently silly. It is possible, too, that many people remembered the unfilled promises of the 1918 election and the failure of the Conservatives, with whom Churchill was associated, to do much to ease the impact of the Depression. The Labour leaders had, by this time, been on the political stage long enough to be accepted as respectable even by many middle-class people, and the wartime plans and controls which had worked so well were socialistic in character. The voters acknowledged Churchill as a great war leader and inspirer of men in times of mortal danger from foreign foes, but for the conquest of domestic evils they clearly preferred to be led by Attlee and his less dramatic officers. A convincing Labour victory required substantial middle-class support for the party, and in 1945 this was forthcoming. The old-middle class had suffered severe setbacks in the First World War and the interwar years, the new-middle class had never been as prosperous and confident as the old and had no overwhelming aversion for socialistic policies, especially ones which promised continuing material progress and security. Therefore, many middle- as well as working-class voters were willing to vote for a party which promised a better future, rather than for one which boasted of its proud past.

Ownership of the means of production, transport, and communications by the people had long been an essential part of socialist doctrine, and practical outlines for public control had already been sketched in by the various government control measures of the inter-war years, but many of the changes brought by nationalization had little effect on society. For example, it is doubtful if the lives of many people were much affected by the formal nationalization of the Bank of England or by the making of a public corporation out of Cable and Wireless Ltd. Even the nationalization of transport facilities and the partial nationalization of iron and steel had few social consequences. Gas and electricity services were nationalized under a system of national and regional boards. No attempt was made to create a unified power service, and later the gas and electricity boards would compete against each other as if they were rival private companies. Early in 1947, in the middle of the winter of the great fuel shortage and the deepest cold since 1881, the coal industry passed into the hands of the National Coal Board. The government, adhering to its policy of making nationalization non-confiscatory, compensated the mine-owners handsomely, paying them over £164 million for their dilapi-dated property which had produced a profit for them for well over a century, which had an abysmal efficiency and safety record, whose equipment had been out of date at the end of the First World War, and whose current production could not keep pace with demand. Nationalization was nevertheless popular in mining areas because it ended the control of the long-resented mine-owners, and because it was felt that the NCB would be a better employer and provide miners with better safety equipment and working conditions.

The socialists hoped, in an idealistic but rather woolly-minded way, that nationalization would usher in an era of fair incomes for everyone and equal opportunities, and stimulate a greater interest of the people in 'their' industries. However, the people soon found that nationalized coal was produced no faster than private coal and that nationalized electricity and gas were just as subject to power cuts and breakdowns as they had been in their non-nationalized past. Workers in national-ized industries found that as an employer, 'the government' fitted easily into the slot which had been occupied by 'the bosses', although the safety record, job amenities, and long-term security were better than they had been in the days of private ownership. Apart from this, as far as most people were concerned, a faceless government simply replaced faceless capitalists. One problem of nationalization which would cause trouble throughout the 1940s and 1950s was that the central government could not cope with its creatures and either ignored or misunderstood the implications of large-scale modern management. Nationalization produced huge new industrial concerns whose corporate structures were of a size few British managers had ever dreamed of, let alone controlled. Few men, if any, in the 1940s had the training and experience needed for their top management and what few there were were also in demand by private industry, which still made up about 80 per cent of the nation's economy. Few of these rare birds were tempted to run a nationalized industry for a poor salary and socialist ideals, especially with MPs and civil servants peering over their shoulders. This deficiency began to be appreciated in the late 1950s and early 1960s when it was recognized that good men would have to be recruited in competition with private industry at high, realistic prices.

The wartime slow-down in building and the bomb damage added to prewar housing shortages, but at the end of the war materials were scarce and construction costs soared. Overcrowding was a serious problem, and if living conditions were to be improved, something had to be done about building a large number of new houses. The 1946 Housing Act empowered local authorities to restrict private building and regulate costs and, most important, the Act allotted government subsidies for local council building projects. By 1950 council building schemes had eased, although by no means solved, the problem by making over 41,000 bomb-damaged houses habitable and constructing over 635,000 new houses. (See fig. 5 for illustration of increased house-building after the Second World War.) To solve the nationwide housing problem, long-range plans were needed which would provide for the expansion of existing communities and the creation of new ones. It was also necessary to keep down construction costs, especially the cost of land, the price of which soared as soon as a new development was planned. The Town and Country Planning Act was passed in 1947 to deal with these problems. It placed all land in England and Wales under the control of local planning authorities which were empowered to resolve disputes about land prices and approve new building projects. The New Towns Act of 1946 was even more innovative, providing for the planning and building of entirely new communities to take some of the pressure off existing population centres. The new towns around London, such as Crawley, were planned under the terms of this Act.

The social reform proposals of the Beveridge Report were acted upon, and a National Insurance Act was passed in 1946. It provided for benefits to be given in cases of unemployment, sickness, maternity, retirement, widowhood, and death—a minimum social security from the cradle to the grave. Echoes of the means test lingered on in the initial provisions of the Act, but the left wing of the Labour Party kept up its pressure against them and in 1948 the National Assistance Act at last abolished all vestiges of the Poor Law, even in the small clauses and fine print. The National Assistance Board was established as the central authority for the nationwide system. The National Health Service Act, passed in 1946, came into operation in 1948, establishing a comprehensive health care system to be run by a combination of national and local government bodies. Hospital and GP services were to be financed directly by the central government, and local authorities were to provide other services to be financed equally by central and local government funds. The variety of institutions involved, the complicated control system established as a result of the need to placate the doctors, and financial and administrative needs produced a highly complex administrative structure. The Health Service also proved to be costly, especially in the early years when vast numbers of people who had been unable to afford health care set about catching up on years of medical neglect. The construction and operation of such a wide-ranging, complex and, above all, costly, health scheme at a time of national economic distress and continued shortages is evidence that the reconstruction years, though drab, were far from being devoid of vision, optimism, and social consequences.

The issue of educational reform in the postwar years was confused by the existence of the 1944 Education Act, the only major piece of peacetime planning legislation to come out of the war years. The Act was a compromise product of the wartime coalition and a hindrance rather than a help to socialists because the changes it provided for were not as far-reaching as the reformers would have liked. Nevertheless, it was a reforming Act, had never been used, and its passage was too recent to make the proposal of new legislation seem feasible. Proposing new legislation before the 1944 Act had even been tried might also have been seen by the people as a delaying device and a repetition of the broken promises which had followed the First World War. Thus, although the Act was not entirely in tune with socialist and even some liberal aims, it was put into operation. It perpetuated diversity in education rather than promoting greater social equality, to the frustration of those who would have liked to see the establishment of a more egalitarian system. The Act did, however, strengthen the existing system of primary education and create a system of secondary education far in advance of anything which had existed before the war.

The Labour Government kept the coalition's wartime promise and put the Act into operation as best it could, raising the school-leaving age to 15 in 1947 and allowing the rest of the system to be operated as money allowed, hoping that it would work at least reasonably well. In practice, fee-paying, direct grant schools and public schools were left untouched, while government-aided local authority schools provided two types of secondary education—academic training in grammar schools and vocational training in secondary modern schools. The Act provided for the establishment of special technical schools, but few were actually set up because the educational system, and the budget, were severely strained by the other changes. Many other provisions of the Act were also neglected because of the shortage of money, equipment, and teachers. The type of secondary education a child was to receive was generally determined by his performance in the 'eleven plus examination', a series of attainment and 'intelligence' tests, which was feared by many children and discussed by many adults. The universities were not immediately affected and would not feel the impact of the Act until the 1950s, when the advance guard of children whose advanced education had been conducted under the aegis of the Act would demand entrance.

In the 1940s the old Empire, which had been in failing health for some decades, finally died, and its attractive but fragile ghost-child, the Commonwealth, was born in a process which illustrates the mixture of idealism and realism which pervaded society in the Labour years. The Statute of Westminster had, in 1931, provided for the legislative independence of the Dominions and recognized a new relationship of 'free association' between Britain and her former colonies. The movement towards colonial independence, especially in Asia, was accelerated by the war, and the Labour Government followed the already established policy of graceful submission to the inevitable and of helping former colonies to independence. The chief problem of the late 1940s was India, where the religious conflict between Hindus and Muslims confused the issue of independence. Negotiations had reached an impasse when Attlee announced early in 1947 that, whatever happened, power would be transferred out of British hands the following year. Under pressure of this deadline, differences were temporarily settled, and from Britain's point of view the transfer of power went smoothly.

In the reign of Victoria, and even of Edward, few people would have dreamed it possible that India, the brightest jewel in the Imperial crown, would be not merely lost or abandoned but resolutely driven away by a socialist Prime Minister who looked like a meek, lower-grade bank-clerk. Yet on a cold and coal-less February day in the mid-twentieth century, the decision was accepted calmly, as if the British people, huddled in their thin utility clothing, worried about fuel shortages and rationing, could not grow impassioned about a strange people in a remote land battling over exotic religions. The *Daily Express* fulminated and fumed, but the majority of the people did not appear to regret the passing of the Empire. Many of them felt it was 'a pity' that the old glory had gone, but most recognized that Empires had had their day, and that Britain lacked both the strength and the will to keep the coals alive.

## SOCIETY IN THE 1940s

On the centenary of the Great Exhibition, the Festival of Britain was held. This was planned by the Labour Government in 1950 to celebrate progress made and to symbolize that the worst of the hardships of reconstruction were over. The Festival, inviting as it did comparisons between 1851 and 1951, inevitably aroused feelings of nostalgia for a glory known to be lost forever. The Festival organizers were conscious of the overwhelming success of their Victorian predecessors, but they could not hope to recapture the mood of the mid-nineteenth century. The Exhibition of 1951 was just as much a reflection of the society of its day as the Exhibition of 1851 had been. This time there were no separate visiting days for rich and poor, upper and lower classes, for by the standards of 1851 the rich were not outstandingly rich and the poor were relatively prosperous. No one worried about whether or not the 'lower classes' would behave decently, as they had long since merged identities with a colourless, classless, larger social group, 'the people'. The solemn, selfconscious pride in world leadership of 1851 had been replaced by a feeling of quiet satisfaction that little Britain had survived another war and was working towards a future that was not just as good as the past, but better. Generally, the visitors at the 1951 Festival came neither to be instructed by modern ingenuity nor to be reminded of faded glories, but primarily to enjoy themselves. Despite the ubiquitous queues and a few bothersome rationing restrictions, they usually succeeded, with the help of the amusement park, a significant addition to Festival features. There was no official recognition of class or prosperity differences in society and none of the self-importance which had characterized the earlier exhibition. This Exhibition was designed to divert, please, and amuse the mass of the modestly prosperous people in this modestly prosperous mass society.

The Festival of Britain was a bright spot marking the end of a decade which on the surface appeared drab and grey but during which many great social changes took place. The late 1940s had been bleak, austere years when the wounds of war had just begun to heal over and when rationing had become a way of life. In some respects, rationing became more severe after the war ended as raw material shortages continued and lend-lease stopped. Bread rationing was introduced in 1946 and potato rationing in 1947. In 1948 the Marshall Plan brought more American economic aid designed to speed European recovery in order to vitiate the attractions of communism. The new aid made it possible to buy the raw materials necessary for rebuilding, and conditions began to improve. Bread, potatoes, and jam came off ration in 1948, clothes and shoes in 1949. Milk and soap came off in 1950, tea and sugar in 1952, but butter, fats, bacon, and meat did not come off until 1954 when all rationing ended. By this time people had been using ration books for fourteen years and had become used to budgeting in coupons as well as in pounds, shillings, and pence.

These were also the years of rose-bay willow-herb, a plant whose name few townsmen knew but whose tall spikes topped with purple flower were familiar to almost all of them. This plant grew vigorously on the bomb-sites which scarred so many towns, bringing an incongruous hint of the wild back to town centres where few wild plants had grown for centuries. During these 'baby boom' years, the generation which would be labelled 'war baby' all its school life grew up, nurtured on government orange juice and cod liver oil and accepting shortages, rationing, and bomb-sites as normal and natural parts of life.

In the forties most people found that there always seemed to be too little coal and meat and too few eggs. They discovered that utility clothing was too thin for real comfort, especially in the cold, snowy winter of 1946–7, when the fuel shortages reduced heating and produced transport failures and electricity cuts. There were 'spivs' who made great profits selling black-market goods, a soaring divorce rate, and a crime wave. The large number of union actions and work stoppages prompted some people to suspect that perhaps powerful unions were the enemies of the people rather than champions of the workers against unjust employers. There were many signs of social stress and national weakness in these years, and yet there was little serious discontent. On the surface, the majority of the people seemed to commit themselves to drabness as if, exhausted by the war, they could survive only at a low emotional level, drawing upon the last reserves of the dogged determination to survive which had sustained them during the long depression and the war. They plodded on, reassuring each other that things could not get much worse and must, therefore, get better if only the present could be survived. Queuing, grumbling, and dreaming, the people waited out a drab present, confident that it was preparation for a better future, especially if the Labour Government fulfilled the promises of its election campaign.

When the war ended, the nation was already heavily taxed and large war debts, plus the government's commitments to an expensive social reform programme, ensured that high taxation would continue. In 1949 taxation was four times as high as it had been in 1938, and the number of people with net annual incomes of over £6,000 shrank over the same period, from 7,000 to 70. The remnants of the nineteenth-century, property-owning, entrepreneurial middle class which had managed to survive the Depression were decimated in the 1940s by high taxes, inflation, and the reduction of income from property, which fell by 15 per cent between 1938 and 1947. The capital-investing, property-owning, old-middle class, always a small proportion of the population even in its heyday, was reduced by the end of the 1940s to an almost insignificantly small segment. Some of the white-collar group, the growing new-middle class, also failed to make much financial progress in these years when salary incomes fell 21 per cent. While middle-class incomes fell, taxes on non-wage incomes remained high, about 35–44 per cent, and the middle classes, both old and new, felt the effects of a two-way pressure on their financial resources. At the same time, wage-earners, the majority of the people, enjoyed an increase in income of about 18 per cent while their taxes averaged only about 13–17 per cent of income. (Figures from Pollard, *The Development of the British Economy*, 344.) There were individual exceptions, but the general trends were for the real income of the propertied and salaried classes to fall while their taxes remained high, and for real wage incomes to increase while taxes on them remained relatively low. There was little change in the distribution of property and many more workers than ever before paid income tax. Nevertheless, in terms of social economics, the working classes rose in the 1940s while the old-middle classes fell and the new-middle classes suffered setbacks.

During the 1940s there was a real improvement in the incomes and living standards of the mass of the people, including those who had suffered most severely in the interwar years. Neither employment nor wage rates fell off after this war as they had after the First World War. Government recovery plans in all fields were acted on and demands for supplies and labour continued to be high, with the result that during the forties most workers worked full-time. The official working day was a little shorter than it had been before the war, but in fact most people worked the same hours as before by putting in a few hours of overtime each week. The employment was so good that by the end of the decade full employment was taken for granted by most of the labour force. Better incomes and steady work enabled the employed not only to enjoy a better standard of living, but also to save and plan for the distant future if they wished. Continued steady employment enabled many people to move from the backwaters of poverty into the modestly prosperous mainstream of working- and new-middle-class life. By the early 1950s unemployment and irregular or inadequate wages, which had been major causes of poverty at the turn of the century, had almost been eradicated, and newer studies concluded that sickness and old age made up 90 per cent of the poverty cases at mid-century. Even without the introduction of the welfare state, it would seem that poverty would have diminished considerably in the forties, given that employment levels had been maintained.

Welfare benefits provided a secure floor to the rising living standards and were of great benefit to the unemployed and unemployable. The improvement in national health was sustained by the new health service which allowed many people to get medical treatment they would otherwise have been unable to afford and ensured that illness placed no drain on the rising incomes of others. Whatever the shortcomings of the theory and practice of the 1944 Education Act, it extended the possible benefits of a higher education to an unprecedented number of new-middle and working-class children. The full social impact of the Act would not be felt until the late 1950s and the 1960s when its first higher-educated wards would enter the labour market. Even before the ration book was abolished, however, university enrolment gave some idea of the potential size of the impact. The number of university students increased in the late 1940s as ex-servicemen resumed their civilian studies. The numbers fell slightly in 1950–1 as this 'bulge' moved out, but in 1952–3 the number of students increased again to over 81,000. This represented an increase of about 30,000 (about 60 per cent) over the number of students in 1938–9. The increase was produced by the operation of the Act, university expansion, increased emphasis on higher education by business and industry, and the higher general level of prosperity which gave more parents the necessary income to allow their children a prolonged education and the opportunity to benefit from the upward social mobility this generally afforded.

The welfare state gave an important added boost to the many social levelling processes which operated in the 1940s. Prosperous people could, and did, benefit from its services, but the introduction of welfare schemes gave them little that they had not been able to buy in the past. The mass of the people, however, had never been able to buy income security, higher education, or adequate medical care, and these services were of enormous benefit to them and a novelty in their lives. Social services were expensive and standard contributions did not meet the whole of their cost. Tax revenue was also used, with the result that the prosperous, who gained few new benefits, paid a larger proportion of welfare costs than did the wage-earning majority, who derived a great deal of benefit from the services. The combination of the social services and the tax system produced a powerful social levelling mechanism. Robin Hood was resurrected from his legend not as an outlaw but as government authority, armed not with bow and arrow, but with statutes, a multitude of buff forms, and steel-nibbed pens.

The welfare state might easily have been merely another experiment in a long history of only marginally effective attempts at social regulation. Workhouses, charitable institutions, and early-twentieth-century welfare services had attempted to combat poverty, but their effects had been very limited and their operations were hated by those who had to resort to them. The welfare schemes of the 1940s avoided many of the pitfalls of earlier schemes largely because of effective planning and the practical application of the principle of universality. Although the poor obviously benefited most, poverty was not a necessary qualification for benefits as it had been in the days of the dole. Many of the benefits, especially from the health and education schemes, went to the fairly prosperous middle classes as well as to the poor. The application of the principle of universality and the wide social distribution of the welfare services meant that the use of their benefits lost the social stigma it had conferred in the past and introduced a new unifying element into working- and middle-class society. Many people, especially the older people with personal experience of the Poor Law and the dole, continued to call National Assistance 'going on the parish' or 'the dole', and to entertain grave reservations about the welfare system. In general, however, the new services were quickly accepted and well-liked. Although some people continued to find collecting unemployment benefit somewhat shameful, this discomfort was nothing compared to the disgrace of the workhouse and the dole. Free education, health care, and sickness benefits came to be regarded as perfectly acceptable socially, indeed, a normal and natural part of the life of all citizens, except for a tiny minority who preferred to follow the old-fashioned habit of paying bills for such services.

Some idea of the extent of the social change which had taken place to date and of the structure of mid-twentieth-century society was given by Rowntree's third study of poverty in York, published in 1951. This study showed that a remarkable improvement in the condition of the lower classes had taken place since his second study in 1936 and an almost incredible improvement since his first study in 1901. The proportion of working-class people living 'below the poverty line' (which had been revised upwards in response to changing contemporary standards) had fallen from 31 per cent in 1936 to 3 per cent in 1950. According to the Rowntree study, if welfare services had not been expanded but had remained at their 1936 level, in 1950 22 per cent of the working class would have fallen 'below the poverty line'. While conditions in York were not precisely duplicated throughout the country, the remarkable improvement in the living standards of the working classes which took place in the first half of the twentieth century is vividly illustrated by comparing the studies of this one city.

As a result of the improvement in the basic living standard and the reduction of poverty, the 1940s were good years for the working classes. Despite the horrors of war, huge national debts and domestic shortages, the loss of Empire and world status, for most people who had not sustained too close a personal loss in the war this was very much a decade of improvement. This improvement, however, came in a decade in which the nation endured another costly blood-letting, bore the costs of reconstruction, and was constantly warned by its leaders that it faced serious problems of all kinds. The forties were, therefore, years of paradox when there was before a majority of the people an incongruous picture of personal betterment amidst national disaster. Many people were well aware that their lives had improved considerably compared to the standards of the confused twenties and the often desperate thirties, but it would have seemed crass to celebrate this at a time when the nation was said to face serious problems and was consciously tightening its belt. The majority of them resolved the conflict between national appearance and personal reality by continuing to play civilian war-games—to queue, to perform culinary sleights of hand, and to grumble—as a matter of social courtesy, even though many of them privately acknowledged that they had less than ever before to complain about. The gap between action and actuality also helps account for the postwar phenomenon that Ernest Bevin called a 'poverty of desire'. The people seemed apathetic, demanding little more than the reasonable fulfilment of the election promises of 1945, and not at all distressed or angered that their social revolution was so slow in coming and so expensive. In reality, as far as many citizens could see, the great 'revolution' had already taken place, and their lack of new demands stemmed less from a 'poverty of desire' than from a slightly stunned surprise that promises which had been mouthed for decades had been kept at last. Never before had political promises been transformed so swiftly into national policies, and most people were content to ruminate over the personal betterment and social levelling those policies had brought, to concede that the nation was in trouble, and to moderate their aspirations lest the changes proved to be a house of cards which would come tumbling down about their ears.

By the early 1950s a few people were ostentatiously rich while some were still degradingly poor, but the majority of the people were standing expectantly and a little apprehensively on the threshold of the good life. Most of them were already enjoying a life which was prosperous and secure beyond the rosiest dreams of their grandfathers, but were not yet sufficiently secure in it to give vent to their enjoyment of it. When the easing of wartime and reconstruction restrictions led to some relaxation in this cautious attitude, the people demonstrated their feelings that at least they had something worth protecting by voting in a Conservative government in the early 1950s. When Macmillan announced 'You've never had it so good' in the late fifties he expressed the feelings many people had had for a long time, and there was a burst of exhilaration as the newly prosperous at last felt able to enjoy their prosperity openly. The jubilation and the celebration of mass prosperity carried over into the 1960s when Britain acquired a new public image as the 'swinging' leader of the western world in such fields as fashion and pop music whose growth was founded on mass prosperity.

# Chapter 8     The Structure of
# Mid-Twentieth-Century Society

In the middle years of the twentieth century the living standards of the mass of the people rose to an unprecedentedly high level. This improvement came, ironically enough, at a time when the nation still faced serious financial problems and its balance of payments and economic future were sources of constant concern. The persistence of economic problems and the improvement of mass living conditions were, in some ways, related. The improvement of standards owed a great deal to rising real wages and the development of a large consumer market. The soaring demand for domestic goods of all kinds increased the imports of both finished and raw materials and reduced the quantity of British-made products available for export. Had luxury imports been fewer and a larger proportion of domestic production been exported, the national economic picture would have looked brighter but some of the improvements in living standards would have had to be sacrificed. Essentially, the choice was between national and individual prosperity. The people chose the latter and paid for their choice in deficits, balance of payments crises, devaluations, and inflation.

## TRANSPORT AND COMMUNICATIONS

The products of the sophisticated mass-consumption economy promoted the development of a society which was more mobile and better informed than ever before. The trend towards increasing mobility had begun over a century earlier with the growth of the railway and had been boosted by the development of cheap newspapers, books, and radio, but the development of the family car and the television set gave mass mobility and communications new dimensions and promoted the establishment of new patterns of life. Car ownership ceased to be the prerogative of a minority and came within the grasp of many ordinary wage-earners, with enormous social consequences. In 1951 there were 2½ million licensed cars on the road, in 1961 just under 6 million, and in 1969 over 11 million. Over the same period more money was spent repairing and constructing roads and motorways, all of which increased the effective range of motor vehicles.

Mass-produced cars became not only status symbols but extensions of the home. They required a constant investment in supplies, services, and equipment to keep them running and a credit to their owners. A new car, like a new house, led to the abandonment of old habits and the formation of new ones. It immediately opened up a wider world for its owners by increasing their range of alternative choices of working, shopping, living and entertainment districts which had formerly been limited by the restrictions of public transport. The long-established pattern of urban separation of home and work was reinforced and extended to more people because car owners could live further away from work and no longer had to live within walking distance of bus stop or railway station. Car ownership also added new elements to the social classification system by offering a new, if imprecise, set of labels. The social gap between owning and not owning a car was more significant than it had been in the past when cars had been beyond the income of the majority of the people, and the names of cars, their age, condition, and equipment could be used to help classify the economic and social standing of their owners.

Most cars were family machines and although some people used them for commuting to work, many vehicles remained in the garage during the week and were used primarily as pleasure vehicles, a fact which car manufacturers recognized by building so-called 'family cars' for weekend excursions and holiday motoring. Cars loosened old neighbourhood ties, but, at least as long as the children were too young to drive, they also tended to draw family members together around a common focus of interest and also to force them into close physical proximity.

The development of the electronics industry led to the production of more and more communications gadgets, the most socially influential of which was the television set. The number of television sets increased rapidly from the 1950s on, and the number of licences doubled between 1958 (6.4 million) and 1964 (12.8 million). In 1954 the creation of the Independent Television Authority officially ended the BBC's monopoly, although transmission did not begin until the following year. ITV, and its commercials, took some time to reach all of the country, but its competition soon had the effect of 'brightening up' BBC programmes. By the 1960s the BBC had recognized the challenge and begun to change many of its programmes and its image. A metamorphosis took place in which the staid old 'aunty' became younger, racier, more irreverent, and lively. The selfconsciously educational function of BBC television was, however, reinforced in 1962 when the transmissions of BBC 2, the 'highbrow' channel, began to spread slowly across the country from the south-east.

Scientific advances enabled television to bring the joys and sorrows of the world into the living room. In 1962 'Telstar', the first trans-Atlantic TV satellite, made possible the first transmissions between Europe and North America, and a few years later the Intelsat system was sophisticated enough to offer live transmissions of test matches between England and Australia—a boon to sleepless cricket lovers in both countries. The technical achievement of international television transmissions was impressive, but the programme content rarely seemed to match. Nations had little to transmit to each other which required instantaneous sound and video apart from spectacular disasters and sports meetings. International 'cultural' transmissions were strained and contrived, and the multilingual inanities of the Euro-vision Song Contest or the Miss World carnival seemed to do little to improve international understanding. The new, brighter BBC abandoned its old TV symbol and its motto, 'Nation shall speak peace unto nation', either to bolster its new image or in despair at the babble.

Television, like radio, acted as a social levelling agent and added to the pool of common experience. It was an important addition to the forces which were producing a more homogeneous national society, helping to flatten accents and stimulate inter-regional and cross-class entertainment interests. By providing readily available home entertainment it tended to discourage the seeking of outside entertainment and provided many families with a new, uniting interest. The influence of the United States was very obvious, as it had been in films, and this was frequently criticized, although there was much more two-way traffic in TV programmes than there had been in films. In the mid-sixties, the levelling effects of radio and television were recognized, and in an effort to promote class and regional tolerance and to sustain some of the diversity of 'regional culture', the local VHF stations of the late sixties were equipped with news readers and announcers with traces of regional accent, as were some TV programmes.

Many of the older communications media faced declining audiences and economic problems in the 1950s and 1960s. The 4,500 cinemas of 1953 fell to just over 2,000 in 1965 as they lost their patrons to the small screen in the living room and were converted into bingo halls or simply allowed to stand empty. Newspapers followed the general pattern of postwar industrial and commercial modernization, and smaller and less profitable concerns went out of business, concentrating more power into fewer hands. A royal commission of enquiry into the concentration of press ownership in 1961–2 reported that three major newspaper groups owned well over 60 per cent of all daily papers. Despite the development of attractive alternative leisure-time pursuits, people continued to read a great deal. In 1950 a Gallup Poll revealed that 55 per cent of the sample taken (a higher percentage than that of any other country) claimed that they were currently reading a book. The popularity, sales, and range of materials covered by paper-backed books increased, and by the end of the sixties there could have been few homes which did not possess at least one Pelican or Penguin paperback.

WORKING CONDITIONS

Working conditions in most occupations were much better than they had ever been, partly as a result of higher legal standards and worker expectations, partly as a result of economic changes. Industrial streamlining, increasing efficiency, and the enormous growth of consumer and service industries vastly expanded the number of technical, white-collar, and service jobs, while the demand for heavy manual labour contracted. Unemployment in many fields, caused by rapid changes in industry, was recognized, albeit inadequately, by the opening of some retraining centres for adults in the 1960s. By 1967 the 'average' worker worked between 40 and 42 hours per week, although in practice fully employed males worked an average of 46.2 hours and fully employed females 38.2 hours. By the mid-sixties five days was accepted as a 'normal' working week, and over half the working population did in fact have a five-day week. Even shop assistants, who had traditionally worked long hours, moved in this direction as the bigger shops hired more people so that they could open a full six days while giving their employees a five-day week. The vast majority of the labour force did not work on public holidays and also had two weeks' paid holiday a year.

Advanced machinery and production techniques, however, made shift work a necessary efficiency measure in many industries. Employers could not allow their expensive machines to stand idle for sixteen hours a day, so in many industries highly trained machine operators were required to do shift work, in the past a mark of relatively unskilled manual labour. For example, companies owning computers tried to get as many hours' work out of their costly machines as they could, while service industries such as garages and restaurants faced a growing demand for round-the clock-services. In the late 1950s F. Zweig investigated the working and domestic patterns of life of employees in selected iron, steel, and light industrial works and found that most workers did not object to shift work. Given their adequate leisure time and comfortable homes, they quickly adapted their domestic arrangements to fit its demands. (*The Worker*, 53–4, 65.)

As workplaces became larger and more mechanized they provided better facilities for the workers. By the 1950s and 1960s the majority of concerns employing twenty or more people had canteen facilities, sometimes with subsidized food. Very many supplied not only protective clothing and equipment for employees but also standard work clothes. Most large industrial and commercial concerns had medical facilities for the treatment of minor injuries and illnesses, and some also provided sports clubs and social and recreational activities. Better safety regulations and machinery which stopped automatically when its protective guards were lifted reduced accidents, while better heating and ventilation systems and better toilet facilities also contributed to the improved health of the workers. Even miners came home with fewer blue scars, clean from the baths at the NCB pitheads. Offices, as well as multiplying, also improved working conditions for their employees. Prestige and the desire of firms to look modern and efficient also played a part in their improvement. Many large, new, stark glass-and-girder office blocks sprang up in major city centres, their forms having as dramatic an effect on the skyline as the employment they provided for large numbers of new-middle-class people had on the old social outlines.

A few people continued to work in miserable conditions, but working life for the vast majority of people was far better than it had been a century, or even two or three decades earlier. Zweig found that the workers in his sample neither hated nor feared their work, as had often been the case a century earlier, and that although a few found it boring and merely tolerated it, the majority enjoyed it. He found that most skilled workers were interested in their work and enjoyed doing it, and although the degree of interest fell off as skill decreased, even the least skilled workers derived some pleasure from their jobs because they enjoyed the company of friends at work. (*The Worker*, 66, 79–80.) The majority of employed people of both sexes were favourably disposed towards their work, too, because they recognized its connection with their improved living standards. The awareness of the relationship between employment and living standards helped to generate a new high level of working-class interest in the state of the national economy and indeed in anything which might affect their employment and wage rates.

The popularity of 'sidelines', part-time jobs and a host of money-making schemes such as selling from mail-order catalogues for commission, testified to the importance many working people attached to the boosting of real income. Many workers in Zweig's sample had sidelines in which they made extra money by helping wives or other family members run small businesses, by raising pigs or poultry, or by doing jobs for friends and neighbours. (*The Worker*, 13, 99.) Skilled mechanical and electrical workers often managed to earn small fees by repairing cars and television sets for their neighbours. The fact that living standards had risen enormously did not dampen the drive to work, but stimulated it. Many people were anxious to work harder than ever to achieve even higher standards and secure them with 'a little nest egg' or 'a bit extra'.

Increasing automation lessened the number of jobs in which physical strength was needed and produced an increasing number of light jobs which were ideal for women. Because women were generally paid at a slightly lower rate than men, female labour was more profitable for employers, with the result that many of the new modernized industries had labour forces which were predominantly female. Food processing and packing plants, clothing industries, electronics and electrical appliance industries, plastics and pharmaceutical industries typically employed a large number of women. In 1901 under a quarter of the labour force had been female; by the early 1960s one-third of it was made up of employed women, and most unmarried girls took it for granted that they would work. The increasing importance of female labour was obvious enough by the sixties to prompt some observers to note that without employed women the industrial and commercial activities of the nation would come to an abrupt halt.

A substantial proportion of the female labour force was made up of married women, many of whom worked on a part-time basis to earn that vital 'bit extra' money. Part-time white-collar jobs in offices or schools were usually hard to find, and most of the part-time, married, female labour force was employed in semi-skilled or unskilled light manual occupations in factories, or as waitresses or cleaners. In the late fifties and early sixties this type of work usually brought in an extra £3–4 per week, about one-fifth to one-quarter of a fully employed male manual worker's wage. The increasing number of married working women (one married woman in 10 worked in 1941, 1 in 3 in

1963) inspired a good deal of comment and speculation about the social effects of female employment. Some investigations into the effects of female employment on families were made, and it was found that women with babies and small children generally stayed at home, but that very many women went back to work as soon as they could find someone to look after the children. Generally an obliging grandmother or other relative could be found, and a few children were lucky enough to find a rare nursery school place. Few cases were found in which children or family were neglected simply and solely because the mother was working, and by the end of the sixties the topic was approached with less emotion and more sense.

Few married women worked because their earnings were vital to family finances. Most worked because they wanted to, either to buy luxuries or to save for the future, or because they enjoyed the change of scene and the companionship which work offered. The scene at the end of a shift at any light industrial plant gave some idea of why women worked and how they felt about their work. Hoards of cheerful, well-fed, well-dressed, happily gossiping women poured out, mounted scooters or bicycles or joined their patient husbands waiting in small but well-cared-for cars. At gatherings of young, professionally trained, married women long and loud complaints could be heard about the lack of child-care facilities for those who lived a long distance from grandparents and relatives and about the lack of opportunities for them to return to work on the equivalent of the manual workers' half-shift.

Average real wages rose 20 per cent between 1951 and 1958, a further 30 per cent to 1964, and generally went on rising slowly to the end of the sixties, when the rising unemployment rate again began to cause some concern. The real incomes of both skilled and unskilled manual workers rose, both in absolute terms and relative to the incomes of non-manual workers, which improved their living standards and at the same time helped close the income/class gap which separated them from the new-middle class. Female earnings also improved, but, despite the equal pay for equal work principle adopted in an increasing number of occupations, their pay generally lagged behind that of men, and the average earnings of women in industry were only about half the male average. Unemployment and low wage rates, major poverty-producers at the beginning of the century, were of negligible importance by the sixties. The mid-century poor were mainly made up of retired people living entirely or mainly on pensions, fatherless families, and the families of low wage earners with a large number of children. Even by the late 1960s, many people continued to face life on less than the National Assistance Board's definition of a subsistence income. The poor continued to exist, and by their existence, to prove that the welfare state had not yet completely achieved its aims and that the ideal society had yet to be formed. Old age pensioners were often undernourished and cold in winter; children in large families sometimes had only barely adequate food and clothing, and some sick people lived, and died, on the drab, penny-pinching lower margins of the affluent society, but for the majority of the people the fifties and sixties were very good decades. Measured against the standards of the past, poverty was only a minor social problem, and the late sixties poor were rich compared to their counterparts even half a century earlier. Poverty was no longer synonymous with starvation, nor did it mean that there would be no help for pain and sickness and no hope for the future, and this alone would mark the first half of the twentieth century as a time of tremendous social change.

LIVING STANDARDS

Increased prosperity was reflected in diet, housing, and possessions. In the nineteenth and early twentieth centuries any increase in working-class prosperity was generally first reflected in increased spending on food because the average diet left ample room for improvement. Despite rising real wages, the percentage of total consumer income spent on food in the 1950s was remarkably stable, and it even decreased a little in the 1960s (from 31 per cent in 1959 to 26 per cent in 1967). By this time the mass of the people had a more than adequate diet and no longer found it necessary, or perhaps possible, to spend additional income on food. On the other hand, many of them were eager to turn their higher incomes into better housing.

'The improvement in housing conditions in the last decade [the 1950s] is one of the most potent factors in the transformation of the working man's way of life' (Zweig, The Worker, 5). Long-standing housing problems had multiplied during the war years, and during the reconstruction years the Labour Government encouraged local authorities to build and rebuild. From the mid-fifties, Conservative governments sought to meet the demand for more and better housing by making private home ownership and building easier, while continuing to provide financial support for local authority building programmes. The Conservatives maintained a good record of house-building, and by 1964 the building industry was capable of achieving their goal of erecting 1,000 houses a day. Massive slum clearance and rebuilding projects were undertaken, and housing estates sprang up all over the country. Bomb-damaged and ancient houses were toppled, and blitzed cities, such as Plymouth, Coventry and Sheffield, cleared the rubble and rebuilt their city centres. According to the 1961 census, there were 16 million dwellings in Great Britain, 6.5 million of which were owner-occupied and 4 million of which were rented from New Town Corporations or other local authorities. Over 96 per cent of all households had piped cold water, 76.5 per cent had a hot water system, over 87 per cent had an indoor water closet, and over 73 per cent the use of a fixed bath. Substandard nineteenth-century housing continued in use, and many improvement projects were not expected to be finished until the 1980s, but the foetid urban and rural dung-heaps where people had lived a century earlier were no more.

By the late fifties, local authorities and private builders were erecting thousands of new houses in all parts of the country which were within the grasp of ordinary working people. People who moved to a better house or flat, whether it was council or privately owned, felt a sense of achievement and a pride in their progress. As Young and Willmott observed (*Family and Kinship in East London*, 127), 'Who can wonder that people crowded into one or two pokey rooms, carrying water up three flights of stairs, sharing a W.C. with other families, fighting against damp and grime and poor sanitation, should feel their hearts lift at the thought of a sparkling new house with a garden.' They boasted of their improved accommodation and stimulated the interest of family and friends in housing, encouraging them to find better housing, too. Some people with high ambitions and steady incomes saved for a deposit on a house and sought loans from building societies, while the less confident and less prosperous waited for council houses on new estates. The waiting lists were often long—the waiting time in Sheffield in the late 1950s was ten years—but many people were willing to wait and to take the probable length of the wait into consideration as a major factor in their plans for the future. Housing became so important that some people deliberately manipulated their lives to create uncomfortable situations in the hope of improving their chances of getting a house quickly. Married couples moved in with parents, knowing that this would produce overcrowding and was below local government standards but hoping that this fact would move them up on the waiting list; others had one more child than they would otherwise have planned for, in the expectation that this would boost them up the list in a similar fashion.

Many young married manual workers in these decades saved a large portion of their weekly income, or the whole of the second income if their wives worked, for the down payment on a house or for major household equipment. Housing and household equipment assumed a great importance in the lives of many people, especially of those who felt that they had done better, not only than their parents, but than they themselves had expected to do. Housing became an important popular status symbol which affected the aspirations of people living in dilapidated housing as well as those who had moved up in the world. People who could not afford to buy a house and who faced a long wait for a council house were often temporarily condemned to live in run-down accommodation earmarked for slum clearance, such as the drab, bleak, gardenless, nineteenth-century terraces of Leeds. Even they took a new pride in their homes, painted the woodwork, attempted improvement projects, and installed bright new curtains, furniture, and equipment. In most cases, workers who acquired better houses acquired along with them new attitudes which had formerly characterized the middle classes. The newly housed and re-housed workers wanted the best household equipment they could possibly afford, more fashionable decorations, neater and more ambitious gardens.

Most people began by aiming at higher standards than their parents had had, but many soon adjusted their sights near or above the standards of their new neighbours, most of whom had themselves set a higher standard than they had had in the past when they moved in. As well as adding new elements of social competition and distinction to the lives of the masses, changing housing conditions altered old patterns of life. The long-established working-class custom of living at the back of the house and keeping the front room (if they were lucky enough to have one) a dust-clothed sanctuary used only in times of death and sickness and visits by the parson disappeared when the front room of the new house became the television room and, hence, a heavily used family centre. Householders of virtually all degrees of prosperity undertook a variety of do-it-yourself decorating, minor rebuilding, and alteration projects. The development and widespread distribution of domestic power tools in the 1960s complemented this trend, and do-it-yourself became an industry with its own retail shops and a host of specialist books and magazines. Increasing numbers of people lavished hours of loving work on their homes, both responding to and stimulating the role of the home as an important status symbol.

A television set became a basic necessity for any reasonably equipped home, and by the later 1950s even many poor homes had a set. In the years of prosperity the ownership of domestic electrical equipment of all kinds became common at all income levels. By the late 1960s virtually every household had an electric iron, 4 out of 5 a vacuum cleaner, over half a washing machine, 2 out of 5 a refrigerator, and 1 in 5 an electric toaster. Electric hairdriers, blankets, sewing machines, small power tools, and food mixers also abounded. Mass materialism of the mid-twentieth century was inspired by motives which were similar to those which had promoted minority, middle-class materialism in the mid-nineteenth century. Neat, well-equipped homes were measures of the success of their occupants, who seldom doubted that they were far better off than their parents had been. Better housing also closed the living standard gap which had always separated the poor working classes from the prosperous middle classes, very many of whom were conscious of being worse off than their parents had been. In addition, the increasing security and prosperity which better housing symbolized stimulated optimism about the future, and more and more semi-skilled and unskilled workers adopted habits of planning and saving and exhibited a degree of pride in achievement which half a century earlier was common only among the middle classes.

Shorter working hours and higher incomes fostered a wide variety of leisure pursuits which soon became vital parts of 'the good life'. An hour or two in front of the 'telly' in a comfortable chair in a pleasant living room must be counted as the chief leisure-time activity of a large segment of the adult population in the mid-twentieth century. Do-it-yourself jobs, decorating, handicrafts, home and car improvement and repair also occupied many hours, so many that Zweig discovered that many men worked so hard at weekends that going to their official work on Monday was a relief and relaxation. (The Worker, 100). Gardening remained enormously popular and the number of amateur gardeners grew as more people moved to new towns and housing estates where, for the first time, they could indulge their horticultural instincts. Dancing, knitting, sewing, listening to and making music, all remained popular hobbies, as, apparently, did reading, because book sales remained high and in the late 1960s almost one-third of the total population belonged to a public library. As television ownership increased, cinema attendance fell off, and after the passing of the Betting and Gaming Act many dying cinemas found a new lease of life in the 1960s as bingo halls. The same Act spawned the betting shops which sprang up all over the country, and the 'gaming house' which provided recreation for more prosperous gamblers. Working Men's Clubs enjoyed an upsurge of popularity in the sixties and began expanding their premises and hiring nationally known, expensive, popular entertainers. By the end of the decade there were almost 4,000 clubs affiliated with the Working Men's Club and Institute Union which had a total of three million members.

By this time the majority of the people had a large enough earnings margin to be able to enjoy an annual holiday, a pleasure which had been almost exclusively an upper- and middle-class privilege half a century earlier. Seaside holidays remained popular and coastal resorts expanded their residential and entertainment facilities. The 1950s and 60s saw a great boom in holiday camps, the giant entertainment factories which had grown up since W. E. Butlin opened his first camp in 1937. As car ownership became more common and as better, lighter, equipment became available, camping, once an occupation for scouts, guides and national servicemen, became a popular way of taking a holiday, especially among families with several small children. The number of holidaymakers seeking sunshine in foreign lands increased sharply from about a million a year in the early fifties to over five million by the mid-sixties. Increasing real wages and the development of cheap mass transport facilities encouraged more and more people to take holidays abroad. Group tours did a booming business in the 1960s, providing travel, accommodation, and food at pre-arranged prices. The package of arrangements minimized the long-standing tourist problems concerning strange languages, customs, and currencies. Among the more adventurous segments of the population, touring in the family car and camping were also popular ways of taking holidays abroad.

SOCIAL FORMS AND STRUCTURE

Increasing prosperity and the operation of the educational reforms of the 1940s and later combined to make education available to more people. Although the educational system continued to favour the children of wealthier and better-educated parents, and to this extent tended to carry forward echoes of the old class system, far fewer children were denied education because they lacked suitable clothing or because they had to leave school as soon as possible to help support their families. Nevertheless, education was a controversial issue in the fifties and sixties because many commentators claimed that only a limited expansion of opportunities and minor social changes had been effected in spite of the glowing forecasts to the contrary which had

been made. By ideal contemporary standards the rate at which inequalities in education were being eliminated seemed inexcusably slow,
but by historical yardsticks the expansion and change of the postwar
years were enormous. In general, the trend was for more children to
stay longer in secondary schools and to acquire a higher degree of
skill or education. The effects of the 1944 Act could most clearly be
seen in the increasing number of univeristy students. The number of
students rose from about 50,000 in 1938–9 to 82,000 in 1954–5, 108,000
in 1960–1, and 211,000 in 1968–9. In 1945 there were seventeen universities, and by the end of the 1960s there were forty-four.

A survey of undergraduates in the early sixties showed that four-
fifths of them were 'first generation' university students, whose
parents had not had a university education, although only one-fifth
of the total number had fathers who were manual workers. Even by
the late 1960s children from well-educated, prosperous, and literate
backgrounds, i.e. from the middle classes, had a considerable educational advantage over working-class children. While the operations of
the educational system were by no means egalitarian and did not
produce as much social levelling as might have been hoped, more
children went to universities under the terms of the 1944 Act than
could possibly have gone there before the war and among them was
an incredibly large number of working-class children. The system had
many faults and needed to be changed if it was to cope effectively in
the future. Many changes, such as the building of comprehensive
schools and the introduction of the Certificate of Secondary Education, were made in the sixties. Although children from middle-class
homes were the primary beneficiaries of the improved social status
education offered, upward social mobility via the ladder of education
by working-class children was frequent enough to make this the theme
of several books, some stage and television plays, and the subject of
reports such as Jackson and Marsden's investigation of the adult lives
of working-class grammar-school children, *Education and the Working
Class* (1962). By the early 1970s, however, it began to seem that the
main problem facing higher education might not be the finding of
new ways to draw working-class children into the system, but the
finding of jobs for university graduates, because by this time the nation
was finding it difficult to absorb all the highly trained young people
the universities were turning out.

Over a century of such fundamental social changes, some alterations
might be expected to have taken place in the basic elements of the
society of the mid-nineteenth century. Certainly with such dramatic

changes in living and working conditions, prosperity levels, and social services, the family could not help but change in some ways. By the mid-twentieth century the extended family group of the mid-nineteenth-century middle-class household had all but disappeared and was considered a 'normal' household grouping by no social class. The strength of the nuclear family (parents and children) had by no means eroded away. The imminent demise of the family was often forecast and many arguments were conjured up to support the contention that, logically, the family would not survive in an age of welfare state and mass society. The family did not die, however, and in some areas a working-class version of the extended family continued to operate, as was shown, for example, by Young and Willmott's study of East London in the mid-1950s. Some investigators, such as Fletcher in *The Family and Marriage in Britain* (1966), have suggested that perhaps the nuclear family was stronger in the mid-twentieth century than it had ever been. In any event, rising mass living standards and the proliferation of small houses ensured that the parent/child grouping would be the typical household unit of all classes.

Rising living standards were, in many ways, beneficial to the nuclear family primarily because consumer goods generally emphasized the importance of the home and the family life within it. The people who lavished their earnings, time, and energy on their houses took it for granted that 'the new house', whether council or privately owned, would be a parents-and-children-only dwelling with no room for servants and space for only temporary accommodation for visiting relatives. Better housing and living standards promoted an atmosphere which was, all other things being equal, more conducive to the development of a closer and more harmonious family life than had often been possible in the past. Status competition undoubtedly introduced new strains into many families, but in the age of material comforts the vast majority of families did not have to cope with the abrasive effects of chronic deep poverty on human relationships. Arguments about earnings, purchases, and the choice of TV programmes might occasionally become bitter, but they were not as traumatic as arguments about the arrangements for sharing a single broken-down bed, the distribution of meagre food allowances, or the rent money for some miserable and degrading hovel.

Zweig concluded that family life was more satisfactory, at least for his sample, than it had been for the previous generation (*The Worker*, 30), and Richard Hoggart described mid-twentieth-century working-class family life as ' . . . in many respects a good and comely life, one founded on care, affection, a sense of the small group, if not of the individual' (*The Uses of Literacy*, 37). Even when the family home did not provide positive attractions for its residents, it was not generally so crowded and squalid as to drive them out, as had all too often been the case in the past. In the later sixties, seven out of eight adults could be expected to be at home on a weekday evening, engaged in some do-it-yourself project, busy with a hobby or car care, or simply watching television. Although households were, in the main, inhabited only by nuclear families, other relatives continued to play an important part in the lives of many people who had not moved far from their home districts. Grandmothers provided invaluable child-care services for working mothers, and although many of the aged remained in their own establishments, their adult children very often made daily visits and were genuinely concerned for their comfort and welfare.

Marriage remained the generally accepted norm for adults, and the mass communications media continued to idealize and popularize the institution, but notions about ideal marriage had changed since the mid-nineteenth century. Marriage was no longer the necessary basis for respectable status that it had been, although everything from taxation to packaged foods continued to be designed for couples rather than single individuals. Divorced people had become perfectly socially acceptable, and although the divorce rate had risen, it had not soared to the anarchy-riddled heights forecast by the opponents of divorce law reform. Marriage was no longer considered vital for the status and comfort of the male and the economic survival of the female. The new ideal stressed personal rather than economic and social fulfilment as the central benefit, and emphasized the emotional happiness of the people concerned. The ideal presumed a degree of equality between the sexes which would have been impossible to imagine a century earlier. It was generally accepted that both would be involved in both major and minor planning, that the wife would work either full- or part-time for at least some years, and that the husband would share in the housework, do some decorating and gardening and help with the washing-up. In its broad outline the mid-twentieth-century home-and-family ideal of all classes had something in common with the traditional, practical working-class home with the poverty, unpleasantness, and violence removed. The contemporary ideal also drew upon traditional middle-class materialism and standards of comfort. This combination seemed to produce an end-product which was in practice a much happier and more satisfying state than the Victorians could have imagined.

The 'average' mid-twentieth-century family unit was much smaller than its nineteenth-century counterpart. The socially acceptable number of children was three or less, and the earlier norm of six, ten, or more was considered unusual, often embarrassing. Domestic architecture reinforced the trend towards smaller families because builders designed houses for families with only two or three children. Larger families faced the prospect of overcrowding or comparatively expensive accommodation. Contraception and low death rates played an important part in producing smaller families, as did increasing prosperity, which encouraged people to choose their priorities with care because they had more options to choose from and more at stake. The change in priorities from children to living standards did not produce an absolute fall in the birth rate in the middle years of the century. The forties saw a sharp postwar increase in the birth rate, which levelled off in the fifties. In the fifties and sixties birth rates fluctuated within a range of about three births per thousand, and the fluctuations were probably due to nothing more significant than interactions of economic change and minor shifts in the age composition of the population.

By assuming responsibility for the welfare and security of each citizen from the cradle to the grave, the welfare state relieved both immediate and extended family members of many of their traditional responsibilities and burdens. Notably, it eased the economic pressure which caring for the old and sick had placed on poorer families in the past. As a result, many people were encouraged to show greater interest in aged or ill relatives in cases in which, in the past, the financial implications of doing so might have been too burdensome.

Between the mid-nineteenth century and the mid-twentieth century the old social structure had become blurred and had dissolved. Poverty and privilege became less pronounced, and the broad majority, not a privileged minority, determined the directions social change would take. The life-style and aspirations of the mid-twentieth-century mass society could generally be described as an amalgam of old-middle- and old-working-class standards and social patterns as modified by economic and technological change. Social divisions continued to exist in the mid-twentieth century, but they were not quite the same divisions nor were they as clearly delineated or as influential as the divisions of the mid-nineteenth century had been. Society was not yet a totally homogeneous mass, but the general trend of the century as a whole was towards the creation of a more uniform society.

The levelling effect of mass communications became more pervasive as technology advanced. By the 1960s virtually everyone had watched dozens or hundreds of films and TV programmes, listened innumerable hours to radio and records, read dozens of books, newspapers and magazines, and shared, through these media, all kinds of experiences and information with thousands or millions of other people. Despite recent counter-trends, the national coverage of radio and television programmes had tended to erode regional and class differences. Middle-class people saw a version of working-class life in such programmes as 'Coronation Street', working-class listeners were fascinated for years by the suburban, servant-studded world of 'Mrs Dale's Diary', and in an overwhelmingly urban nation the popularity of the rural antics of 'the Archers' was almost startling.

The reduction of extremes in income and the general rise in the living standards of the mass of the people led more and more people to live in increasingly similar surroundings and to accept increasingly similar settings as the background to a 'normal' way of life. A suburban landscape of semi-detached houses surrounded by little gardens came to be accepted as the normal domestic habitat of most people. The difference between council and more expensive private development was merely one of degree, not of kind. Regional differences in building styles and materials melted away as the mass prefabrication of parts and materials increased to keep pace with the need for large quantities of relatively cheap housing. Similar forces led to people looking more alike. Chain stores, especially Marks and Spencer, by outfitting everyone from duchess to dustman's daughter, probably did more to change the personal appearance of the people and to make all classes look more or less alike than any other single force in the twentieth century. Mass manufacture and distribution of all kinds of goods led, in a similar way, to the development of a 'mass society' in which people of all classes and income levels ate similar kinds of food, owned similar domestic appliances, and even washed their clothes in similar detergents.

The descendants of the exclusive aristocracy of the mid-nineteenth century were no longer so exclusive, partly because economic realities meant that they could no longer afford to be so insular, partly because social and political changes had brought new types of people into their ranks. The increasing costs and problems of running large estates coupled with high tax rates and heavy death duties to force the aristocracy into closer contact with the common people. Some of them took jobs in business and industry, while others were obliged to open their homes and parks as museums and pleasure grounds for the people, whose half-crown entrance fees and purchases of tea, scones, and ice-cream enabled the aristocrats to keep up their family estates. So many were forced to commercialize their estates in this way that 'stately homes' became almost a new business arena in which rival owners vied with each other in introducing new attractions, such as fun-fairs and lions, to draw the masses which their ancestors had despised, patronized, or feared. Commoners even entered the House of Lords after life peerages were established to strengthen the Lords' contemporary role as the advisory House. Politicians and specialists in many fields were given lifetime titles, which enabled them to sit in the Lords and add the weight of their experience to its deliberations. Even the monarchy was pressed into closer contact with the mass. The increasing prosperity which enabled common men to visit the homes of aristocrats also enabled them to visit the palaces of the monarch and to attend royal events such as the trooping of the colour and formal openings. Television took up where radio had left off in bringing the royal family into the living rooms of ordinary people, and the reduced importance of the constitutional role of the monarchy in the age of mass democracy led it, almost as a measure of self-preservation, to attach greater importance to its social role and to attempt to show the people in more graphic ways that it had first-hand experience of their problems and was genuinely concerned for their welfare. On the whole, the monarchy adapted to social change very well, so well that a survey in the 1960s revealed that Prince Philip would be the people's choice if they had to choose a dictator.

The rural population was by this time only a tiny segment of the total, and the urban majority determined the shape and development of society. Although they were outside the mainstream of national life by virtue of their rural residence, country people were affected and carried along by the forces which affected the urban majority, much as the quieter margins of a stream are influenced in their direction by the main body of water which moves swiftly along the centre of the channel. Cars and television brought them to the world and the world to them just as they did for townsmen. Mass production, electrification, and social welfare programmes changed the pattern of their lives too, improved their living standards, gave them more domestic comfort, and developed their liking for the good life. Mechanization and sophisticated farming techniques even increased their leisure time. The introduction of new forces of social change was often delayed in many country districts, the rate of change was slower and the significance of the changes was sometimes much less than in towns. For example, rural workers always tended to work longer hours and be less well paid than urban workers at any given time. Nevertheless, changes did take place and rural society was pulled into new shapes by the same inexorable forces which determined the development of the dominating urban society.

It became increasingly difficult to draw class distinctions along traditional lines as people of all classes looked more alike, had incomes within an increasingly narrow range, and shared a roughly similar pattern of life. No easy, new social indicators appeared while the old ones were vanishing. The domestic servant, a valuable class indicator in the nineteenth century, was valueless in this respect in the mid-twentieth century. By the late 1960s, less than 5 per cent of all households employed regular domestic help of any kind, and less than one per cent had a resident servant. On the other hand, one household in forty received local-authority home-help service at some time each year to enable its members to cope with emergencies such as illness, maternity, or old age, but this service bore no relation to class, only to need. Contemporary attempts to make precise social classifications and establish formulae for the determination of social class have ranged from the tortuously complicated to the absurdly trivial, but no generally acceptable scheme has appeared. While becoming less important, the whole class structure has certainly become far more complex or has, perhaps, when viewed in a historical context, become irrelevant.

Despite the increasing complexity of class definition, many people continued to think of themselves and others in the old terms and, in so doing, complicated the question still further. Interviews, letters to editors and other public forums in the 1950s were flooded by complaints from self-proclaimed middle-class people who wanted to prevent the country from being ruined by 'them'—the lower classes. The gist of these complaints was that welfare benefits paid to the grubby-handed workers were draining the life-blood out of the taxpaying middle classes and that the scruffy members of the mob would swarm into the new council houses, squander national assistance and family allowances, keep coal in the bath, clog the plumbing, and chop up the doors for firewood. By the 1960s this variety of old-middle-class virulence seemed to be fading, probably partly because middle-class people realized that in reality they benefited as much as anyone from health and education services and partly because 'they' proved to be decent people after all. Little reciprocal bitterness seemed to emanate from people who described themselves as 'working class'. This group complained about a more powerful 'them', but this seemed to be less an expression of sincerely felt hostility than the continuation of wartime grumbling habits and a fulmination against a variety of malicious powers which included the government, 'people in authority', and the clerk at the gas board who always got the bill wrong. Many self-classified working-class people were aware that upward social levelling was taking place although they continued to classify themselves socially as working class. Many, however, were quick to add, with some truth, that 'everyone' worked and so 'we're all working-class now'. Although many people continued to use them, the old class labels had lost clear meaning because the ways of life they had originally implied had disappeared.

The society of the mid-twentieth century, though prosperous, was far from being free of strain. Persistent economic uncertainty and the failure to find any secure niche for Britain in the postwar world worried many people who realized that the higher living standards were grounded on rather fragile and shallow foundations. The failure to find a new political role in a world dominated by the American and Russian super-powers was also disturbing. The Commonwealth seemed never to materialize into a viable family of nations, while joining the Common Market, although becoming a reality by the early 1970s, remained repellent to many people, especially to those who saw the plan as an immediate threat to their standard of living. Fear of what the massively destructive new weapons of war would do to Britain and the world if another war came troubled many people, especially in the 1950s and early sixties when marches under the slogan of 'Ban the Bomb' became almost a new social obligation among the young. The steady inflation which accompanied rising incomes occasionally troubled members of the new-middle and working classes but was a constant worry to the remaining remnants of the old-middle class who were still trying to live on their more-or-less fixed income from investments.

While the old lines of social division were becoming less and less meaningful, many new divisions were being suggested in the sixties. Society may redivide along lines of skill, education, and training, as was forecast by Young (*The Rise of the Meritocracy*) and others. The development of a meritocratic society, however, depends on a sustained demand for well-educated, highly skilled people, but by the early seventies the schools of higher learning seemed to be overproducing people or the demand to be flagging. Another possibility is a division along age lines indicated by the apparently widening gulf between young and old, the 'generation gap' of the 1960s. The 'angry young man', whose prototype was Jimmy Porter in John Osborne's 1956 play *Look Back in Anger*, criticized society and its values, especially those typified as 'middle class'. In the 1960s the young seemed to go beyond mere criticism to the creation of a culture of their own whose values and social divisions were divorced from anything their parents said they had known or experienced. In 1963 the Beatles burst upon the English scene and quickly became the heroes of the young, and, until the first shock had worn off, the horror of middle-aged and elderly people. The 'youth cult' produced many other phenomena including mini-skirts, kipper ties, multi-coloured shirts, and Carnaby Street fashions. By the mid-sixties, the sub-culture of the young had become international. The success of the new 'culture' was due partly to the international popularity of American musical forms and largely to the mass-production economy which churned out cheap records, record-players, radios, clothing, and all the other paraphernalia demanded by the young of the prosperous society.

Another social rift began to develop in the postwar years along colour lines. After the war, Commonwealth immigrants were attracted to England by the bright promise of full employment and a better way of life. They provided much-needed labour in lower-paid occupations which many English workers were beginning to disdain—jobs in public transport, local authority services, and hospitals. Their strange accents, unfamiliar customs and foods, and, above all, the easily identifiable, dark, damning colour of their skins, stirred the native English mistrust of foreigners and made the immigrants difficult to assimilate into the main body of society. People living in areas with a large immigrant population felt uneasy in any event, and especially in times of economic stress feared that the immigrants would compete for their jobs, accept lower wage rates, and threaten the good life their earnings brought. The workers, now enjoying a high standard of life, reacted to real or imagined danger from below in much the same fashion as the old-middle class had reacted to upward pressure from the workers a century earlier—with fear, resentment, animosity, and demands that official steps be taken to suppress the danger. In the 1950s and 1960s fear and hostility mounted on both sides of the colour issue. Violence erupted in some places; public pressure led to the establishment of new immigration controls, and Enoch Powell emerged as the political spokesman of anti-immigrant resentment. Meanwhile, second and third generations were born, no longer immigrants, but brownskinned Englishmen who faced a difficult and uncertain future.

Many of these disturbances and social divisions were not unprecedented. A 'generation gap' undoubtedly existed between the 'lost generation' of the interwar years and their parents; 'angry young men' in literature, rock and roll, and the mini-skirt closely parallel the literature of social realism, the jazz craze, and the short fringed dresses of the twenties. Other social phenomena like racial strife, however, have no exact earlier parallels, and whether they are momentary disturbances or permanent features of the English social scene remains to be seen. In the late 1960s the welfare state came under increasing attack from all sides. The advocates of continued social levelling and government collectivist reform questioned the effectiveness of the welfare state, while the advocates of private free enterprise and government economy questioned its cost. Some people wondered if mass production and widespread prosperity had, in effect, taken over the functions of the welfare state and rendered government-sponsored programmes for citizen welfare and security redundant. This idea seemed a curious one in view of the fact that, across the Atlantic at this time, the mass production, mass prosperity state *par excellence* began to wonder how much longer it could manage without nationalized health services and guaranteed minimum incomes. The lack of any dynamic new directions in government social planning may signify that the government collectivist phase of social reform is drawing to a close, just as utilitarian, evangelistic social reform faded in the late 1870s, and that the advocates of a more powerful government social planning agency and more social levelling are flogging a dying horse. The discovery and definition of challenging new social goals may again be necessary, as it was in the last decades of the nineteenth century, and perhaps somewhere in the statements of contemporary demographers, ecologists, pacifists, or Common Market supporters lie the beginnings of what will prove to be that redefinition of goals.

# Figures

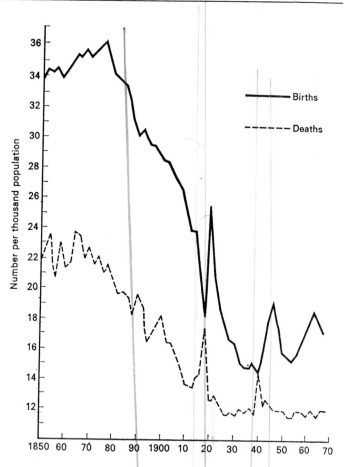

*Figure 1* Birth and death rates in England and Wales, 1850–1969
(alternate even years)

*Source:* Mitchell & Deane and *Annual Abstracts of Statistics*

NOTES

1 The birth rate increased erratically from 1850 to the early 1880s probably in response to increasing national prosperity in general and rising real wages in particular.
2 The most obvious and dramatic shift in the birth rate line occurs between the 1880s and the First World War, when the rate fell from the middle 30s to the low 20s per thousand, reflecting a whole series of shifts in society and especially declining family size at the turn of the century.
3 Sharp and erratic shifts in the birth rate line during and immediately after the two great wars offer one illustration of just how profoundly the wars affected society.
4 The overall steady fall in death rates from the mid-nineteenth to the early twentieth century illustrates the improvement in diet, general standard of living, urban sanitary conditions, etc.
5 The fairly stable and low death rate levels in the 1920s and 1930s suggest that although the Depression caused untold misery, the palliative measures, especially the dole, meant that there was little starvation and excess death.
6 The operation of the national health service undoubtedly plays a part in keeping the death rate low and stable after the late 1940s.

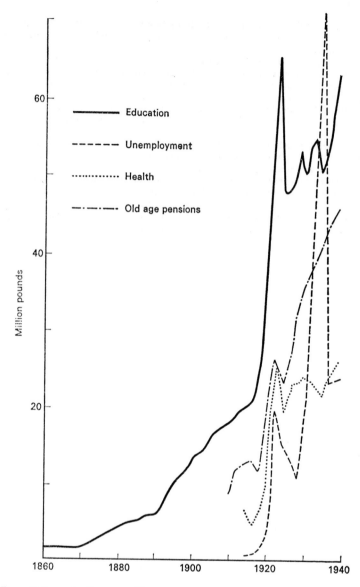

*Figure 2* Some indicators of increasing government activity and expenditure, 1860–1938

*Source:* Mitchell & Deane

NOTES

1 The low level of expenditure on education and the lack of expenditure on other basic social services in the mid-nineteenth century contrasts sharply with the amounts spent on the variety of basic services that the government supplied by the 1920s and 1930s. This contrast helps illustrate the unprecedented extent to which the government was participating in, and affecting the direction of, social change by the early twentieth century.

2 Unemployment, health, and old age pension payments which enter in the first two decades of the twentieth century follow and reflect the social questioning and investigations which took place at the turn of the century and the attempts of the Liberal Party to adjust national policy to cope with the problems revealed.

3 The dramatic surge in the graph for unemployment pay in the 1930s reflects the extent of unemployment during the Depression.

4 Graphs for government expenditure on social services are not extended beyond 1940 because expenditure and range of services increased so dramatically in the following decade that a graph on this scale would have been quite inadequate, while a change to an appropriate scale would have rendered the graphs for the vital period of initial expansion covered above rather small and meaningless.

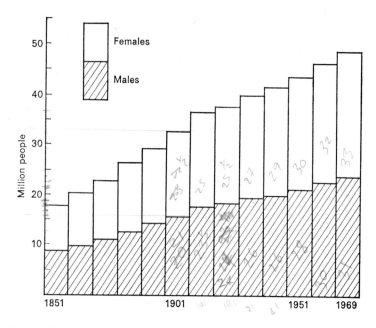

*Figure 3* Population of England and Wales, 1851–1969

*Source:* Mitchell & Deane and *Annual Abstracts of Statistics*

NOTES

1 The steady increase in population throughout the period can clearly be seen in this block graph, as can the fact that the population more than doubled between 1851 and 1969.
2 The slight but persistent excess of females over males is also evident throughout.

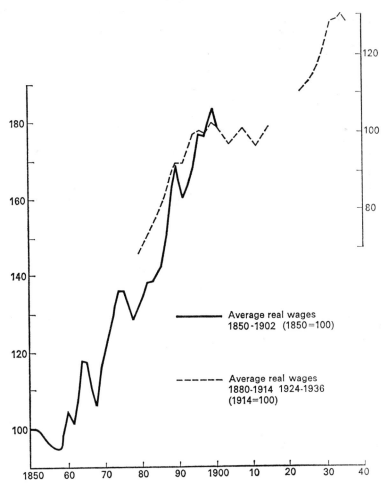

*Figure 4* Real wages index, 1850–1936

*Source:* Mitchell & Deane

NOTES

1 Real wages are extremely difficult to determine for a variety of reasons (for example, lack of material in the nineteenth century, unemployment and inflation), and very detailed and complicated work is needed before a reasonably accurate index can be produced. It is also very difficult to produce an index on the basis of the same criteria over a long period. The above graph is an attempted compromise between reliability and length of time.

2 Average real wages (real wages reflect purchasing power, as opposed to money wages, which alone are rendered meaningless by changes in prices) 1850–1902 are based on the figures in Mitchell & Deane which have as their source G. H. Wood, 'Real Wages and the Standard of Comfort since 1850', *Journal of the Royal Statistical Society* (1909). Average real wages 1880–1936 are based on the figures in Mitchell & Deane which have as their source A. L. Bowley, *Wages and Income since 1860* (C.U.P., 1937).

3 The two sets of calculations are based on different criteria and take as their base level (expressed as 100) real wages in different years. Hence they have been overlapped at a suitable point, partly to provide some continuity between the two, and partly to illustrate the differences which can occur between two relatively reliable sets of calculations.

4 The gap in the second section of the graph reflects the impossibility of assessing real wages when both prices and money wages are disrupted by war and its aftermath.

5 Despite all the difficulties involved in real wages calculation, the possible inaccuracies, and the divergence at the overlap, it is clear that between the 1850s and the 1930s there was a considerable and generally fairly steady increase in real wages which was reflected in the improvement of the living conditions of the working classes.

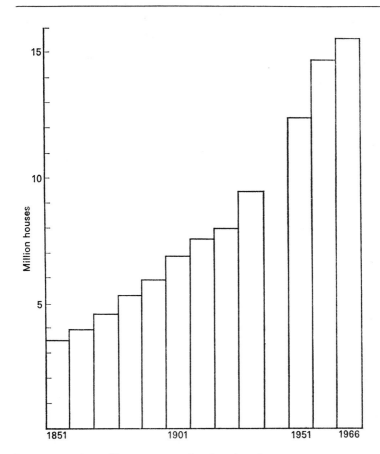

*Figure 5* Number of houses in England and Wales, 1851–1966

*Source: Annual Abstract of Statistics 1970*

NOTES

1 The tremendous increase in the number of houses between the 1850s and the
  1960s reflects the increase in population over the same period and also suggests
  the rapidity with which the built-up area expanded during this time.
2 The gap for the 1940s is due to the fact that it was impossible to determine the
  number of houses for most of this decade as a result of the destruction, damage
  and disruption caused by bombing in the Second World War.

# Bibliography

Primary sources are too numerous to list in a short bibliography. Among the most important are Parliamentary Papers, Acts of Parliament, Census Reports, newspapers and periodicals. There are many novels, plays, and poems which are useful as sources or which provide illustrative material. However, only those which have been referred to in the text have been listed in the bibliography. Statistical materials, figures for graphs, etc., have been taken from the invaluable collection in B. R. Mitchell & P. Deane, *Abstract of British Historical Statistics* (Cambridge University Press, 1962), and from the relevant *Annual Abstracts of Statistics* (HMSO), unless otherwise stated.

The following bibliography is very brief and should be supplemented with the excellent bibliographies provided in many of the volumes listed.

Adams, W. E. *Memoirs of a Social Atom*, New York, 1968.

Altick, R. D. *The English Common Reader: A Social History of the Mass Reading Public 1800–1900*, Chicago, 1957.

Appleman, P., Madden, W. A., & Wolff, M. *1859: Entering an Age of Crisis*, Indiana and London, 1959.

Bagehot, W. (ed. St John-Stevas, N.). *Bagehot's Historical Essays*, London and New York, 1965.

Banks, J. A. *Prosperity and Parenthood: A Study of Family Planning among the Victorian Middle Classes*, London, 1964.

Blythe, R. *The Age of Illusion. England in the Twenties and Thirties, 1919–40*, London and East Orange, N.J., 1964.

Booth, C. *Life and Labour of the People of London*, 17 vols, London, 1902–3.

Bowley, A. L. *Wages and Income in the United Kingdom since 1860*, London, 1937.

Briggs, A. *The Age of Improvement*, London, 1960; New York, 1965.

Briggs, A. *Victorian Cities*, London, 1963; New York, 1970.

Burn, W. L. *The Age of Equipoise: A Study of the mid-Victorian Generation 1852–67*, New York, 1964; London, 1968.

Burnett, J. *Plenty and Want. A social history of diet in England from 1815 to the present day*, London, 1968.

Burnett, J. *A History of the Cost of Living*, London, 1969.

Carr-Saunders, A. M., Jones, D. C., & Moser, C. A. *A Survey of Social Conditions in England and Wales as Illustrated by Statistics*, London, 1958.

Central Office of Information. *Britain: An Official Handbook*, 1969.

Checkland, S. G. *The Rise of Industrial Society in England 1815–1885*, London, 1964; New York, 1965.

Clark, G. S. R. Kitson. *An Expanding Society: Britain 1830–1900*, London, 1967.

Cole, G. D. H. *Postwar Condition of Britain*, London, 1965.

Cole, G. D. H., & Postgate, R. *The Common People 1746–1946*, London and New York, 1961.

Crewe, Q. *The Frontiers of Privilege: A Century of Social Conflict as Reflected in 'The Queen'*, London, 1961.

Dangerfield, G. *The Strange Death of Liberal England*, New York, 1961; London, 1966.

Daniel, W. W. *Racial Discrimination in England*, Penguin Books, 1969.

Deane, P., & Cole, W. A. *British Economic Growth 1688–1959: Trends and Structure*, London and New York, 1962.

Disraeli, B. *Sybil, or the Two Nations*, New ed., London and New York, 1954.

Dodds, J. W. *The Age of Paradox. A Biography of England 1841–1851*, London and Westport, Conn., 1953.

Ensor, R. C. K. *England 1870–1914*, London, 1936.

Escott, T. H. S. *England, Its People, Polity and Pursuits*, 2 vols, London, 1883.

Escott, T. H. S. *Social Transformations of the Victorian Age*, London, 1897.

Fletcher, R. *The Family and Marriage in Britain*, Penguin Books, 1969.

Freeman, T. W. *The Conurbations of Great Britain*, London, 1959.

Gissing, G. *New Grub Street*, Penguin Books, 1968.

Glass, D. V. (ed.), *Social Mobility in Britain*, London, 1954; New York, 1963.

Gloag, J. *Victorian Comfort: A Social History of Design from 1830–1900*, London, 1961.

Graves, R., & Hodge, A. *The Long Week-end: A Social History of Great Britain 1918–1939*, London, 1947; New York, 1963.

Hobsbawm, E. J. *Industry and Empire: an Economic History of Britain since 1750*, London and New York, 1968.

Hoggart, R. *The Uses of Literacy. Changing Patterns in English Mass Culture*, London and New York, 1957.

Houghton, W. E. *The Victorian Frame of Mind 1830–1870*, New Haven, Conn., 1957.

Hynes, S. *The Edwardian Turn of Mind*, Princeton, N.J., 1968.

Jackson, Brian, & Marsden, Dennis. *Education and the Working Class*, London and New York, 1962.

Johnson, W., Whyman, J., & Wykes, G. *A Short Economic and Social History of Twentieth Century Britain*, London, 1967.

Lewis, R., & Maude, A. *The English Middle Classes*, London, 1953.

Lipson, E. *The Growth of English Society: A Short Economic History*, 4th edn, London and New York, 1959.

Lockwood, D. *The Blackcoated Worker*, London, 1958.

Lynd, H. M. *England in the Eighteen-eighties: Towards a Social Basis for Freedom*, London and Clifton, N.J., 1945.

Macmillan, H. *Winds of Change 1914–1939*, London and New York, 1966.

Marcus, G. *Before the Lamps Went Out*, London, 1965.

Marsh, D. C. *The Changing Social Structure of England and Wales*, London, 1965.

Marwick, A. *The Deluge: British Society and the First World War*, New York, 1965; London 1967.

Marwick, A. *Britain in a Century of Total War: War, Peace and Social Change 1900–1967*, London and Boston, Mass., 1968.

Mathias, P. *The First Industrial Nation: an Economic History of Britain 1700–1914*, London and New York, 1969.

Money, L. G. C. *Riches and Poverty*, London, 1905.

Moorhouse, G. *The Other England: Britain in the Sixties*, Penguin Books, 1964.

Mowat, C. L. *Britain Between the Wars 1918–1940*, London and Chicago, 1955.

Muggeridge, M. *The Thirties: 1930–1940 in Great Britain*, London, 1940.

Orwell, S., & Angus, I. (eds). *The Collected Essays, Journalism and Letters of George Orwell*, 4 vols, London and New York, 1968.

Pollard, S. *The Development of the British Economy 1914–1950*, London and New York, 1962.

Quennell, P. (ed.). *Mayhew's London* (selection from *London Labour and the London Poor, 1851*), London, 1949.

Routh, G. *Occupations and Pay in Great Britain 1906–60*, London, 1965.

Rowntree, B. S. *Poverty: A Study of Town Life*, London, 1901.

Rowntree, B. S. & Lavers, J. *Poverty and the Welfare State,* London, 1951.

Ryder, J., & Silver, H. *Modern English Society, History and Structure 1850–1970*, London and New York, 1970.

Sampson, A. *Anatomy of Britain*, London, 1962.

Sampson, A. *Anatomy of Britain Today*, London, 1964.

Saunders, A. M., & Caradog Jones, D. *A Survey of the Social Structure of England and Wales*, London, 1937.

Shanks, M. *The Stagnant Society*, London, 1961.

Sissons, M., & French, P. (eds). *The Age of Austerity 1945–1951*, London, 1964.

Taine, H. (translated and introduced by Hyams, E.). *Taine's Notes on England*, London and New York, 1957.

Taylor, A. J. P. *English History 1914–1945*, London and New York, 1966.

Thompson, F. M. L. *English Landed Society in the Nineteenth Century*, London and Toronto, 1963.

Walbank, F. A. *England Yesterday and Today: In the Works of the Novelists 1837–1938*, London, 1949.

Wells, H. G. *Tono Bungay*, London, 1909.

Williams, Raymond. *Culture and Society 1780–1950*, London and New York, 1963.

Williams, William M. *The Sociology of an English Village: Gosforth*, London and New York, 1956.

Young, G. M. *Victorian England: Portrait of an Age*, London, 1954.

Young, Michael. *The Rise of the Meritocracy 1870–2033*, Penguin Books, 1963.

Young, M., & Willmott, P. *Family and Kinship in East London*, London, 1962.

Zweig, F. *The Worker in an Affluent Society: Family Life and Industry*, London and New York, 1961.

# Index

Workhouses, 24, 26–7
Working classes, 2–3, 5, 8–9, 18, 24–8, 52, 65, 66–7, 73, 102, 109, 138, 161, 170, 172, 182
Working conditions, 25, 26, 53, 95, 125, 166, 167
Working hours, 53, 159, 166, 181
Working Men's Clubs, 174

X-rays, 82

'Yellow backs', 43
York, 73, 161
Youth cult, 112, 183
Youth hostels, 135

Zeppelins, 79